Gerasa

Philadelphia
(Amman)

PEREA

Bethany
Beyond Jordan

River Jordan

Sychar
(Jacob's Well)

Jericho

Jerusalem

Bethlehem

Antipatris

Lydda

Emmaus

JUDEA

Hebron

Azotus

Joppa
(Tel Aviv)

Beer-sheba

NEGEB

Wilderness

Gaza

MEDITER

EGYPT

D1234436

The Holy Land

THE
HOLY LAND

by
G. Frederick Owen

Member of
The American Schools of Oriental Research,
Jerusalem, Amman, and Baghdad

Foreword by
Col. James B. Irwin
Astronaut on the Apollo 15

BAKER BOOK HOUSE
Grand Rapids, Michigan

Reprinted 1977 by Baker Book House Company

ISBN: 0-8010-6661-1

Library of Congress Catalog Card No. 77-076289

Printed in United States of America

Contents

The Eastern Tableland

Foreword

It has been my very great privilege to go to the moon and to the Holy Land!

As a small boy I gazed at the friendly moon on its best summer nights and almost fancied myself walking over its plains and along the foothills of what seemed to be its mountains. It seemed so very real to me that as a young lad I used to point to the moon and say, "I'm going to go up there someday."

I also attended Sunday school classes and learned of that wonderful country called Palestine and of its interesting places such as Mount Sinai, the Mount of Beatitudes, Bethlehem, Nazareth, and Jerusalem. Abraham, Moses, Joseph, David, and Jonah interested me, but the story of Jesus and how He loved all people —even me—enough to die on Mount Calvary to pay the penalty for our sins touched me very deeply and caused me to want to visit that land where all these things took place. I took part in the Christmas program at our church every year. At 11 years of age I made a public decision for Christ, and my desire to go to the Holy Land increased. Now that I am a man in mid-life and have gone both to the moon and to the Holy Land, I like to parallel the two exploits.

On July 26, 1971, we left the planet earth on Apollo 15 to explore space and the moon. We circled the earth a couple of times at 18,000 mph, then directed our spacecraft toward the moon. At a distance of 50,000 miles, we maneuvered our spacecraft so that the earth appeared in my window. I looked out and couldn't believe my eyes. I called to my colleagues, Dave and Al, and very quickly they floated over. All of a sudden there were three heads—six eyeballs glued to the window—viewing our home—the spaceship earth—looking like a Christmas tree ornament hanging in the blackness of space. It was the most beautiful sight we would see on our voyage—a sight that made us deeply appreciative of the creation of God, keenly aware of *His* precise control, and moved by *His* love.

The major purpose of our landing was to explore the mountains of the moon. We landed at Hadley Base, on the edge of Mare Imbrium (Sea of Rains) and at the foot of the towering Apennine Mountains—mountains that were 15,000 feet above our campsite. I was astonished when I first saw the lofty mountains—I was reminded of a favorite ski resort.

While exploring the area around our campsite, I was conscious of another Force—not visible, but definitely there—a Force that answered prayer, guided our footsteps, and inspired our thoughts to new heights—the very presence of God.

We were guided to the "Genesis Rock"—a unique rock that is said to date back to the earliest beginning of the moon. It was sitting on a dust-covered pedestal rock—glistening white and practically free from dust so that we could see it long before we picked it up. Singularly enough, the rock is composed of a material known on the earth for centuries as moonstone. We found this rock on the Apennine mountain slopes, a long way from our temporary home, Falcon, which appeared like a speck down in the valley.

We returned with a wealth of new knowledge about our moon, but for my personal life the greatest discovery was God's presence on another planet. The total experience caused a deeper spiritual awakening in my life that gave me new direction and a mission when I returned to the spaceship earth. Sharing God and His Son, Jesus Christ, became my new mission on the spaceship earth.

You can imagine my great delight when I learned that I would be able to visit the Holy Land with my family during Christmas, 1972. Since I had never visited the Middle East, where the great religions had their birth, there was a high degree of anticipation—would the spiritual experience be as wonderful as that felt on the moon? This was to be another discovery voyage for Jim Irwin.

8

As a goodwill ambassador to the Holy Land, there were many semiofficial meetings with government officials and many speaking engagements. We arrived in Amman, Jordan, after an eventful flight—including a forced landing outside Damascus. There was little delay before we began our drive down into the depths of the Jordan Rift Valley, across the Allenby Bridge, by Jericho, and up into the Judean wilderness. I felt like a pilgrim as we wound our way up through the wild, barren mountains to Bethany and on to Jerusalem, the City of God.

We spent our first day traveling to the lowest place on the earth, the Dead Sea, and with Prof. Yigael Yadin as our guide, we visited the magnificent site of Masada with its tragic, breathtaking past. On our return, we inspected the site of Qumran where the far-famed Dead Sea Scrolls were produced and near where they were found.

On Christmas Eve, Mary and I attended a reception held by Mr. Elias M. Freij, mayor of Bethlehem. Mr. Harold Wilson of England and I addressed the reception, representing our countries. That evening I addressed the crowd of pilgrims gathered in Bethlehem square and shared the Christmas story and my personal story. I thought back to my youthful days when I participated in the church Christmas program. I had come a long way. After the program, the mayor took our family to the revered birth site in the Church of the Nativity, where we prayed together as a family in that very holy place.

On Christmas morning I spoke at the Garden Tomb. The stark reality of the empty tomb impressed me anew with the fact of Christ's resurrection.

From Jerusalem, we drove north through Samaria and had a drink from Jacob's well. That night we slept peacefully on the shores of the Sea of Galilee. The next day we lunched on St. Peter fish, and that evening I shared my moon experience with those at Kibbutz En Gev, across the sea.

It was a very winding road to the top of Mount Tabor from where we could see into the Plain of Esdraelon (Armageddon) 9 and to the Mediterranean. We had lunch with the mayors of Upper and Lower Nazareth, and then the Israeli Air Force insisted that I also have lunch with them at a base just west of Nazareth before we flew across the Plain of Armageddon to Tel Aviv. What a beautiful plain for the world's last great struggle!, Mount Carmel was a tranquil sight as the sun sank into the Mediterranean.

After two functions in Tel Aviv we drove back to Jerusalem. It was about midnight, a clear desert sky, and a half moon that was just hanging above the steeples and minarets of the Holy City. The moon was inclined so that it appeared to be a golden goblet pouring out its blessings upon the City of the Great King. A most remarkable and memorable sight! When on the moon we had to look directly overhead to see the earth and then it was a half earth—the size of a marble. Now, from the earth, we saw the moon in its stirring beauty.

We had an opportunity to visit with Mrs. Golda Meir and her grandchildren. I presented her a flag of Israel which we had flown to the moon. With her I shared my feeling of the presence of God on the moon. She told me that she had experienced a very similar feeling when on Mount Sinai.

The time went very quickly and before we knew it, it was time to return to Jordan, so we retraced our travel through Jericho.

The people of Jordan were very gracious to us. King Hussein and Prince Hassan took care of our desires, including a flight to Aqaba and then a helicopter flight to Petra. Of course, the final journey into Petra was by jeep. That fascinating city carved from the sandstone canyons captured our imagination, and we were loath to leave. Once back in Aqaba, we visited with the king and Queen Alia at their beach house.

Prince Hassan arranged a personal tour to Hassan Air Base, where I briefed the pilots on my mission. They scheduled a scramble takeoff of two F-104s and a flyby in my honor. I visited the hospital at Aijalon and returned by helicopter to Jordan University, flying over the very well preserved city of Jerash.

10   The final evening was the most exciting opportunity. I addressed the royalty of Jordan and presented to the king the flag of Jordan that we had carried to the moon.

What a privileged and happy man I am to have been to the moon and to the Holy Land. God revealed himself to me on the moon, and many times I felt closer to Him when in the Holy Land because I had walked where Jesus had walked.

As I look back on both experiences, I can see many similarities and differences regarding the moon and the Holy Land. The stark, barren nature of the moon is reflected in the barren badlands of the Wilderness of Judea. The isolation found here provides a place and time to reflect on the purpose of our lives. I can understand why Jesus went into this Wilderness as part of the preparation for the grand ordeal of His life.

Rocks seem to be everywhere—on the moon and in the Holy Land. On the moon, we found the "Genesis Rock"; and in the Holy Land, three of the most magnificent temples in history have been placed on the great rock on Mount Moriah. Only a few men have walked on the mountains of the moon, while many mighty souls have walked upon the heights of the Holy Land, and they are embroidered with the emblems of the most profound history known to man.

The moon is devoid of life in any form. The richest Life on earth was found in the Holy Land. The Son of God came down to visit the spacecraft earth and to impart His plan for our lives. The moon may occasionally cast light on the earth, but the Spirit of Jesus Christ can illuminate all our darkest hours. God has given man the hope and inspiration to "reach out and touch the face of God."

I have now read Dr. Owen's book *The Holy Land* and am much better able to relive my meaningful experiences in that land. I only wish I had had the opportunity of reading this book before I made my trip.

The scriptural injunction is "Go and walk through the land, and describe it," and Dr. Owen has spent a lifetime researching this part of the world and has the talent to give a total picture combining geography, topography, and the rich heritage of its ancient past. The book covers the entire area of the Holy Land 11 —Lebanon, Israel, Jordan, and Syria. It begins, not in Jerusalem, but in the northern city of Ras Shamra. From there you will travel south, going into all sections, sites, and cities of that marvelous land—from Phoenicia to Petra.

I know you will cherish the experience of the Holy Land under the expert guidance of Dr. Owen. I now look forward to another visit because I feel like an expert after reading this book, *The Holy Land.*

—James B. Irwin
Astronaut, Apollo 15

*

The Coastal Plain

*

CHAPTER 1

The Land of Canaan

The land of Canaan!" That is
what all Bible readers think of when they think of Palestine in its
morning years. And Canaan's land it became when Canaan, the
grandson of Noah, came from Babylon about 2900-2800 B.C. and
"staked his rights" on the coastal plains north of Mount Carmel.
His 11 sons became the progenitors of the people afterwards
known as Canaanites.[1]

14

Sidon, the firstborn son, not only had the honor of having
the first Canaanitish city called by his name, but inherited all the

originally inhabited coastal strip and ruled over the Sidonians, who later were called Phoenicians.[2] His 10 brothers settled over Palestine and Syria, each taking homesteads wherever it seemed to please his fancy and suit the convenience of all concerned. Wherever they went, they were known as Canaanites, and the entire country became known as "the land of Canaan."

Eight centuries of occupation and expansion had firmly fixed this in every mind when Abraham came this way.[3] For nearly 1,000 years they wrote with Babylonian cuneiform script, then either borrowed or carved characters of their own and formed them into the Phoenician alphabet and passed them on to the world.

The Sidonians planted a string of cities and built highways along the seaside from Mount Carmel in the south to Byblos and Ras Shamra in the north. Fertile but narrow was their coastal strip. The snow-crested mountains shut them in on the east; the Great Sea crowded them on the west. Necessity nudged and opportunity urged. From the sea they caught fish; from the sands they made glass; from the murex shells they extracted dye; and from the worms they obtained silk. The challenge of the sea was accepted when they hewed timbers for their ships, carried cargoes and mails, established commercial relationships with the peoples of the then known world, and courageously sailed the seas until trade became their delight and glory.

The Phoenicians founded proud and prosperous colonies in Carthage, Malta, Sardinia, Tunis, and Spain; then broke out of the Mediterranean and sought their fortunes beyond the Gates of Hercules. The Azores, Madeira, the British Isles, and other faraway shores saw their sails, heard the keen barter of their merchantmen, and recognized them as the most famous mariners of ancient times. But their religion was that of Baal and Ashtaroth (Astarte). To these deities they "made horrible sacrifice of manhood, feminine purity, and child life."[4] Their religion destroyed them. Succeeding generations have admired their genius but revolted against their religion.

15

Some of the chief cities and leading points of interest in Phoenicia are: Ras Shamra (Ugarit), Arvad, Byblos, the Dog River, the Pass of the Conquerors, Beirut, Sidon, Zarephath, the River Leontes or Litany River, Tyre, and the Ladder of Tyre.

Ras Shamra, known in ancient times as *Ugarit,* was a thriving commercial and religious center with its Canaanite beginnings in the Early Bronze period—probably about 2900 B.C. It was located on a hill a half mile from a small harbor and served as a seaport junction between the Mediterranean and the Euphrates. Copper, tin, timber, purple dye, and other riches of the then known world passed through its port for long generations. In the 15th and 14th centuries B.C. it enjoyed unusual prosperity, but about 1350 B.C. it was shocked by an earthquake which devastated the city and port. Afterwards it recovered and enjoyed a measure of prosperity under Hittite and Egyptian influence until about 1200 B.C., when it was invaded from the north and left in ruins.

In modern times it appeared as an attractive mound three-fifths of a mile in diameter and 65 feet in height. In 1828, a Syrian was cultivating his field on top of the mound when his plow struck the roof of a fine-vaulted tomb containing many valuables. This led to 10 carefully directed archaeological campaigns which uncovered temples for worship, schools for learning, a palace with its royal archives, counting houses for commerce, a wealth of materials in storage jars, magnificent vases, many kinds of weights, a pantheon of gods, a pile of 74 well-preserved tools and weapons, and a temple library containing hundreds of clay tablets written during the 15th to 14th centuries B.C. Many of these tablets were written in the conventional cuneiform script, but more than 600 tablets were written with 30 characters or letters which formed an alphabet of the early Semitic language closely related to the Hebrew. Many of the homes were built around an open court and had many rooms, including bathrooms and other sanitary facilities.

Arvad, now called Ruwad, was an ancient Phoenician city, located on a small island two miles off the coast, directly south of Ras Shamra. The Arvadites were descendants of Canaan—close relatives of the people of Tyre, for whom they served as mariners, pilots, and guards (Ezek. 27:8, 11). The city was first mentioned in the Amarna letters of the 14th century B.C. and later appeared

16

engraved on the Assyrian Bronze Gates of Shemaneser III (858-824).

Byblos, 25 miles north of Beirut, was a small settlement as early as 2900 B.C. and was among the first cities developed by the Canaanites. It had a small but adequate harbor. In the Bible it was known as Gebal (Ezek. 27:9). In Phoenician mythology, the nearby castle-crowned rock was where the strikingly handsome Adonis lived and was loved by Astarte, the beautiful goddess of love and fruitfulness. While hunting, Adonis was wounded by a wild boar and perished before Astarte could save him. Here in later years, the Phoenicians and Greeks of the Adonis cult gathered each autumn to mourn with Astarte over the death of her lover, and each spring, when the goddess of fertility prevailed, they met for mystic festivals.

> *Astoreth, whom the Phoenicians called Astarte,*
> *Queen of heaven, with crescent horns;*
> *To whose bright image nightly by the moon*
> *Sidonian virgins paid their vows and song.*

Byblos was the intellectual center of the ancient Phoenician world and was known as the City of Books because the Phoenicians imported crude papyrus from Egypt and refined it into writing materials for documents, accounts, and chronicles. In Greek the word *byblos* meant papyrus, and this city was the intermediary source of their papyrus supply; therefore they called it Byblos. And later through the Latin *biblia* came our word *Bible*—the Book of Books. Thus the papyrus industry at Byblos gave to the world the word *Bible*.

From here, during the 14th century B.C., the governor of Byblos wrote 13 of the Tell El Amarna letters to the ruling Pharaoh of Egypt. Here the medieval Crusaders first tasted sugarcane.

The excavations carried on in the ruins of this ancient city have disclosed some most interesting facts that have to do with the language, religion, commerce, and customs of the people—especially during the 14th to 12th centuries B.C. In the necropolis royal tombs were found containing funeral offerings—of gold, silver, bronze, and alabaster. On the sarcophagus of Ahiram, king of Gebal (1000 B.C.), was an inscription in the earlier form of Hebrew writing, and at other places in the ruins were found inscriptions in the cuneiform and hieroglyphic scripts.

Some miles southward from Byblos, the **Dog River** penetrates a picturesque mountain defile and empties into the beautiful Bay of St. George. The spot teems with historic interest, but the interest centers not in the river itself nor in the valley through which it flows. On the cliffs facing the sea, upon the ragged faces of which have been carved a series of wonderfully fascinating inscriptions, are memorials of "the conquerors of antiquity who

High on the cliffs south of the Dog River are a series of carvings and inscriptions, apparently memorials to various conquerors.

have passed this way, and, in passing have stopped to leave the indelible stamp of their achievements."

There are upward of a dozen inscriptions, one or two in Latin and Greek, but the majority commemorating the valor of the Assyrian monarchs, among whom are Shalmaneser II and Tiglath-Pileser III. In a panel cut deep into the rock is the seal and unmistakable hieroglyphic inscription of Rameses II, who passed in his triumphant progress against the Hittites to Kadesh and dedicated tablets to the great gods of Egypt. Singularly enough, beside the finest of Rameses' Egyptian panels, there was added, about 670 B.C., that of the Assyrian King Esar-Haddon in cap and curly beard, who passed in the reverse direction with his Assyrian host to overrun Palestine and enslave Egypt.

The Crusaders, the Saracens, the Turks, the French, and the British have inscribed tablets which tell of their military achievements. Here, side by side, graven upon this towering rock cliff, some of these have "looked out over the same restless sea for almost three millenniums—mid springtime and harvest, dawn and sunset, storm and calm."[5]

What an illustration is here given of the march of the military might of the ages; yet the slow, passing centuries have exacted their due. In many instances, while the general outlines are very apparent, the cuneiform characters of Babylon and the hieroglyphics of the Pharaohs are now scarcely discernible.

Some few miles southwest of the passageway of the conquerors, lifting itself tier upon tier above the Mediterranean Sea, lies the port city of **Beirut** upon which nature has lavished rich gifts. Myriads of fronded palms stand here in their stateliness. Pine, fir, and cedar are reminders of the distant past. Orange, almond, and oleander blossoms waft their fragrance out over the sea, across the colorful landscape, and up the snow-capped Lebanons which serve as a distant, though fitting, background.

On the seaward side the azure bay—resting in its quiet beauty; or tossing its white, billowy, spray like dust into the air; or heaving its great swells to the consternation of landing tourists —completes a picture of irresistible charm for all types and moods of humanity. One contemplates the past with all its grandeur and glory, as well as its wreckage and its ruin.

Beirut was old even among the Phoenicians, being surpassed in age only by Sidon and Byblos. Some think it the Beroth of Samuel and Ezekiel. Alexander the Great captured it from the Phoenicians. The Romans named it Berytus after the daughter of Emperor Augustus. She must have been possessed of exquisite charm and beauty that this place should have reminded them of her.

It is mentioned in the Tell El Amarna tablets of the 15th century. Strabo, Pliny, Ptolemy, and Josephus attest its importance in their time. Under the Romans, Beirut became a mighty military center, the seat of the celebrated school of law, and an outpost of Latin culture in the Greek-speaking and Hellenized Orient. To it students flocked from almost all parts of the known world. Some were said to have passed by Athens and Alexandria to study law at Beirut. It continued as a seat of learning until A.D. 551, when the city was largely leveled by an earthquake, followed by a tidal wave.

In afteryears the city was rebuilt and steadily grew in importance to a position of first place among Syrian and Palestinian cities as a commercial, religious, and educational center. Thousands of young men and women came to study at Beirut's four main universities: Lebanese, French, Jesuit, and American. The last was the largest in the Middle East; in the years immediately preceding the civil war, it had more than 3,000 students from 44 countries and 20 different religious groups. The Syrian Protestant College and many other smaller institutions of learning also have constituted an important factor in the development of the entire Levant.

Cultivated and earnest professors and teachers have devoted themselves with marvelous diligence, ability, and fidelity to the work of educating the young men and women who came here from all areas known as Bible lands. Teachers, ministers, doctors, lawyers, and businessmen are now scattered throughout these eastern Mediterranean countries, and the majority are the products of these splendid institutions of learning. Beirut became recognized as an educational center second to none in the Middle East, and it is hoped that the devastation of the war will not have crippled beyond recovery this monumental facet of this once beautiful city.

Not long ago, Beirut had also become an "oasis of pleasure," with its 86 banks, 15,000 hotel beds, hundreds of dazzling new apartment buildings, along with 500,000 visitors who spent some $50 million each year in Beirut and the surrounding country. That picture has changed drastically and tragically but hopefully not beyond the possibility of recovery.

Leaving the city and going south along the Phoenician Plain, one passes through that fair forest of pines—the famous "snow-bar" which yields some of the world's most delicious pine kernels.

Stretches of red sand which skirt Beirut to the south, lead on to the vast olive garden reputed to be the second largest in the world. Numerous villages, made picturesque by pines, dot the plains or cling to the hillsides. Pastures and grainfields cover the floor of the valley. Millions of leafy mulberry trees, kept to a moderate height, remind one that he has come to the home of the renowned silk industry of Lebanon. But alas! The scientific process by which "silk" is manufactured has all but put the silk-worm out of business. Many of the hillsides are carefully terraced and sown with wheat and barley or planted with vines, figs, or mulberry trees.

Passing through a scenic area broken here and there by villages, olive gardens, and orange groves, the road enters the village of **El-Jiya**, where the Mohammedans have a white-domed shrine in honor of the prophet Jonah, whom they say was cast up onto the shore in this vicinity by a whale. From here he is said to have taken the most direct road to Nineveh.

On nearing the city of **Sidon**—20 miles south of Beirut—the plain widens to almost five miles. The city and its environs lie in an almost Edenic setting of green gardens, grain, and orchards, watered by the aid of a great waterwheel slowly turning its 21 ponderous wooden frame, raising its jars from hidden depths, and emptying them in wearisome succession into a small tank.

From here the water is led off to nourish the growths of palms, pomegranates, plums, almonds, bananas, apricots, figs, olives, melons, citrons, pears, peaches, cherries, apples, and oranges.

Beautiful for situation is this mother city of the Phoenicians. Three streams flow into the plain, bringing the elixir of life worth millions. In older times an aqueduct came down from the mountains, bringing an abundant supply of cool, refreshing water from the copious spring known as the Fountain of the Cup. The display of skill evidenced in this ruined water system shows advanced knowledge of engineering in those distant days.   .

Sidon was one of the older cities of the world, being mentioned both in the Book of Genesis and in the Homeric poems. It was celebrated for its purple-dyed fabrics, its silverware, its manufacture of glass, and its shipbuilding industry. In Solomon's time there was none that had "the skill to hew timbers like the Sidonians."[6] They assisted Solomon in his preparations for the building of the Temple. They also brought cedar trees from Lebanon to the sea and sent them on rafts to Joppa for the building of both Solomon's and Herod's temples.

Homer extols the purple-dyed garments woven by the Sidonian women, and praises the silver and metal work as famous beyond all others of the kind in the world.[7] These luxuries were used by the rich of Europe, Asia, and Africa.

According to Strabo, Sidon early achieved fame because of its proficiency in philosophy, science, and art—but especially in astronomy. For wealth, commerce, luxury, vice, and power it was unequalled in the Levant until Tyre outstripped it, and Shalmaneser conquered it in 725 B.C.

Paul came by Sidon when on his way to Rome and was allowed "liberty to go unto his friends" there and to eat and drink with them.[8] During the two centuries of the Crusades, Sidon was in the hands of the Christians several times, once for 25 years, but in A.D. 1291, it passed into the hands of the Mohammedans.

22   Archaeologists have unearthed a remarkable sepulchre near here containing a number of exquisitely carved marble sarcophagi. They are believed to belong to some of Alexander's

high military officials who fell in the Battle of Issus and the Siege of Tyre. One especially fine sarcophagus is thought by some to have belonged to Alexander himself. It is now displayed in the Constantinople Museum as the "sarcophagus of Alexander the Great."

Successive waves of conquest have swept away almost all signs of the ancient city. "Sidon the Great," as it was called by Joshua, has long since been spoiled. Only the ruins of the fine old 13th-century castle of Louis in the upper portion of the town, a few columns, broken statues, sarcophagi, and smaller bits of architectural remains attest the city's former fame. Encircled by the sea and standing on a rock a little way from the mainland are the ruins of a 12th-century fortress, *Qal-at-el Bahr,* which can be reached only by a narrow bridge of stone.

The Sidon of a few decades ago was so poorly maintained that travelers frequently spoke of it as the place where the "king of fleas" held world court. But conditions have steadily improved until Sidon (Saida) is now a growing town where some 40,000 people carry on various forms of light industry and cultivate extensive gardens and orchards which produce vast quantities of fruits and vegetables. Considerable credit is due Gerald Institute, a unit of the Syrian Protestant Mission; two American high schools; and Dr. Shabb's excellent, 24-bed hospital—all founded under Christian and American auspices.

Along the old Roman thoroughfare, eight miles south of Sidon, is **Zarephath** or **Sarepta.** Zarephath means "Melting Houses," which indicates it as a place of furnaces—a chief center for the far-famed glassworks of ancient Phoenicia. Its greatness, however, lies in the noble lesson of faith taught by the plain, rugged prophet Elijah and the obedient, generous-hearted widow. Here in an atmosphere rank with Baalism, the Lord, through Elijah, multiplied the barrel of meal and the cruse of oil, neither of which failed for a full year; and here the prophet raised the widow's son to life. Oh, what divine loftiness alongside low, groveling, licentious Baalism! 23

God might have sent Elijah to be entertained by one of the glass magnates or a wealthy merchant of Zarephath, but why should the Almighty do rash things? Their smug smartness would have caused them to reveal the secret and fail to receive the honor of feeding and concealing the plain preacher, thus spoiling God's plan. What blessing and renown they missed! What fame the widow received! And, a lesson of obedient faith she taught the more sophisticated world.

Sarepta (Zarephath) is located on a promontory within a small but attractive plain close to the shore. Its ruins are scattered over the plain at intervals for more than a mile. A rather flourishing city it must have been in its glory days. But now its human habitation has all gone. A new village called Serepta lies two miles inland under the shelter of the hills. Kind nature spreads its mantle over the environs of the old site. Its crops, its flocks, and its flowers give it a pastoral scene of beauty and restfulness that impress the many who pass this way.

The way now becomes sacred ground, consecrated not only by the touching visit of the great prophet of Israel "unto a woman that was a widow," but still more by the footprints of One greater than Elijah, who came into the Gentile region of the coasts of Tyre and Sidon and awakened in the Phoenician mother that instance of noble and persistent faith. "Have mercy upon me, O Lord, and heal my child," her plea continued, until her body, like a filthy rag, was humbly thrown at His feet, while her brown, fevered lips uttered that effective plea, "Lord, help me."

On being advised of her lowly station, she gave ready assent, yet in her persistence made the most humble plea ever recorded: "The dogs eat of the crumbs which fall from the master's table." Christ's immediate commendation and verdict was, "O woman, great is thy faith: be it unto thee even as thou wilt."[9] Her plea was granted; her child was saved. With what emotion one reads of this Syrophoenician woman and of the great multitudes from Tyre and Sidon who followed Him. Only eternity will reveal the enduring results of that divine visit to Phoenicia!

The landscape holds one's interest with irresistible force as you proceed southward. On the right hand are the deep blue waters of the Mediterranean, while the left is bounded by the majestic Lebanon Range "crested by *Jebel Sunnin* with its

24

whitened crown." Patches of barley and wheat green the landscape. Halfway between Zarephath and Tyre the **Leontes** or **Litani** River empties into the sea. It is the finest river in all Phoenicia but is little utilized, except in its upper reaches where only a small portion of water is taken from it as it flows southward from Baalbek through the fertile Valley of Beka'a, between the Lebanon and Anti-Lebanon ranges.

The main street of ancient Tyre

It is with mingled emotions that one looks upon **Tyre**, the "crowning city situated at the entry of the sea." Being founded by a colony from the city of Sidon, this proud imperial mistress of the commerce of the then known world was called "The daughter of Sidon . . . whose antiquity is of ancient days."[10] The murex shell, from which they extracted the world's most famous dye, was found here in abundance in ancient times, and so great was the production and sale of the royal dye that it is usually thought of at the mention of Tyre.

Who has not heard how Tyrian shells
Enclosed the blue, that dye of dyes
Whereof one drop worked miracles,
And colored like Astarte's eye
Raw silk the merchant sells?

In Joshua's day it was "the strong city."[11] During the days of David and Solomon, Tyre enjoyed the time of her greatest power under Hiram, whose wisdom and sagacity "enhanced her reputation as a powerful commercial center and as a good and peaceful neighbor." Hiram not only made a league of mutual friendship and assistance with David, but established splendid trade relations between Tyre and Israel. He furnished both material and men for the construction of Solomon's Temple at Jerusalem, and every three years Hiram's and Solomon's fleets sailed together to foreign lands and returned with "gold and silver, ivory, apes, and peacocks." In Ahab's day there was no belle that suited him for a wife like Jezebel, the daughter of the king of Tyre.

One of the later kings of Tyre, Pygmalion, gave his sister Elissa or Dido in marriage to a priest of Astarte. The priest attempted to usurp the throne but lost his life. His widow and a party of sympathizers fled by sea to the north coast of Africa, where they bargained for land and founded the city of Carthage, famous in the Punic Wars and in the period of the Early Church.

The situation of Tyre seemed, in many respects, the most ideal in all the ancient Levant. A small island largely composed of rock, about three-quarters of a mile from the mainland, not only gave the city its name—"the rock"[12]—but made possible a port and a place of refuge such as were denied other ports in much of this eastern Mediterranean world.

The original Tyre was built on the mainland, but New Tyre soon raised its proud and defiant ramparts on the island. The builders made use of limestone from nearby quarries, cedars from the Lebanon mountains, red and gray granite from Egypt, ivory from Chittim, and "every precious stone gathered from afar." The best engineering and architectural skill of the day made of it a city of strong walls and high towers, and a thing "of perfect beauty."[13]

A dip in the rocks from the hills enabled the engineers to send a vigorous subterranean streamlet under the sea to the rock island, where it was brought to the surface and furnished a never-failing supply of cool, refreshing water, in time of both peace and war. The island city was never troubled by want of water and therefore could withstand the longest and most severe sieges.

From its position, Tyre outstripped Sidon, its parent city, and became the mart of nations and a "merchant of the people for many isles." Its ships were among the most beautiful ever seen in the blue waters of the Mediterranean. The boards were of fir, the masts of the cedars of Lebanon, the oars of the oaks of Bashan, the decks of ivory, and the sails were of the costly blue and purple linens of Egypt and the isles of the sea. Many of their mariners were renowned for their knowledge of sails and the sea, some were scientists and philosophers, others were soldiers. Above all they were tradesmen and merchants of the first rank.

With various foreign lands they trafficked in slaves, horses, mules, sheep, goats, apes, peacocks, gold, silver, ivory, ebony, tin, lead, acacia wood, purple-dyed fabrics, and cedar chests in which to place them; also wheat, barley, oil, honey, precious spices, balm, wine, and wool.[14] So famous did the merchant city of Tyre become and so glorious, that seafaring men of other countries joined her marine and became her men of war. She became "the renowned city, which was strong in the sea"—a perennial "world's fair" into which came the merchandise of the then known world.

The greatness of their riches, the volume of their merchandise, the beauty of their city, and the keenness of their wisdom caused the heart of her king to be lifted up in pride. He said, "I sit in the seat of God in the midst of the seas." And as it was with the prince, so with the people. In their pride, in their loftiness, they became jealous of God's chosen people, they rejoiced at Hebrew adversity. With Jerusalem's fall, Tyre burst forth in a song of exultation: "Aha! She is broken that was the gate of the people, her traffic and her wealth are turned to me. I shall be replenished now she is laid waste."[15]

The merchants of Tyre even purchased Hebrew captives and

sold them as slaves. These insults sealed her doom with God. Their proud, haughty spirit only presaged their fall. Ezekiel prophesied that Tyre was to be fought against, decline, and be destroyed.

In keeping with this prophecy came Shalmaneser III, king of Assyria, in 725 B.C., and besieged Samaria, then came up to Tyre and destroyed its mainland; but even with five years' effort was unable to crush the island city. Following this unsuccessful siege, the people rebuilt all that Shalmaneser had destroyed and enjoyed prosperity for 150 years.

Then came Nebuchadnezzar, king of Babylon, in the year 571 B.C., with a vast army well supplied with horses, "engines of war," and with ships. Mighty was that army that strove year after year for 13 years. The mainland city went down, and many maidens and men were taken, and "every head was made bald and every shoulder was peeled." The siege was exceedingly severe, yet out on the fortified rock the flag of Tyre waved proudly to the end. Tyre was humbled, but Nebuchadnezzar gained not the "crowning city . . . for the service that he had served against it."[16]

Under the Persians, who succeeded the Babylonians, the glory of Tyre "was sadly dimmed." Then, in 332 B.C., the city was besieged by Alexander the Great. With comparative ease he took charge of Tyre on the mainland, but the inhabitants retired to the island stronghold, and having command of the sea, defied all the efforts to take their city. Surrounded by mighty walls and with ramparts fronting the mainland to a height of 150 feet, withdrawn from the shore, the task seemed no small one even for Alexander.

A general of the land, Alexander, began the stupendous task of filling up the channel between the island city and the mainland. In this he employed the materials which had made up the mainland city, and in so doing, the prophecy of Ezekiel was fulfilled: "They shall lay thy stones and thy timber and thy dust in the midst of the water."[17] The site of the old city was left bare, yet the causeway was not entirely completed.

28   A storm destroyed much of the causeway. The forces of nature seemed to fight against the famous conqueror, but he

pushed the work with even greater vigor. Immense quantities of trees were used in the new structure, but opposing Tyrian divers swam out and attached grappling hooks with which the defenders then pulled them away into deep water. Fireships were floated against the wooden causeway, and when they crept up near, the defenders poured molten lead and red-hot sand upon Alexander's men. But alas, despite all setbacks, the causeway was finished and Alexander's legions ascended towers and scaling ladders and poured into the place where no other soldiers had been able to enter. A few of the inhabitants escaped by boat, but immense numbers were massacred, 2,000 were crucified or hanged on the seashore, and 30,000 were led away captive and sold as slaves. Fuller says that Alexander's armies "which did fly into other countries were glad to creep into this city."

Rising again from its wreck and ruin, the city staggered to a respectable position but never again enjoyed the prominence it once held. Christ considered it a city of the past. Many people did live here, however, some of which heard Christ and became His followers. Paul, when on his way from Ephesus to Jerusalem, tarried here seven days; and when he departed, the Christians accompanied him until they were out of the city; then, after a prayer on the seashore, they returned home while Paul went on to Jerusalem where he should be bound.[18]

The Moslems took the place during the 7th century; the Crusaders wrested it from them during the 12th; and it remained in their hands for more than a century and a half. When the Crusaders lost Palestine, Tyre was among the last strongholds to be surrendered; but when they saw they were losing all, they had prayers and left the city "without the stroke of a sword, without the tumult of war," and embarking in their vessels, abandoned the city to be occupied by their conquerors. On the morrow the Saracens entered, "no one attempting to prevent them, and they did what they pleased." The fortifications were razed to the ground, and from this blow Tyre has never recovered.

Approaching Tyre today, one will find a small, poorly arranged town located, for the most part, on the sands covering the mole or causeway built from the mainland by Alexander. The inhabitants are chiefly fishermen who make the rocks and sands "a place for the spreading of nets." The crowning city, with "heaped up silver as the dust, and fine gold as the mire of the streets," is all changed now. Her walls are destroyed; her towers are broken down. Her markets and her merchandise, and her stately ships, with masts of cedars from Lebanon, benches of ivory, and sails of blue and purple from the isles of Elishah, are no more.

Only shafts of gray and red granite columns, capitals of many kinds of marble, and fragments from the buildings of many generations protrude from the debris, lie in the water, or are buried in confusion. Three cities of the Crusaders lie beneath several feet of debris; below this is what remains of Mohammedan and early Christian Tyre. The Tyre of the Phoenicians and early Canaanites lies below these ruins.

The glory of Tyre thus departed. The prophetic voice has been verified: "I will cause the noise of thy songs to cease; and the sound of thy harps shall be no more heard. And I will make thee like the top of a rock: thou shalt be a place to spread nets upon: for I the Lord have spoken it, saith the Lord God."[19]

> Now on that shore, a lonely guest,
> Some dripping fisherman may rest,
> Watching on rock or naked stone
> His dark net spread before the sun,
> Unconscious of the dooming lay
> That broods o'er that dull spot, and there
> Shall brood for aye.

In the neighborhood of Kanah, a village just a few miles southeast of Tyre, there is a large Phoenician sepulchral monument known as the Tomb of Hiram, King of Tyre.

The pedestal of the tomb is made of three layers of grey limestone, each three feet thick, the top stone extending slightly beyond the other two. The tomb or sarcophagus which rests upon the pedestal is 12 feet long, 6 feet wide, and 6 feet high, and is made of a single block of stone. A heavy lid, which consists of one solid block three feet thick, rests upon the sarcophagus. A large hole in the eastern end of the tomb indicates that vandals have broken into it, probably to secure the royal jewels and precious stones that were interred with the body. Here is the way they entombed Hiram, king of Tyre.

Ras el Nakoura, or "The Ladder of Tyre." Some few miles south of the site of the ancient city the rough hills crowd the sea in bold cliffs, thus forming the natural boundary between modern Lebanon and Israel. Once the steplike passage across these steep, jagged rocks overhanging the sea gave name to the place. Conquerors have marched their men and pulled their chariots and war machines across the Ladder, and travelers have dreaded the crossing; but today one passes on a well-surveyed road which robs it of its old-time dangers. You ascend on the Syrian side and descend into the beautiful Plain of Acre, on the Israeli side.

CHAPTER **2**

The Beautiful Plain of Acre

At *Ras el Nakoura,* one reaches the border line between Lebanon and modern Israel. Soon after leaving the custom house and the border patrol station, you enter the Plain of Acre which sweeps southward for some 20 miles until Mount Carmel lies athwart the way.

The Plain of Acre derives its name from the ancient and picturesque city of Acre. Being 20 miles in length, and having an average width of about 5 miles, the entire area comprises some 60,000 acres. Its eastern boundary is formed by the foothills of

32

the Galilean mountains, its western boundary by the Mediterranean Sea and the beautiful crescent-shaped shoreline of the Bay.

Out across the plain eastward, many springs and two rivers leap from the Galilean hills, or enter from the far-famed plain of Armageddon. The once famous *Belus River,* now known as *Nahr Naman,* is about 3 feet deep and 100 feet wide. It rises in the upland region north of Nazareth, meanders across the north central portion of the plain, drives a number of mills, and finally flows into the bay a few hundred feet south of Acre.

Entering in from the Plain of Armageddon through the pass at *Tell el Kassis* is the *Kishon,* "that ancient river" which runs close by the foot of Carmel, then breaks away for the last two miles and leisurely enters the bay just northeast of Haifa.

The volume of these streams varies with the wet or dry seasons, yet they are always augmented by living springs which rise from the nearby hills. Other splendid springs have, through the recent centuries, been permitted to run uncontrolled over the plain and create unhealthy marshland. Reeds and rushes, thorns and thistles, wild flowers, shrubs, and a few date palms have encumbered the ground and made it famous for its beauty, its fertility, and its longtime idleness.

Between the bay and the plain a broad belt of yellow sand forms a smooth beach, which for centuries has constituted a hard and firm roadway over which kings and conquerors have often led their armies, and pilgrims have trudged on toward the fulfillment of their sacred ambitions.

The history of the Plain of Acre dates back to the earliest Canaanitish settlements on the shore of the Mediterranean. Following the Hebrew Conquest, many of those fertile acres were assigned to the tribe of Zebulun. "Zebulun shall dwell at the shore of the sea, and he shall be a shore for ships."[1]

In a larger sense, however, it may be said that the plain lay within the territory of Asher. Perhaps there was too much of the trader instinct in the seacoast tribesmen and too little of the tiller of the soil, for the people of Zebulun and Asher dwelt among the Canaanites and apparently made little use of these fertile farmlands.

The Phoenicians recognized many things of value about the plain and put it to fair use. Their principal industries were the making of purple dye from the murex shells, and the manufacture of glass from the white sands found in such great abundance along the beach of the Bay of Acre. Pliny, the historian who wrote about A.D. 60, says that the Phoenicians discovered the value of these sands for glassmaking when a merchant ship landed near the mouth of the river Belus.

The ship's cargo consisted of natron, a natural alkaline crystal, usually called saltpeter, found in Egypt. When the crew lighted a fire, they used lumps of natron from the cargo to prop up their kettle. What was their surprise to find afterwards a stream of crystal running from their campfire! The heat acting on the natron and on the sand had caused them to fuse and form glass.[2] This, however, could not have been more than the beginning of the glass industry among the Phoenicians, for the art of making glass was well known in Egypt from much earlier times. But the industry grew to large proportions and was widely used by the Phoenicians as shown by the large quantities of beautiful glassware found in excavations, and wherever Phoenician tombs have been opened. Acre was probably a principal center for the industry, as debris from the glass furnaces is frequently found about the city, particularly in the wadies between Acre and *Kafr Yasif*.

During the Maccabean Wars of the second century before Christ, the Maccabean leaders and the kings of Syria had various encounters on this plain. Paul passed this way as he went to Jerusalem in A.D. 60.[3]

During the Middle Ages vast numbers of pilgrims came this way. In 1163, Benjamin of Tudela visited Acre, where he found nearly 200 Jews. In Haifa he found Jewish tombs but no Jews. On the plain he found no Jews, no tombs, and few signs of life at all. The plain often played a large part in romantic war episodes of men of the Cross. In 1192, Richard the Lion-hearted encamped on the plain in the well-known palm grove where he contracted

34

a malarial fever which detained him four weeks and gave rise to reports of his death.

During the four centuries of Turkish rule in Palestine (1517-1917), Omar Zahar and Ahmed Pasha el Jezzar made themselves famous as rulers in this area. The latter developed the plain, brought water to Acre by means of a very fine aqueduct, constructed the great White Mosque, built an enduring Turkish bath and the splendid White Market, and became responsible for strengthening of the massive stone fortifications and port facilities, much of which stand today as a mute testimony to the enduring quality of his work and that of the Crusaders.

Napoleon Bonaparte fought on this plain in the year 1798, but he and his 13,000 men faced failure and left these plains in the hands of Ahmed Pasha el Jezzar, who died in 1802 and was buried in the great mosque of Acre. When the British assumed control in 1918, the plain was unoccupied save for those who lived in Haifa and Acre and small groups of malaria-stricken Bedouin, with a few *fellahin*.

In 1881, Menahem Ussishkin visited Palestine and dreamed of a day when Jewish people would purchase the lands constituting the Plain of Acre. The lands, he said, should receive back the biblical name—**Emek Zebulun**—according to Gen. 49:13. He was annoyed by the Germans in Haifa who told him Jews could not work the land! He felt they should at least have a chance to try.

Theodor Herzl, the father of modern Zionism, envisioned a day when great ships would lay anchored in the roadstead between Acre and the foot of Carmel. Cupolas, minarets, and grey old castle walls would outline in delightful Oriental silhouettes against the morning skies. The gracefully crescent-shaped bay would be unchanged. But to the south there would be thousands of white villas in green gardens. The whole area from Acre to Carmel would be one great park. The summit of Carmel, too, would be crowned with beautiful homes. A magnificent city would be built beside the sapphire blue Mediterranean. The massive stone which went into the construction of the harbor would make it the safest and most convenient port in the eastern

Mediterranean. Every kind of craft, flying the flags of all nations, would lie sheltered there.

When the late Sir 'Abbas Effendi 'Abdu'l Baha stood on Mount Carmel on February 14, 1914, and looked across the Plain of Acre, he said:

> In the future the distance between Acre and Haifa will be built up and the two cities will join and clasp hands becoming the two terminal sections of one mighty metropolis. As I look now over this scene, I see so clearly that it will become one of the first emporiums of the world. This great semicircular bay will be transformed into the finest harbor, wherein the ships of all nations will seek shelter and refuge. The great vessels of all peoples will come to this port, bringing on their decks thousands and thousands of men and women from every part of the world. The mountain and the plain will be dotted with the most modern buildings and palaces. Industries will be established and various institutions of a philanthropic nature will be founded. The flowers of civilization and culture from all nations will be brought here to blend their fragrances together and blaze the way for the brotherhood of man. Wonderful gardens, orchards, groves, and parks will be lighted by electricity. The entire harbor from Acre to Haifa will be one path of illumination. Powerful searchlights will be placed on both sides of Mount Carmel to guide the steamers. Mount Carmel itself, from top to bottom, will be submerged in a sea of lights. A person standing on the summit of Mount Carmel, and the passengers of the steamers coming to it, will look upon the most sublime and majestic spectacle of the whole world.[4]

As a first step toward reclaiming this unusual plain, the government set aside a large acreage in the well-drained area northeast of Acre, where they established a very large and up-to-date experiment station for the encouragement of agriculture, horticulture, and animal husbandry. The very finest breeds of horses, mules, cattle, hogs, sheep, goats, turkeys, chickens, and ducks are kept and cared for along scientific lines for the express purpose of lending every encouragement possible to the people of the country who will accept any help toward improving their herds, their poultry, their fruits, and the grain of their fields.

During the years in which this experiment station has been in operation, they have proved that bananas, dates, oranges, olives, almonds, grapes, figs, and loquats are well adapted to this section. Both large and small grains and a great number of vegetables thrive on the plain, some of which may be produced for export.

The outstanding move, however, to reclaim the Plain of Acre had its beginning in 1925 when the Haifa Bay Development Company purchased 11,750 acres of this land between Acre and Haifa, and in 1928 resold it to the Jewish National Fund and the Palestine Economic Corporation. It was to be held for the Jews for all time and there was to be no speculation.

The Jews named it Emek Zebulun in conformity with the biblical dictum, "Zebulun shall dwell at the haven of the sea."[5] They took upon themselves the heroic task of reclaiming the plain. This required courage and skill, seeing much of the area was little more than "an oasis of scrub in a wilderness of malaria," a place where millions of mosquitoes carry death as they wing their way across the plain.

Bronzed young Jews, with pickaxe, spade, and dredging machine, dug channels, lined them with concrete, and forced the waters to obey the orders of engineers. Thus the swamps and marshy wastes were drained, death-bearing mosquitoes were destroyed, and the plain leveled and rendered healthy and habitable.

They then employed Prof. Patrie Abercrombie of Liverpool University, who mapped the entire area, surveyed a road across the plain, and divided the land into three zones. Nearest to Haifa was the industrial zone of 4,000 acres, which included about one-third the area. Here they constructed a variety of plants, including oil refineries; steel, concrete, chemical, and glass works; foundries; railway and machine shops; flour mills; woolen mills; canneries; and many other manufacturing and industrial concerns.

The second area was given over as a residential zone where, far from the maddening crowd and away from the noise and bustle of the busy city, the tired worker might occupy his own home in the workers' suburb, while next to him was a settlement for a "middle class," and on beyond was a settlement for the

German Jewish families. Beyond the residential zone is located the agricultural land from which come a rich variety of fruits, vegetables, and dairy produce for the town and residential neighborhoods.

A strip of green trees lies between the industrial and residential zones. This serves as a park, stretching for more than a mile, accomplishing much toward keeping out the smoke and smell of industry from the homes as well as providing a place of rest and quiet when the day's work is done. A splendid drainage system has been completed, the scourge of malaria has fled, the sand hummocks near the sea are being utilized, and practically all of the plain is reclaimed and presents a most charming spot.

The plain, as it now appears in its springtime freshness and buoyancy, presents a *partial* fulfillment of the dreams cherished by the Jews, the Persians, the Frenchmen, and other farsighted world leaders.

When seen from Mount Carmel, there is the highly industrialized area with its hum of economic activity; the pleasant residential sections with their groves of lofty cypress; the rich orchards; the fresh streams; the long reach of perfectly level beach, with men and animals and machines diminishing in the distance; and the broad bay, with its boats and ships, opening out upon the boundless sea. All these combine to excite the mind, enliven the scene, and impress one with the pathos of prophecy.

When out on the higher, less-developed portions of the plain, one feels an irresistible fascination in the enjoyment of a wild beauty spread far and near. Here and there are somewhat broken low ridges, as if to show that nature loves variety. In the springtime there are patches of wheat and barley; then thick bush, arbutus, and wild flowers of the most exquisite red, blue, and yellow spring up in rich luxuriance among the emerald carpet. Along the eastern border are a number of native villages, both in the plain itself and on the slopes of the hills. Thus there meet on this beautiful plain the ancient and the modern—the intriguing past, and the prospect of the future luring man on to a nobler place to live and love and labor.

The three better-known cities of the plain are: Achzib, Acre,

38

and Haifa. *Achzib,* now known as *Es Zib,* is an ancient Phoenician port which crowds the shoreline north of Acre. Twice mentioned in the Bible, this town was regarded as the northern limit of the Holy Land after the return from the Babylonian Captivity. Today it is a native village with little order and less ostentation. Nearby is a thriving Jewish colony.

The ancient city of **Acre,** sometimes called *Acco,* occupies the northern promontory of the Bay of Acre. When viewed from a distance, it is the most picturesque city of Palestine. Historical associations carry its story back to the days before the children of Israel were in Palestine. It is listed on the Egyptian monuments as one of the towns that Thotmes III conquered when he made his famous and exceedingly successful campaign against the Canaanites just after 1500 B.C. Later it was mentioned in the Tel el Amarna letters. And Sennacherib enumerates it among the Phoenician towns he took in 702 B.C.

Acre, along with its surrounding plain, was allotted to the tribe of Asher, but the Israelites were unable to drive out the inhabitants of the place. It never fell to the Jews until during the Maccabean Wars. It was at Acre where Jonathan Maccabaeus met his enemy, Trypho, for an interview, was made a prisoner, and his bodyguard of 1,000 men was massacred, and Jonathan himself was later put to death.[5]

When Pompey invaded Palestine, he made it, along with several other coast towns, a free Greek city-state. Paul refers to his stay in the city of Acre on his way from Damascus to Jerusalem. During the years from A.D. 67 to 70 Vespasian and Titus used Acre as a port of landing and an important military section in their campaign against Galilee and Judea. Josephus mentions the city many times, for it was in nearby Jotapata that he lived and was eventually taken captive by the Romans. Al Harira, a famous Arab poet of about A.D. 1100, praised Acre as "a pleasant meetingplace of the ship and the camel, where lizards may watch the leaping sea-fish, where the camel-driver communes with the sailor, and the fisherman astonishes the tiller of the soil with stories of the sea."

39

The Crusaders made of it their chief port of invasion and

principal base of supplies. Here they fought some of their fiercest battles and eventually suffered one of their saddest defeats. For it was near here that Khalil, the Mameluke Sultan, who reigned in Cairo, swore by the name of Allah in 1291 that he would exterminate the last of the Christians within the limits of his dominions. Gathering an army of 200,000 men, he pitched his camp before the walls of Acre. The Christian forces defending the city were sufficient in size, but division of counsel, confusion, and feverish excitement so enfeebled their efforts and weakened their wills that they turned to the sea for escape.

Thousands gathered their few belongings and hastened to

The fortified seawall of Acre (ancient Acco)

the wharf where they embarked. Only 12,000 knights and warriors were left to defend the stronghold. These held out for 33 days until the Mameluke warriors effected a breach in the walls and began to pour into the city. The inhabitants left in the city were quickly butchered or seized as slaves. The knights fought until there were only seven left to tell the tale of destruction. Thus the fate of the Crusader Kingdom was sealed with the final fall of Acre.

The present city covers an area of 50 acres and is surrounded by walls and fortifications which date from 1750 to 1840 but are for the most part built on Crusader foundations. The only entrance is through the Tower Gate to the southeast.

The strong seawall along the south front of the city is built of very large stones, many of which bear the marks of the Crusaders. The bold western seafront with its loopholed battlemented walls is strong, long, and impressive. Both the north and the east walls have a double line of fortifications and are surrounded by a moat. Places of interest to be seen inside the city are: the Crypt of the Church of St. John (13th century), the Great Mosque of Jezzar Pasha, and the arsenal containing large stones of early 19th-century munitions of war.

A beautiful white marble gateway, novel in style, stood before one of the Crusader churches in Acre. But after a siege of one month, in A.D. 1291, Sultan Khalil of Egypt stormed Acre and carried the gate away to Cairo, Egypt, where it now spans one of the main thoroughfares of that city. The gateway is especially interesting, seeing it is the only perfect relic now left of the many churches built by the Crusaders at Acre.

The external appearance of Acre today is "preeminently picturesque" when viewed from Mount Carmel across the bay, from the deck of a ship, or on a calm, bright, moonlight night when God's lanterns are in the sky.

One mile east of Acre is "Mount Turon," an artificial mound 96 feet high, which dominates the city of Acre and overlooks the plain. Here the great Crusader, Richard the Lion-hearted, 41 encamped in 1191, and here Napoleon planted his batteries in vain in 1799.

Looking across the city of Haifa and its beautiful harbor from the slopes of Mount Carmel.

Haifa, "The Gateway to Israel and the Middle East," is situated between Mount Carmel and the southern end of the Bay of Acre, and not far from where the ancient river Kishon merges into the bay.

Its situation, from a commercial point of view, is the most ideal of all cities in Palestine or Syria. It has before it the most beautiful bay in eastern Mediterranean countries; to its rear is the magnificent Mount Carmel range which juts far out into the sea, forming the best natural breakwater of the entire Levant. Nearby is the fertile Plain of Acre extending away to the foothills where an unlimited supply of fruits and vegetables may be produced.

Many have marveled that the ancients constructed no large city here to accommodate their imports and exports. But such seems to be the case, for there is no certainty that either the Canaanites or the Hebrews had any kind of a city at this exact location. The Greeks and Romans had a small place called Sycaminum (Sycamore) somewhere in this area. The Crusaders, under Tancred, besieged and stormed a comparatively small town here in A.D. 1100. Eighty-seven years later it fell into the hands of Saladin, but was afterwards assaulted and destroyed by Richard the Lion-hearted. Traces of these ruins remain to the present time in the excavated mound of ancient Shikmona.

The present city, however, owes its origin to Omar Zahar, the leader of a strong Bedouin group, who, in 1761, established his seat of government at Acre. Marching his army along the curvature of the bay, he attacked and destroyed a small rebellious town situated just below the northwest point of Mount Carmel, and transported the survivors to the present location, where he built a castle and surrounded the town with a wall. The gates and portions of the old wall stand today, and in this section there are native bazaars conducted in real Oriental style.

The city of Haifa made phenomenal progress during the British occupation from 1918 to 1947. Seeing its possibilities as a commercial city for imports and exports, the British made soundings in the bay and decided on Haifa as *the* deepwater port of Palestine.

In 1927, the contract for a very fine harbor was let to Messrs. Rendel, Palmer, and Tritton for a consideration of £1 million sterling (then U.S. $5 million). After further surveys and an elaboration of plans, one-quarter of a million pounds was added to the original contract price. The first steps toward building the port were taken in 1929, when the engineers opened the stone quarries near Athlit, the Crusader stronghold south of Mount Carmel. The work was fairly well completed in 1933, but has since been extended so as to provide quay space for more ships.

The main breakwater of the harbor is about a mile and a half long. The cost of this breakwater was the largest item of the project. It is formed of natural blocks of quarried stone, graded according to size, the largest weighing some 12-15 tons, being placed on the seaward side. It contains more than 1 million cubic yards of stone and is surmounted by a concrete parapet, with ballards at intervals for end-on moorings for cargo steamers. The other breakwater, known as the lee breakwater, is formed by prolonging the existing railway jetty, and is about half a mile long. It is of less massive structure than the main breakwater. In all, the breakwaters total nearly two miles in length and inclose an area of nearly 300 acres of sheltered water, within which a score of steamers, up to 30,000 tons, can lie at moorings.

A deepwater berth about 1,400 feet long, to accommodate three or four large steamers, was provided, and at the eastern end an oil dock was formed to accommodate the famous Iraq Petroleum Company and other large oil concerns. The port has ample rail and road access, and a site is reserved for a maritime station, which, in time, is to act as the terminal for the proposed Haifa-Baghdad railway. Huge transit sheds allow orange growers to load and unload in stormy weather with little risk to their wares.

The sands dredged from the harbor were placed between the city and the harbor, thus forming a considerable area of newly made land. This was arranged according to modern methods of town planning, and in time the wide streets were lined with some of the world's most beautiful and most modern commercial buildings. Thus traffic was relieved in the congested streets and alleys of the old city, more spacious shopping and social centers were provided, and a new and striking appearance given the city of Haifa. As Israel's northern metropolis, Haifa is now the largest in area and second largest in population.

To enter this beautiful Holy Land harbor, in the eventide of a spring day after a long voyage, one is half encircled by the yellow and white sands of the crescent-shaped bay and sees Mount Carmel like a sentinel on guard keeping watch above the hush of the waves. He feels the soft winds of this congenial clime and is overwhelmed with the consciousness of having come to a pleasant port.

CHAPTER **3**

The Excellency of Carmel

$\mathbf{J}$utting out into the Great Sea and lying between the Plain of Acre and the Plain of Sharon is a long, bold promontory known as Mount Carmel. In naming it Carmel, the ancients regarded it as "The Park," or "The Garden of the Lord." Its excellency was proclaimed in story and in song.

Carmel runs inland from the sea 15 miles and is from 3 to 8 miles wide. At its extreme northwestern point, which extends out into the sea, it is 500 feet high; and about a mile and a half due south of Esfiya, 10 miles away to the southeast, it reaches its highest point of 1,810 feet. From there it gradually falls away to the Plain of Armageddon.

Its general shape is that of a triangle with its apex pointing northwest, but this is seldom noticed, seeing the important portions of the mountain appear as a long, rugged ridge oriented northwest to southeast. Its massiveness reminds one of a huge, houndlike creature which, having crossed the great Plain of Armageddon, has lain down beside the Kishon "with a firm foothold upon the sea."[1] But this creature impression is gained only from its general form when one views it from afar. At close range it pleases and fascinates.

A high road runs along its central watershed, and from this extend fairly long parallel spurs, divided in places by narrow, winding valleys. All along the top of this rugged ridge one finds outcroppings of a thin layer of chalky limestone overlaid by a thin layer of soil, studded here and there with stunted pine and scattered flowering bush. Farther down the mountainsides one finds hard, gray limestone, covered for the most part by a rich, red soil which is remarkably productive. Here grow a few large oaks—reminders of its ancient glory. Anxious to preserve these, the government has set aside this area as the Haifa-Carmel National Park.

In ancient times the royal vineyards of King Uzziah were located on Mount Carmel, and it was used for the production of fruits and flowers for various purposes. Throughout the Old Testament, Carmel stood as a symbol of vast productiveness and quiet, fixed beauty enveloped in an atmosphere of refined sacredness. It received unstinted praise, and its beauty and usefulness were far famed.

Along with Sharon, Lebanon, Tabor, and Bashan, it was regarded as reflecting the favor of the Lord. Of all the praise given, it was quite deserving; for it alone, of all mountains of the Levant, extended far into the sea and formed a natural, crescentlike bay which was one of the finest and most beautiful known to man.

46 Carmel was the first of Israel's highlands to receive the moisture that came from the Mediterranean Sea, and its dews were usually quite heavy throughout the summer months. Therefore

in Israel's glory days it was clothed with grand forests, vast olive orchards, productive vineyards, flowering shrubs, and myriads of wild flowers.

Much of its grace and parklike beauty passed when men of various wars and Turkish axmen cut away its fine forests, thus permitting heavy rains to wash much of its soil to lower levels. Yet just as time heals the hurt of life, so nature has slowly, yet faithfully, worked toward restoring its beautiful trees, renewing its soil, and replacing its flowering bushes and shrubs, while more and more wild flowers have ever sprung up with the passing seasons.

Today there are ruined sites, ancient cisterns, millstones, and oil and wine presses to attest its former productiveness. And, too, there are olive groves and vineyards, carob and oak, pine and plane trees which thrive at various places on the mountain. Carmel's wonderful array of flowering and perfumed shrubs, such as bay, storax, linden, arbutus, and innumerable others, waft their fragrance through the air and verily set the mountainsides aflame with beauty throughout the spring and far into the summer. A thousand glades on Carmel are graced with flowers of every hue; such as crocus, cyclamen, tulip, and "the lily of the field" which bloom in wild profusion. The best of Carmel's beauty comes in the spring, yet it remains quite green and beautiful throughout the year; for when the rain-bearing winds from the Mediterranean cease in May, then come the heavy dews which keep it refreshed throughout the summer months.

Otto van Richter declares, "There is no mountain in or around Palestine that retains its beauty as Carmel does; its groves are few, but they are luxuriant; no crags are there, nor precipices, nor rocks for wild goats." And the famous Belgian traveller, Van de Velde, declares, "I have not found in Galilee nor along the coasts nor on the plain any flower that I did not find on Carmel." The wild flowers of Carmel, when properly dried and pressed, never lose their color. Pope sang of it: "Carmel! thy flowery top perfumes the skies."

47

Solomon beheld Carmel's graceful form and verdant beauty and likened it to "the head of a bride." "Thine head upon thee is like Carmel, and the hair of thine head like purple; the king is held in the galleries."[2]

Mount Carmel's natural beauty, however, was but a dim shadow of its spiritual beauty and fertility, for its chief renown was as *a place of worship*. It was considered a fit sanctuary for those who stood in awe before nature at its best, or for those who bowed down before the Maker of heaven and earth and the beautiful sea that sang at the foot of that glorious headland which lifted itself far out above the waters of the beautiful Mediterranean.

Here came the ancient Canaanites worshiping their gods on the quiet and sunny summit of Carmel. Then came the mighty prophet Elijah who established a school of the prophets here and trained many young men for the work of the Lord.

Along the coast northward at Sidon, Baal and Ashtaroth were worshiped without restraint in all the abominations of those foul, debasing, and immoral idolatries. The king himself was the priest, and his royal daughter the priestess. And in order not to marry out of royal line, Ahab, the young king of Israel, passed by the daughters of Israel and yielded to the flirtations of Jezebel, the worldly, fastidious daughter of the king of Tyre. He took the heathen enchantress to wife. When at the royal courts at Samaria and Jezreel, she lived in luxury but not in idleness. She sat down to her table to eat and to drink; she rose up to pervert the truth and to seduce the people away from what pure worship of God as remained among them.

Temples of Baal were created, priests with highly colored robes burned incense, "high places" were built, images were set up, altars of Baal and Ashtaroth became numerous both at the court and upon those picturesque hills and mountains of Samaria.

When this Baal worship had almost ruined Israel, then came Elijah, that stern yet holy man of God, representing God's prophets, as Moses had represented God's law. With a mission from God to Ahab and Jezebel, this strange yet powerful prophet came

to check the widespread abominations of the court and the people. Suddenly, without warning, he confronted the king and declared: "As the Lord God of Israel liveth, before whom I stand, there shall not be dew nor rain these years, but according to my word."[3] When no dew nor rain had come for three years and six months, and Ahab and Israel had time to think, then Elijah reappeared as suddenly as he had gone away.

In dramatic style, Elijah said to Ahab, "Now therefore send, and gather to me all Israel, unto Mount Carmel, and the prophets of Baal four hundred and fifty, and the prophets of the groves four hundred, which eat at Jezebel's table." The king obeyed the request of the plain, powerful man of God. In brief time there were gathered all the 850 leaders of the Baal cult and a vast concourse of the people along with Ahab to a vast natural amphitheater on the southeast brow of Mount Carmel.

Here on this mountain, poised between the countries of Israel and Phoenicia, the lone prophet of the Lord stepped before the king and the vast assemblage of people and said, "How long halt ye between two opinions? If the Lord be God, follow him: but if Baal, then follow him." The people being speechless, Elijah continued,

> I, even I only, remain a prophet of the Lord; but Baal's prophets are four hundred and fifty men. Let them therefore give us two bullocks; and let them choose one bullock for themselves, and cut it in pieces, and lay it on wood, and put no fire under: and I will dress the other bullock, and lay it on wood, and put no fire under: and call ye on the name of the Lord: and the God that answereth by fire, let him be God.[4]

The altars were prepared, and there followed the strange, weird scene of the priests hysterically calling in vain upon Baal. They leaped upon the altar, they cut themselves, and cried out hour after hour for the fire from heaven, but none came. Then near the time of the evening sacrifice, while the sun was lowering over Mount Carmel and the Mediterranean, Elijah repaired the altar and calmly stood before God and quietly prayed, "Hear me, O Jehovah, hear me, that this people may know that thou, Jehovah, art God."

Then the fire fell from heaven, and the water with which the sacrifice had been drenched was licked up, and the burnt offering and the wood were consumed. The awe-stricken people fell on their faces and cried out. "The Lord, he is God! The Lord, he is

God!" At the foot of the mountain where ran the river Kishon, the priests of Baal were slain, and the water ran red with their unhallowed blood.

The prophet withdrew from the crowd and bowed himself to the earth in prayer. After a time he asked his servant to go to the highest point on the mountain and look toward the sea for signs of rain. Over and over he went and returned until on his return the seventh time he reported seeing a small cloud arising out of the sea "like a man's hand." Elijah then said to him, "Go up, say unto Ahab, Prepare thy chariot, and get thee down, that the rain stop thee not."

Then the heavens grew black with clouds and wind, and there was a great rain, and Ahab mounted his chariot and drove off in furious haste toward Jezreel. "And the hand of the Lord was on Elijah: and he girded up his loins, and ran before Ahab to the entrance of Jezreel."[5] How vivid the landscapes into which the narrative fits perfectly!

High up on the southeast brow of Carmel, 1,685 feet above sea level and 13 miles from the sea, is a natural amphitheater and a rude quadrangular structure of hewn stones known by everyone as *El Mukhrakah,* or "the burning of the Lord." There, says tradition, is the place where Elijah met the idolatrous priests of Baal, the favorites of Ahab and Jezebel, and gained the day for the Lord Jehovah. Nearby is the spring from which the water for sacrifice was obtained. Beneath flows the river Kishon, which the Arabs call *Nahr el Mukhattar,* "The River of the Massacre," which, of course, harks back to the slaughter of the priests of Baal, and perhaps also to the destruction of Sisera's host.

At the bend of the stream, at the nearest point to the place of sacrifice, there is a "tell" or ancient townsite, which is called Tell el Kassis ("The Hill of the Priests"), and this most probably was the place where they either executed or buried the priests of Baal.

Traditions and miraculous stories of the prophet Elijah became so common during succeeding centuries that he readily became the patron saint of various Jewish, Christian, Mohammedan, and Druze communities over Palestine and elsewhere.

Mount Carmel itself, because of the mighty manifestations of divine power, became a kind of memorial to Elijah, a symbol of religious power, a shrine and a place of retreat to which many would resort. Pythagoras, the Greek philosopher and astrologer, spent some time here during the fifth century B.C.; and Tacitus, the Roman orator and historian, tells us that an altar to the God of Carmel stood on top of the mountain, and that Vespasian caused the oracle to be consulted in A.D. 69, while on his Palestinian campaign.

The northwestern promontory overlooking the sea came to be considered one of the most sacred parts of the mountain. Here, it is said, the prophet Elijah, "wearing the yellowed shawl of wisdom" and bearing the mighty presence of God, chose these heights overlooking the sea and built a school of the prophets. The spot now held in greatest veneration by Christians, Arabs, and Druzes, is a "grotto" about 15 feet long and 12 feet high, where the prophet is said to have resorted for prayer and security. Over this grotto there now stands a magnificent church, and adjoining it is the Carmelite Monastery. Farther down the mountainside toward Haifa is the great gilt-domed Temple of the Bahia—one of the quietest and most picturesque spots of this area.

Being a place of beauty, where grow so many trees, flowering shrubs, and wild flowers, and extending out into the sea and lifting its head 500 feet above the water, Mount Carmel is by nature a cool, quiet retreat and an ideal residential area for those who can afford such luxury of life, and for thousands of others who come for a brief time to escape the midsummer heat of other less-favored sections of Palestine. A number of Jewish towns and villas are located on the sides or on the summit of Carmel, the most flourishing of which is villalike Carmelia with its beautiful homes and contented people—in fact, the entire central and western portions of Mount Carmel are now well settled with elegant homes, hotels, and pensions.

Hadar Hacarmel, "the splendor of Carmel," is built on the slope of Carmel and at the same time is really within the municipal boundaries of Haifa. The first step towards the forming of

Hadar Hacarmel was the erection of the Hebrew Technical Institute building in 1912. Other educational institutions of various types, including public and private kindergartens, elementary and secondary schools, colleges of music, and public libraries, soon followed. The first homes in Hadar Hacarmel were built in 1920. Then from 1924 to 1939, its population grew to 36,000. Today it is a large, compact, garden, resident city of detached villas of individual design with front lawns, clean concrete houses, tree-lined boulevards, comfortable boarding houses, hotels, hospitals, and thousands of dwellings. It is one of the chief centers of Jewish public and cultural life for Haifa and the surrounding area.

Somewhat higher on up Carmel lies Achuzat Sir Herbert Samuel, named after the first high commissioner for Palestine, and known simply as *Achuza.* It is a gardenlike settlement with about 5,000 inhabitants and a great future.

Yaarot Hacarmel, the settlement highest on the mountain, has an area of 2,000 acres, where enterprising laborers cultivate the soil and work to acquire plots of land of their own. Other newer homes and building projects almost completely take up all available building sites on the western half of Mount Carmel. Two or three picturesque Arab villages stand well back eastward on the mountain.

A rare experience is in store for any who may on a spring day stand on Mount Carmel, at one of its highest points, and forgetting self and life's small demands, just open wide the heart and eyes and see one of the grandest countrysides that may ever fall into man's view. Northward lies the picturesque Bay of Acre with its crescentlike beach of yellow sand; and on beyond the ancient city of Acre with its massive gray walls, rare-lit domes, white minarets, and gleaming cupolas, one sees through the haze the white Ladder of Tyre. To the northeast are the fertile hills and vales of northern Galilee, the Lebanon mountains, glistening in their whiteness, and snow-clad Mount Hermon standing in its majesty

—the "chief" of all the mountains of the Holy Land.

Eastward is the grand sweep of the Plain of Armageddon, the hills of Lower Galilee, the wooded slopes of Tabor, Mount

Moreh, Mount Gilboa, with here and there between the gaps, the mountains of Bashan and Gilead on the other side of Jordan.

To the southeast lies the imposing mound of mighty Megiddo and the hilltops of Samaria, with the mountains of Ebal and Gerizim standing out in bold relief.

To the south is the lovely Plain of Sharon with her scattered forest, her vast orange groves, her thriving colonies, and her coast of yellow sand glistening in the sunlight. Southwestward, almost at your feet, lies the battered ruins of Athlit, the last stronghold of the Crusaders.

Westward is the boundless expanse of the Mediterranean Sea; stretching on out as far as the curvature of the earth will permit the eye to see are the blue green waters, shadowed by passing clouds and brightened by the many white sailing ships that gracefully pass during the course of the day. Then at eventide, when the sun dips into the waves, the firmament is fired to a burnished gold, then turns to a lilac and purple, while one dark streak of crimson lines the horizon and fades as the sun sinks into its reddened sea and the glory of the day passes away.

> So when, deep sinking in the rosy main,
> The western sun forsakes the Syrian plain;
> His watery rays reflected luster shed,
> And pours this latest light on Carmel's head.

CHAPTER **4**

The Fertile Plain of Sharon

The Plain of Sharon begins just south of that western portion of Mount Carmel that juts out into the sea. It sweeps southward for some 62 miles to the river Rubin, 7 miles south of Joppa (Tel Aviv). At first the plain is only a few hundred yards wide, then widens to from 1 to 4 miles for about 18 miles, until one approaches the ancient city of Dor,[1] after which there is a gradual increase in width to 10 or 11 miles. This increase in width is maintained until just north of the city of Lydda, where the plain broadens to 13 miles as it connects with the Valley of Aijalon.

54

Sharon is the largest and finest plain west of the Jordan River. Much of its surface is level and well watered; other portions are agreeably varied by sandy ridges, isolated hills, or even chains of hills which afford slightly elevated positions for villages, upland fields, and forests.

Its western border is fringed by the white foam of the sea. But under that foam, the entire coast is underlain with, and composed of, deep beds of coarse, soft sandstone. The perpetual wash of the waves disintegrates and crumbles it into sand and pushes the sand onto the shore, where it is dried by the sun and driven inland by the wind. For long centuries this process has continued, until an almost unbroken ridge of yellow sand stretches along the coast, tending to obstruct the outflow of streams. It is gradually creeping inland at the rate of approximately 3 feet per year. At some points it rises as high as 50 to 60 feet and has covered almost everything in its path for as much as two to four miles. Seeing the steady inundation of the Holy Land's most valuable acres, the Jews in recent decades have become alarmed and planted trees in its path and in places constructed walls and other obstacles to halt the oncoming scourge.

From the sea to the mountains there is a fairly gradual ascent of nearly 200 feet in the elevation of the plain. When the extreme eastern limits of the plain are reached, a fringe of olive groves beautifies the border and demonstrates nature's kindly manner of modifying abruptness.

The Plain of Sharon is traversed by a number of streams of considerable size, which rise in the mountains and flow westward across the plain. The most important of these are the *Crocodile River,* the *Dead River,* the *Salt River,* and the *Auja River.* These four streams are perennial, being fed by springs either far up in the mountains or at their foothills.

The **Crocodile River** rises in the southwestern extremity of Mount Carmel and, from the marshes of the Plain of Dothan, flows westward through wide pastures, by flourishing farms until in its meandering it has crossed most of the plain, then turns slightly northwestward and flows into the sea five miles south of Dor and two miles north of the ruins of Caesarea. The natives call it the *Zerka* or Blue River. Several mills are located on this fine stream, fish abound in its waters, and crocodiles were taken from it as late as 1902.

Now the marshes have been drained and the celebrated Crocodile River canalized. The climate of this region resembles that of Egypt, and the Jewish people grow rice and sugarcane. Here was once located the Roman circuit of the town of Crocodipolis, and many antiques can still be found in the area. The colonists have made a little museum which grows from year to year.

The **Dead River,** known by the natives as *Nahr el-Mefjir,* has its rise on the Plain of Dothan. After flowing across the Plain of Sharon, it empties into the sea two miles south of Caesarea.

The **Salt River,** known by the Crusaders as *Iskanderuneh,* or Alexander's River, drains the center of the plain and enters the sea two miles south of the Jewish colony of Natania.

The **Auja River** is known as the shortest river in Palestine, being less than 10 miles in length, yet it is also the largest river west of the Jordan. It is formed by the confluence of a number of lesser streams, but it has its main source at the large, fine spring at Antipatris, known as *Ras el-Ain.* It is a deep stream with flowers and Syrian papyrus along its banks, and the only genuine pines in Palestine dot the higher banks of its upper course. For long centuries it has had sufficient depth for sailing vessels to make their way some miles inland up this stream. Now much of its waters are being pumped in large pipes southward to irrigate the Negeb.

The river *Rubin* properly belongs to the Plain of the Philistines, as it touches the Plain of Sharon only at its outlet to the sea.

"Sharon" means "The Forest Country," or "The Plain of the Forest." Josephus describes the Plain of Sharon as "The Place Called the Forest." Strabo is said to have called it "a great forest," while the Crusaders called it "The Forest of Assur." Even as late as Napoleon's day, he called it the "Forest of Meski," from the village of Miskieh.

Of the forests which were so very dense in those distant days, there remains only one large oak grove covering an area of about eight square miles in the extreme northeast section of the plain. In going southward, however, one encounters scattered clumps of oak, carob (husks), tamarisk, willow, cyprus, sycamore, eucalyptus, ash, and palm trees. Smaller shrubs are more plentiful.

The soil on most of the plain is now extremely rich, varying from bright red through chocolate brown to deep black, with a few breaks and gullies between low-lying hills. Ninety percent of the area, aside from the sand-blown coastline, lends itself to intense cultivation. And like California and Italy, both its climate and soil are favorable to the growth of cereals, melons, citrus, grapes, olives, and almost every kind of fruits, and flowers. Their specialty is the production of the far-famed Jaffa oranges. Normally the citrus fruit industry exports $75 million to $80 million worth of citrus fruit annually, and more than half of this is grown on the Plain of Sharon.

Millions of flowers of various kinds are cultivated for the

57

Packing the famed Jaffa oranges for shipment

A field of commercial flowers on the Plain of Sharon

markets, and a great variety of wild flowers are scattered over the fields and meadows of the plain—poppies, anemones, narcissus, gladiolus, phlox, daisies, myrtle, and pimpernels. During the spring months the air is well populated with bees and butterflies. The rose of Sharon and the lily of the valley once grew here, but no one now is quite able to positively identify either of these flowers. The word translated "rose" in our Bible is believed by some to have been the narcissus. It blooms here in abundance and is carried around for the benefit of its perfume, yet it is not a true rose. The general consensus is that the lily of the valley is the scarlet anemone, which colors the ground in unforgettable beauty here and elsewhere in Palestine in the late winter and spring. The name *shushan*, translated "lily" in the Scripture, is now used by many of the people as they speak of this flower.

The beginning of man's habitation on this fertile Plain of Sharon is somewhat obscure, yet here and there one finds indication of Egyptian, Canaanitish, and Babylonian influence from two to three thousand years before Christ. In the middle of the 16th century B.C., Egyptian history mentions a conquest of Palestine which is followed some 35 years later by another. During the early 14th century B.C. the Tell El Amarna letters show Palestine to be still subject to Egypt, but they speak of the *Habiru* or Hebrews who were then entering and overrunning the country.

For a time, during the second millenium before Christ, the Philistines and Canaanites occupied this plain, depending on which was the stronger. In time, however, the Philistines overcame the Canaanites and completely ruled the plain. The Isrealites gradually settled here.

During the reign of King David, around 1000 B.C., the Plain of Sharon was the feeding grounds for the royal flocks and herds, and during Solomon's reign the king's table was supplied with meat and other delicious foods from this fertile plain (1 Kings 4:11; 1 Chron. 27:29). Isaiah describes Sharon as a fold for flocks, and its prosperity and excellency was symbolic of the excellency of God.

With Alexander's invasion the Philistine coast and cities were opened to Greek influence. Greek trade came through the harbors; Greek men settled in all the cities; Greek institutions arose; old deities became identified with Greek gods. Though the ancient Philistine stubbornness persisted, it was exercised in defense of civic independence from Greek ideas, Greek manners, and Greek morals.

Coming in 63 B.C., the Romans built roads, drained various areas, sowed fields, protected the forests, planted a string of cities, and developed the plain until under Herod the Great it became the pride of the country. From being merely a place for game, farms, and fruit, it arose to almost first place of importance. Even the capital of Palestine was moved to Caesarea, which was sometimes called "Little Rome."

Across this plain ran the great highway of the nations, and connecting roads were built between such important cities as Jerusalem, Neapolis, and Sebaste in the interior, and Acre on the north and Gaza on the south. The commerce of Damascus, Persia, and India passed this way to Egypt and the colonies of northern Africa. This traffic, along with the constant movement of troops backward and forward, must have made this plain one of the busiest and most populous regions of Syria.

Few places in Palestine are so closely connected with the apostolic history as this tract of coast between Gaza and Acre, and especially the neighborhood of Caesarea.

However, the glory of Rome finally collapsed and the rising power of the Arabs seized the glorious Plain of Sharon in the seventh century. Together with overthrowing the excellency of Rome, the Arabs overthrew the glory and excellency of Sharon, for under the Arabs the plain greatly deteriorated and fell to ruin.

Again deterioration swept over the plain as the Turks, in A.D. 1517, conquered all the lands in the Near East. The Turks permitted the Arabs to occupy the plain, and little effort was made to rebuild it or even to maintain the cities and fields already developed. The rivers and wadies stagnated in many places as debris and sand stopped their flow. Mosquitoes and other insects thrived in these swamps, and soon entire sections of the plain became malaria-infested. The plain deteriorated still farther, being sparsely inhabited by people who only took from the land and did nothing to replenish the woods or fertilize the soil.

The Plain of Sharon is strewn with the wrecks of bygone centuries. Ruined cities, red and gray granite columns protrude above the sands or lie sprawled in the water's edge. These ruins carry us deep into the historical past. Mighty civilizations have been there, but now the Jews are constructing many cities and making a veritable garden spot of most all the plain from north to south. Its cities during the past and present have played and are now playing a large part in the history and development of the plain.

Of the past, there remains the memory and the historic ruins of such cities as Athlit, Dor, Caesarea, Antipatris, Joppa, Lydda, and Ramle. The present modern cities include such important places as Tel Aviv, Benyamina, Hadera, Herzliya, Tulkarm, Raanana, Sarona, Petah Tikva, Mikweh Israel, Rishon Le Zion, and scores of thriving colonies and picturesque villages.

Athlit is located eight miles south of Mount Carmel, slightly west of the coastal road from Acre to Jerusalem. The city site is on a cape which projects about a half mile into the sea, terminating in a compact and rocky promontory. Some have seen in it the

60

appearance of a "clenched fist"—a grim headland thrust out in perpetual defiance. And much of the history of the place would harmonize with such a thought.

Athlit was the last stronghold of the Jews in their fight for independence in A.D. 130, but with the Jewish defeat all was left in ruins until the coming of the Crusaders, who saw it as an ideal location at which to check the enemy's forays from Mount Tabor, some 30 miles east. In 1217, they began the construction of one of the most important crusading strongholds in Palestine, the Castle of the Pilgrims, which, when finished in 1218, was one of the strongest and finest of the Latin castles.

This imposing four-story castle fortress, of which ruins remain today, stood in the center of the rocky promontory between two bays. This site afforded a double port facing north and south and forming a natural breakwater, the only such port possible along the Palestinian coast. A stage on the road from Acre to Jerusalem, it was at times used as a port of entry for pilgrims, whom the Templars escorted inland.

The huge outer walls of the castle were of sandy, porous limestone, 15 feet thick and 80 feet high. They were strengthened by great towers and pierced by three impressive gates. Graceful arches adorned the spacious rooms, from which large windows opened toward the sea. On the highest point of the rocky promontory these men of the Cross carved out of the solid rock a beautiful, spacious banqueting hall, then crowned the lovely place with a magnificent church. One great wall shut out these buildings from the mainland, and outside this great wall ran a deep moat into which the sea flowed, completely surrounding the stronghold.

The place contained extensive stables accommodating 250 horses. Iron horseshoes have been found in the ruins. There were also good wells of water. The surrounding country was well watered and possessed vineyards, orchards, and pasturelands. The nearby waters were well stocked with fish, the coast held splendid salt pans, and the forest afforded an abundance of game and fuel.

Around the harbors and about the castle grew up the city of

Athlit, which became a town of considerable importance. Its contented and prosperous inhabitants were not exposed to the ravages of war, for the place was never besieged and scarcely threatened. At last, however, when the battle of Hattin had been lost and Acre had fallen, Athlit could not resist independently. The Crusader leaders assembled in the great banqueting hall for their last conference. After praying earnestly and committing themselves to the care and protection of Almighty God, they embarked in their ships on that August night of 1291 and sailed away for Cyprus.

Dor, now known as Tanturah, six miles south of Athlit, occupies the site of the ancient city of Dora, as it was called by the Romans. In early times it was a Sidonian colony, but later became a royal Canaanitish city with several outlying towns. Its soldier inhabitants fought against Joshua in the battle of Hazor. Dor, along with its daughter towns, was allotted to the children of Manasseh, who were unable to expel the Canaanites, but who finally compelled them to pay tribute (Josh. 17:11-13). The city was much fought for because of its coastal position and its rich supply of murex shellfish, so valuable in the manufacture of the famous Tyrian purple dye.

During Solomon's reign, "Judah and Israel were many, as the sand which is by the sea for multitude, eating and drinking, and making merry," and the demands of the king's table for one day was "thirty measures of fine flour, and threescore measures of meal, ten fat oxen, and twenty oxen out of the pastures, and an hundred sheep, beside harts, and roebucks, and fallowdeer, and fatted fowl." The wise king had 12 officers who lived in as many districts of Palestine, and were each responsible for one month's provision for the king and his household. One of these officers was *Ben-Abinadab,* who lived in Dor, and was son-in-law to Solomon. His must have been a comparatively easy and pleasant task, seeing the fertile fields about Dor produced so abundantly, the pastures sustained such vast flocks of sheep and herds of cattle, and the nearby woods abounded in wild game of almost every kind (1 Kings 4:11, 20, 22-23).

A wild beauty pervades the environs of the place today. Old

ruins protrude, tombs and quarries abound, with here and there a low, wet bog. Stretching away eastward are fields and woods, and strewn on the nearby beaches are many murex shells which remind one of the ancient glory of the city.

Caesarea. Two hundred years before Christ, Caesarea was known as "Strato's Tower," and today the ancient name in the Arab form, *Kaisariyeh,* still clings to the ruins on the seashore about 30 miles north of Jaffa, 25 miles south of Mount Carmel, and 55 miles northwest of Jerusalem. The change from "Strato's Tower," where some few ships landed, to the Caesarea of which Tacitus speaks in the first century A.D. as being "the head of Judea," was made by Herod the Great in his desire to build a strictly Roman town on the seaside that would be suitable for a port and a stronghold of naval power, as well as the capital of the country.

The city was begun in 25 B.C., and its construction required 12 years.

Herod was known for enlarging and beautifying cities, but his special care was bestowed on Caesarea, for he named it after Caesar, and made it a model of Graeco-Roman civilization. It was to become the official residence of the Herodian kings, and of Festus, Felix, and other Roman procurators of Judea, as well as the headquarters of the military force of the province. Under the Roman governors, Caesarea was a vast and crowded metropolis.

The city was constructed of white marble, red and gray granite, and other expensive materials brought from afar. King Herod spared no expense. Most sumptuous palaces, spacious public buildings, airy courts, attractive bazaars, and long, wide avenues were characteristic of the place.

In the north part of the city was constructed a magnificent theater building; in the south quarter, a great amphitheater accommodating 20,000 spectators; and near the east gate, in a slight depression, a hippodrome 1,000 feet long. The Romans were eager for sports, and Herod intended that ample provision should be made for their overdeveloped instinct in this direction. 63

Herod erected spacious quarters for those who sailed the seas and an appropriate base for the Roman legions of the Levant.

Crowning all was a grand palace for himself and those Roman governors who should rule after him. An abundant water supply was brought to the city by two aqueducts; one was a double conduit of great size. Nor did he neglect to provide sanitation and convenience, for a complete system of underground sewerage carried the refuse into the sea. An elaborate subterranean passage for both people and transport led directly down to the wharf and the seaside. The substantial walls of this Herodian city enclosed 400 acres. Outside the walls were villas and gardens, for peace was assured when Rome ruled.

But "the greatest and most laborious work of all" was the magnificent harbor, "always free from the waves of the sea." To make amends for the absence of a natural haven, Herod had his engineers pass out to where the water was 20 fathoms (136 feet) deep and let down "vast stones" 50 feet long, 18 feet broad, and 9 feet thick, and thus effect the construction of a double harbor 200 yards each way. It was excellent workmanship, and all the more remarkable because the place itself was not suitable for such noble structures. The whole coastline is singularly ill-fitted for the formation of harbors.

A pier was also constructed, 130 yards in length and 200 feet wide, which was adorned with splendid pillars and several towers, the largest of which was called *Drusus,* after Drusus, the son-in-law of Augustus Caesar. There were also arches formed in honor of the seamen, and nearby residences constructed for their convenience.

Around the entire haven was a splendid walk which was most appropriate "to such as had a mind to that exercise." Along this elevated circular haven there were many edifices constructed of highly polished stone, and towering above them all was a temple that stood out in bold relief—a spectacle for all who sailed near Caesarea.

Caesarea was a great city during the lifetime of Jesus and Paul. Its harbor, its buildings, and its fine streets were famous among the world's seaports. All its streets led to the harbor and were intersected by straight, parallel avenues.

It was the military, commercial, political, and sporting capital

Portside ruins of what was once the magnificent harbor of Caesarea

of Palestine, and as such was to harbor many a strange person and event. Built with unheard-of pomp by Herod the Great, it was further embellished by Herod Agrippa for Bernice, for whom this city was a favorite resort. She came here with King Agrippa to hear Paul tell of his conversion experience on the Damascus road; she also came here with Titus.

It was here that Cornelius, the devout Roman centurion, heard from heaven and sent for the Apostle Peter (who was at Joppa, 31 miles down the coast) and became one of the first Gentile converts to Christianity.

Here, too, Herod Agrippa donned the robes of silver tissue,

entered the theater, and made an oration before the people who flatteringly hailed him as a god. Proud to be accorded divine attributes, the king accepted the blasphemous homage only to be stricken down in violent pain and carried from the theater (that his grandfather had built) to his palace, where after five days he died, "worn out with pain."

Here Paul stopped for a few days in the home of Evangelist Philip, who had four daughters that prophesied. Later he was brought here as a prisoner and kept for two years, previous to his going to Rome. It was here before Felix and Drusilla, the Roman governor and his attractive wife, that he made a noble defense in which he "reasoned of righteousness, temperance, and judgment to come," and received that pathetic answer from the governor, "Go thy way for this time; when I have a more convenient season, I will call for thee." And later, before Festus and King Agrippa, he delivered that celebrated oration which made Festus declare that much learning had made him mad, and Agrippa say, "Almost thou persuadest me to be a Christian" (Acts 26:28).

It was here that Vespasian, the father of Titus, was proclaimed emperor. Here, in the old circus building, Titus, after the fall of Jerusalem in A.D. 70, celebrated his victory with games and contests in which over 2,000 Jewish prisoners were killed as gladiators in the arena.

The dissensions between the Jews and the Syrians here led to a great massacre of the former, which brought on the rebellion and the Roman war. A council was held here in A.D. 95, when the city was the seat of an archbishop. In the third century it became the metropolis of the Christian bishops of Palestine and the home of Origen and of Eusebius, the illustrious church father, and the author of Onomastikon, an important research work on Palestine geography. In A.D. 548, the Jews and Samaritans united in taking up arms against the Christians. In the year 639, the city was taken by Abu Obeida and remained in Mohammedan hands for nearly 500 years.

66   In the year 1035, it was visited by the traveller Nassiri, who describes it as an agreeable city, irrigated with running water and planted with date palms and oranges, sweet and bitter. It

was surrounded by a strong wall, either built or restored by the Mohammedans during their first occupation.

In 1101, King Baldwin seized Caesarea, put the inhabitants to the sword, and among the booty *discovered a green glass bowl,* made of a single large emerald, which he and his fellow Crusaders believed to be the veritable Holy Grail used at the Last Supper.[2] The Crusaders then settled in the place in their own manner, making a portion of the city into a small medieval fortress. Saladin took it from them in the year 1187, but the Crusaders recaptured it in 1191. Louis rebuilt the citadel and the walls, and it stood for long years. But Sultan Bibars of Egypt took it in 1256 and partially destroyed both its walls and buildings. At times it has tried to rise again but has failed.

Today Caesar's city, built with unheard-of pomp by Herod the Great, lies in extensive and intricate ruins. Across its fields of sand lie broken pottery, fragments of granite and marble columns, shattered portions of gates and castles. Desolation "laughs at the mightiest works of man, turning beauty to ashes and strength to destruction." Among the many things of interest found during excavations at Caesarea were: a Roman amphitheater, a Crusaders' cathedral, a cache of 3,700 bronze coins at the site of a 3rd century B.C. synagogue, two crusader seals of the 13th century, and an inscription bearing the name of "Pontius Pilate," the infamous governor who washed his hands before the multitude and permitted the mistrial of Jesus the Messiah.

Antipatris (Ras el 'Ain). On the eastern side of the Plain of Sharon, just above the large collection of fountains which serve as the main source of the Auja River, lies a high mound which holds the remains of ancient Antipatris. It was built by Herod the Great as a pleasant residence town and named after his father, Antipater.

Lying as it did, 42 miles along the Jerusalem highroad which led down to the seaside capital of Caesarea, it afforded a most convenient place for statesmen, churchmen, and military personnel to break the journey when traveling between these two most important cities.

Seventy mounted troops and 200 foot soldiers accompanied

the Apostle Paul when he was sent as a prisoner along this road. After a rest at Antipatris, the foot soldiery returned to Jerusalem, while the 70 horsemen continued with Paul to Caesarea, 26 miles away. Parts of the old Roman road have been uncovered near Antipatris and remain unto this day. Water from the fine springs here irrigate nearby fields and gardens, and some is pumped to Jerusalem for part of its water supply. And a larger volume is carried away in a huge 48-inch concrete pipe to furnish water for the thirsty Negeb more than 40 miles southward.

Joppa, one of the oldest cities in the world, is said to have derived its name from the Hebrew *yafe,* which means beautiful. Others say it was named after Japheth, son of Noah, who established the city after the Flood. It is situated on a 116-foot-high promontory which juts out into the Mediterranean Sea and appears like a flower garden nestled among great orange gardens, fig trees, and date palms. For long centuries Joppa has been a strange place and thoroughly Oriental.

It is mentioned by the *Mohar* of Egypt, who travelled in Palestine during the 14th century before the Christian era, and in the Tell El Amarna tablets of the 15th century. It is among the list of towns enumerated in the Temple of Karnak as having been conquered by Thotmes III during the 16th century. One record describes what is probably the origin of the Ali Baba story, of a general named Thutia, who commanded the army of Thotmes III and introduced 250 picked warriors into the city, concealed in earthen jars. These warriors bound the garrison and let in the beseigers.

Only occasional mention is made of the city in the Bible. Josh. 19:46 mentions the city as bordering on the territory of Dan.

Joppa was the port where the prophet Jonah took passage for Tarshish, when he was running away from the job which the Lord had assigned him. Cuneiform inscriptions have been found recording Sennacherib's capture of the city in 702 B.C.

In Solomon's time, Joppa was the port of Jerusalem, to which Hiram, king of Tyre, sent the cedars of Lebanon on rafts, and from there King Solomon's men took them up to Jerusalem. Again in the days of Zerubbabel, when the second Temple was built, "cedar trees were brought from Lebanon to the sea unto Joppa, according to the grant that they had of Cyrus, king of Persia" (2 Chron. 2:16; Ezra 3:7).

Alexander the Great stormed the town in 333 B.C., after which it passed from hand to hand. During the Maccabean Wars the local inhabitants turned upon the Jewish residents in the city and took 200 of them out to sea in boats and solemnly drowned them. This event caused Judas Maccabaeus to lead his army down and avenge them by burning the ships. Jonathan and Simon fortified the place and dug a harbor for foreign trade. Joppa soon became the most Jewish town on all the coast, and the only seaport the Jews possessed.

In 135 B.C., Antiochus took Joppa, but the Roman Senate ordered him to restore the town and its port to the Jews. In 63 Pompey took Joppa from the Jews and made it a free town, but Julius Caesar ordered all that had previously belonged to the Jews to be given back to them, and Joppa was restored to the high priest Hyrcanus. In the struggle between Herod and Mattathias II, Joppa remained faithful to the Jews; and when Herod returned from Rome to become king of Judea, it was necessary for him to take Joppa by storm.

In New Testament times Joppa was chiefly associated with the work of the Apostle Peter. It was here that he raised Dorcas to life and later received the great vision of clean and unclean beasts, together with his call to Cornelius at Caesarea and the Gentile world at large, while lodging in the house of Simon the tanner. The house now shown as the original is probably on the site of the one where Peter lodged.

After Herod built Caesarea with its spacious harbor, Joppa fell from its position as chief harbor of Palestine. Being a purely Jewish town, however, and maintaining close relations with Jerusalem, it continued to be a prominent place until the fall of Jerusalem in A.D. 70. After this it became a rendezvous for pirates and was finally destroyed by Vespasian.

It soon rose up again and became the seat of a Christian 69 bishop, but was captured by the Arabs in 636, after which it sank to the level of a small and insignificant place. Being on the coastal road along which the Christian and Moslem armies marched, it experienced many a bloody conflict during the period of the Crusades. It was here that Richard the Lion-hearted is said to have jumped into the sea in full armor and fought his way to land. Following Crusader days, the place suffered varying fortunes and misfortunes, but once again became the harbor of Jerusalem in the latter part of the 18th century.

Napoleon Bonaparte captured the city in 1799, and was faced with a predicament upon finding 2,000 prisoners surrendered to him after a gallant resistance. His generals and soldiers objected to sharing any of their limited food with these "Arabs and Jews." He was pressed for time, too. Influenced more by the clamor of his men than by the appeals of his prisoners, he lined them up on the beach and had them massacred. Returning later on his retreat, he occupied Joppa again, and by chance or fate the regiment which did the massacring was quartered in the hospital and ground recently used by lepers. The horrible disease fastened on them, and only seven escaped.

Joppa has been dealing with the outside world for many centuries, but the native life here has not seemed to have been affected. There are many narrow streets in which the merchants have their tiny shops, funished with small stools upon which men sit smoking their curious pipes (narghilas), bargaining and gesticulating. The bazaars present a lively picture, teeming with life from all Asia Minor and bringing together so many races and languages and products that one cannot help but be interested.

The gardens of Joppa, surrounded with stone walls and cactus hedges, stretch inland about a mile and a half and are over two miles in extent north and south. Palms, oranges, lemons, pomegranates, figs, and bananas are grown in profusion, water being supplied by means of numerous deep wells.

The gardens are skirted by vineyards on the south. On the southeast is the land belonging to the Mikveh Israel, or Jewish Agricultural Alliance, 780 acres in all, of which a third is reclaimed land. The work here has developed into one of the finest agricultural colleges in Israel.[3]

On the way from Joppa to Lydda, about half a mile out, is a

fountain which is one of the finest specimens of Saracenic architecture in Palestine and a memorial of a thoughtful and kindly governor, Abu Nabat. It is built of white stone in the form of a parallelogram, and *inside the center cupola* lies the sarcophagus of the founder with an inscription in Arabic calling upon all who gather about to offer a prayer for him who provided this fountain for the free use of every passerby.

Jaffa is said to have had a population of about 8,000 before it was taken over by the Jews in 1948, a majority of whom were Moslems, but Greeks, Latins, Armenians, Maronites, Protestants, and Jews were found there. The place had a trade with Egypt and the north in silk, oranges, sesame, and other such products. The annual value of the fruit crop alone was said to be $10,000. However, since the Jews took control, much of the city is being rebuilt. Only a small portion retains its ancient appearance, and only a few thousand Moslems and Christians live here.

The Plain of Sharon, as a whole, is now thickly dotted with modern cities, towns, and colonies. These colonies began to be planted on the plain during the latter part of last century. Now there are more than 100 colonies—mostly Jewish; yet there are two Christian German colonies and one Greek colony, along with some Arab villages. The most of these began as agricultural colonies but in time developed some kind of an industrial quarter to supplement the colonists' income. *Herzliya* built luxury hotels; *Natanya* developed its picturesque beach to attract tourists and became famous for its diamond-cutting and polishing industry; *Michmoret* went in for fishing; *Mishmar-Ha-Sharon* grew gladiolus for export; *Ramot-Hashavim* became famous for its poultry farms.

Other colonies constructed hotels, rooming houses, restaurants, cafes, and established factories for producing cement, wine, and olive-wood products. A few of the colonies have grown into flourishing towns and cities. In between the colonies are rich and fertile citrus groves, olive orchards, and grape vineyards. And there are people, many people on the Plain of Sharon. One Jewish physician said to me, "Almost everybody desires to live beside the sea."

CHAPTER 5

The Plain of the Philistines

The Philistines! Strange how that people who passed along the highway of history so long ago should cling to our modern-day thinking, and the name be perpetuated by modern sociologists who suppose they find the Philistines' counterpart in a certain nondescript group who infest modern social circles. From whence those ancient Philistines came, and whither they went, has offered about as much inducement for speculation as has any people of ancient time.

No final word has been spoken, yet after decades of patient

research it has about become the consensus that these people descended from one Mizraim, the son of Ham, whose two sons, *Casluhim* and *Caphtorium,* settled on a Mediterranean island which became known as Caphtor or Crete.[1] Some unknown catastrophe left only a remnant of them, who migrated to their distant kinsmen, the Egyptians, who permitted temporary settlement on their coast.

Being soon sized up as desirable frontier fighters, they were offered a free hand by shrewd Pharaoh for conquest in southern Canaan, with the understanding that they would become the guardians of Egypt's north frontier.[2] Varying fortunes accompanied the Philistine effort at conquest, but in time the country which became known as the Philistine Plain was a strip of land which extends from river Rubin *(Nahr Rubin)* to the river of Egypt *(Wady El Arish),* a distance of about 50 miles. Its average width is 12 to 16 miles, or slightly greater than that of the Sharon Plain, especially that portion which lies between Gaza and the *Wady El Arish,* which is the famous pastoral region known as the kingdom of Gerar in the time of Abraham.[3] The well-known trade route from Asia to Africa ran directly through the center of their country and passed by their leading cities; thus the Philistines could justly be styled "the guardians of the gate to Egypt." The Philistines were a tall, well-proportioned, warlike people. They went to battle in chariots of iron, armed with helmets, shields, swords, and other weapons of artistic workmanship.

Israel avoided their way as danger-fraught and God-forbidden, when she left Egypt for Canaan. Such a formidable enemy to be met after a long desert trek was too much, even for Israel. But later, when Israel had entered by the east, she listened to Joshua's final address, and then, in the fresh rush of enthusiasm, took Ekron, Askelon, and Gaza. But they soon lost these because they could not drive out the intrepid Philistines who fought with "chariots of iron."[4]

Amos declares that the same Power planted the two nations in the land—the one on the coast and the other on the Central Mountain Range—yet they never seemed to be at peace with one another.[5] Their outlook, their ideals, and their mission in life were poles apart. War, commerce, agriculture, stock raising, pagan worship, and the pursuit of personal pleasure absorbed the Philistine mind. Israel seemed destined for a higher purpose; yet the Bible makes no mention of a Philistine being changed at heart and taking the upward path that leads to nobler achievement here and eternal life hereafter. Too often they are merely represented as the proverbial enemies of Israel.

The Philistines pushed and horned the Israelites at intervals and grew so strong and independent that Ramses III attacked them in battle about 1190 B.C.[6]

The Plain of the Philistines is drained from east to west by four principal streams: *River Rubin, Sukerir River, Wady el-Hesy,* and *Wady Ghazzeh* with its tributary, *Wady esh Sheriah.* Some of these streams are perennial, but none are very large, except when swollen by winter rains. Much of the water from these winter rains, however, makes its way toward the sea along the top of the underlying rock. In a few places these waters break out and come to the surface as springs, but for the most part they remain 25 or 30 feet underground, which means that an inexhaustible supply of fresh water is found by digging wells of moderate depth.[7] Abraham and Isaac, in their day, dug wells in the Gerar section, but today there are thousands of wells scattered over the plain, and more will be dug as needed.

The soil on the plain is generally fertile, suitable for the production of grain, melons, grapes, figs, olives, dates, and the various citrus fruits. The crop for which the plain has long been known, however, is that of grain, the plain from Ekron to Gaza being one of the best grain districts in Palestine. In ancient times cargo ships from Greece and other countries put into the old port at the mouth of *Wady Ghazzeh* and were loaded with the grain of this plain. In fact this district was long known as "the granary of the Near East."

In ancient times there stretched for many miles, in every direction, a sea of grain, which in the warmer days of late spring, as harvest approached, would be like so much tinder.[8] It must have been into such fields as this that Samson loosed the foxes with firebrands tied between their tails and burned the grain-fields of the Philistines.

The land of the Philistines was originally divided into five districts, over which five "lords" ruled in as many cities—*Ekron, Gath, Ashdod, Askelon,* and *Gaza.* Each of these cities had a cluster of "towns" about it which were subject to the ruling city.

Ekron, celebrated for the worship of Beelzebub, stood in the center of the plain, slightly north of the ancient valley of Sorek.

There seems no reason for doubt that the present Arab village of *'Akir* answers to the ancient Ekron. That city was the northernmost of the five cities of the lords of the Philistines and was situated near the southern border of Sharon; while the other four cities lay well within the territory usually ascribed to the Philistines. Here, in ancient Ekron, Samson was betrayed by Delilah, the infamous Philistine beauty.

Afterwards it became remarkable in connection with the capture of the ark by the Philistines, which was sent back from Ekron upon a new cart drawn by two milch cows. These being left to their own course took the "straight way" to Beth-shemesh, the nearest point of entrance to the mountains of Judah. In coming, therefore, by the present road from Ekron to Beth-shemesh, one almost follows the track of the cart on which the ark was thus sent back. After David's victory over Goliath in the Valley of Elah the Philistines were pursued to Ekron. At a later day, the prophets uttered denunciations against it, along with the other cities of the Philistines.

The Ekron of the Bible was built of unburnt bricks, which within a comparatively few years were reduced to dust. The only remains of the ancient city are represented in the stones of hand-mills, two marble columns, and a stone press. The present Ekron was only a mud hamlet until a few years ago when the Jews purchased the ground, where they have built a thriving colony which they call by that name.

Gath was the home of Goliath, the famous giant whom David slew with a sling and a stone. The place fell into disrepute and has been so much forgotten that its name has disappeared, and the site cannot be, or has not been, definitely ascertained. Tell-es-

Safiyeh, a fine mound in the western portion of the Valley of Elah, has long been pointed out as the probable location, but considerable uncertainty abounded and no excavations were ever carried forward there. In 1955, the Jews founded Kiryat-Gat (town of Gath) far south of here, near a conspicuous mound which they supposed to be the biblical Gath.

Ashdod, the military pride of the Philistines, was located midway between Ekron and Askelon, on a low, rounded hill overlooking the sea. Being known for its military strength and for its sacredness in connection with the temple of Dagon, the Philistines, on capturing the ark of the covenant, hurried the ark to their temple. The following morning the people found the image Dagon fallen and broken to pieces; thereafter they had less faith in it.

In 760 B.C. the prophet Amos denounced Ashdod's inhabitants.[9] Isaiah says that Sargon, king of Assyria, sent Tartan, his general, who took the city of Ashdod.[10] For a long time the critics disputed this positive statement, because of secular history making no mention of such a king; then, in 1842, M. Botta began excavations at Khorsabad. The first monuments brought to light were those of this vanished Sargon. As one of the most magnificent of the Assyrian conquerors, he possessed a palace which was scarcely excelled in ornamentation by any royal edifice. Later, Mr. George Smith discovered an octagonal cylinder recording the very conquest mentioned by the Hebrew prophet. Sargon's inscription read: "In my ninth expedition to the land beside the great sea, to Philistia and Ashdod I went . . . the cities of Ashdod and Gimzo of the Ashdodites I besieged and captured."[11]

Ashdod withstood siege longer than any city in history, when Pharaoh Psammeticus (633-609 B.C.), the first king of the 26th dynasty, kept his armies before its gates for 22 years ere the standard of Upper and Lower Egypt flew over the city. How strange are the vicissitudes of war. Men and maidens were born "with the enemy at their gates, grew to maturity, married and had their families—all with the menace of red death ever before them. Shut up within the city, the camp fires of the Egyptian glimmering every night in the warm dusk of the Philistine eve-

76

ning, or sputtering beneath the lash of the heavy rains of winter."[12]

Likewise young men entered on their military career in the Egyptian army, were assigned trench duty at Ashdod, finished their full years of service with their initial venture yet unsuccessful. Such sieges went far toward breaking up the military might of the Philistines. And of fulfilling the prophecy of Amos who, as God's prophet, had said, "And I will cut off the inhabitants from Ashdod . . . and the remnant of the Philistines shall perish" (Amos 1:8).

In the year 163 B.C. Judas Maccabaeus cleared the city of idols, and 15 years later Jonathan and Simon burnt the old temple of Dagon.[13]

During the Greek and Roman period Ashdod was known as *Azotus,* and it was here that Philip began his evangelistic tour after he had brought about the conversion and baptism of the treasurer of Ethiopia, "a eunuch of great authority under Candace, queen of the Ethiopians."[14]

Today the city mound rises high over the surrounding country, being covered on its very top with fields of lentils, and bordered with olives, figs, and other semitropical fruits. The secrets of the interior remain yet to be divulged by a thorough archaeological expedition, the process of which would be thrilling and the results enlightening. An Arab village nestles at the foot of the mound eastward. But in 1958, the Jews began to build a new town four miles north of the biblical mound, and to make of Ashdod Israel's newest Mediterranean port. Large docking facilities were built, and soon its population grew to 24,000 with splendid prospects for the future.

Askelon, 10 miles north of Gaza, was the second seaport city of the Philistines. Having no inlet of the sea or natural harbor in which vessels might be sheltered, its walls were so arranged as to stretch around the water's front like "a deeply bent bow" with the sea in the position of the bowstring.

Askelon was wealthy and had a varied history. It was here that Samson collected the necessary articles to pay his wager with the Philistines. Here the mayor of the city made golden figures of mice to send with the ark of the covenant to Jerusalem, in an effort to propitiate God in relieving the Philistines of an awful scourge that must have been similar to the bubonic plague.[15]

Out from the port of ancient Askelon went large stores of food and provision shipped to Egypt, Greece, and other Mediterranean countries. Among the Tell El Amarna tablets there is a letter from "Ita, prince of Askelon," informing his overlord, the king of Egypt, that he had furnished all the "victuals, drinks, cattle, sheep, honey, and oil" that he had required. Considering it a central city of extreme importance, David, in his lament over Gilboa's tragedy, said, "Tell it not in Gath, publish it not in the streets of Askelon."[16]

Just previous to the Christian era, the place became famous as the birthplace of *Herod the Great*, who honored his native city by erecting magnificent buildings, "baths, costly fountains, and a cloistered court." But Askelon's history was not to be written in such peaceful paragraphs. Fierce and bloody battles were to be fought around and within those half-circled walls. The conflict between the cross and the crescent brought days of trial and disaster, when both Godfrey and Richard held it for a time, then Saladin. The city being lost and won like a pawn, and destroyed and rebuilt like a plaything, its ruin was at last sealed, and it never arose to any prominence. The city whose name had been known in every land in Europe came to be known as a place of "utter desolation," where fragments of massive walls marked outlines of the once proud and famous city of the Philistines and of Herod the Great.

A few years ago, an Arab owner of land within the ruins of Askelon was cutting a towing path to enable a camel to draw water from a well when he found some bronze figures. Subsequently, Mr. J. Ory, inspector of the Department of Antiquities, carried out soundings and found a hoard of bronzes, including human figures, animals, and weights. One figure, thought to represent Isis nursing Horus, still had on its face the original gold leaf with which it was covered. It was thought probable that most, if not all, the figurines were similarly gilded.[17] Further excavations laid bare so many walls and interesting ruins that historical

Askelon has now been made a national park to which visitors pay an entrance fee.

Gaza, the most famous of the five Philistine confederate cities, and one of the oldest cities in history, was located two and one-half miles from the sea, on a well-rounded hill rising some 60 feet above the surrounding plain. Situated on the great coastal highway between Egypt and Mesopotamia and at a junction of the trade route from south Arabia, it was one of the ideally located caravan cities and an important commercial and military center when Moses led the Israelites out of Egypt to Canaan.

Markets, traffic, and trade have always been the very life of the city; yet Gaza exported more than she imported, for the gardens, orchards, olive groves, and extensive grainfields north and east, stretching away for miles and billowing like the waves of the sea, supplied the local demand and furnished cargoes for the outgoing ships bound for Phoenicia, Greece, and the islands of the sea.

It was here that Samson took one of his first steps on the downward road. Here, when the Gazites attempted to trap him, he "took the doors of the gate of the city, and the two posts and went away with them, bar and all, and carried them to the top of a hill," which tradition says is the prominent but isolated hill of *El Muntar,* southeast of Gaza. Here, too, he was forced to come when the Philistines "put out his eyes, brought him down to Gaza," and "he did grind in the prison house." Often he must have thought of his godly mother and the angel who talked to her of God's plan for his life—"If I only had . . ." Here he made vows to God and his strength returned. Then one day while making sport for the Philistines, he asked to be led to the two principal pillars of the great temple of Dagon. On removing these, the building crashed and killed both himself and the leading lords and ladies of the Philistines (Judg. 16:20-30).

The Philistine gods were Dagon, Baal-Zebub, and Astarte. The manner of worship directed toward these false deities debased and sensualized the worshippers. Unchaste goals and gross materialism gradually swallowed up the Philistines. Their cities are now but dust and their name a curse, while noble ideals and a sense of the sacred mission not only preserved Israel but caused them to give to the world sacred law, ennobling literature, fearless prophets, and the Messiah who pointed the path to higher realms and imbued men's minds with a spiritual ideal that should outlive the ages.

Gerar, where both Abraham and Isaac sojourned for a time, dug wells, and prospered under the generous treatment of "Abimelech king of Gerar" (Genesis 20 and 26), has long been identified with *Tel el Jemmeh,* about eight miles south of Gaza. The mound was partially excavated by W. J. Phythian-Adams (1922) and Sir Flinders Petrie (1927). In the former excavation four city levels were found, extending from the Patriarchal to the Roman period. In one short season Dr. and Mrs. Petrie uncovered seals, scarabs, jewelry, idols, weapons, household utensils, agricultural tools, grain pits, a "sword furnace" where iron implements were sharpened, and a large variety of pottery. Nothing was found that identified the site as Gerar.

More recent surveys have led many very good authorities to believe that Gerar should be identified with *Tell Abu Hureira,* which lies on the banks of Wady esh-Sheriah, 11 miles southeast of Gaza. On this 40-acre mound is found an abundance of pottery which indicates prosperity during the Patriarchal period. Anywhere one may dig here he will find an abundance of water 20 to 30 feet beneath the surface.

CHAPTER 6

The Shephelah

The term *Shephelah* means the "low hills" and is applied to the group of irregular hills lying between the Plain of the Philistines and the central range of the mountains of Judea. The term "the hills" was first applied to this section in the Book of Joshua,[1] and later the Talmud merely designated it "the Shephelah."[2] The Bible refers to this section 18 or 20 times under the general name Shephelah. In this wide sense Shephelah included much of the territory originally given to the tribe of Dan.[3]

This region measures about nine miles from east to west, and extends from the Valley of Aijalon on the north to Wady esh-Sheriah on the south. It is entirely separated from the Central Mountain Range of Judea and has a topography different from that of any other section in Palestine. Its hills, with open valleys between, vary in height from 500 to 1,000 feet above sea level and are usually covered with marl, clay, pebbles, and soft, chalky limestone, with here and there an outcropping of fragments of black like flint.[4]

The Shephelah is more than barren hills. Its agricultural life, its historical background, and its valleys with their cities teem with interest.

The inhabited villages and cities of the Shephelah are frequent. The soil, in its own way, is some of the richest and most productive. Its special adaptation is to olive groves and grain. The olives are usually grown on terraced hillsides which have been built up with stone retaining walls. Grainfields abound on the more level areas. There are also a few mulberry, sycamore, and scrub oak trees growing here and there. In recent years the rougher areas have been reforested with a variety of trees.

The Shephelah is refreshed by the sea breezes, receives a fair amount of rainfall, and is blessed with numerous springs in areas where there is an outcrop of hard limestone. In fact, almost all the area is underlain with a sheet of very fine water, and any number of wells may be dug only a few feet below the surface of the ground and will yield an abundant supply of spring water.

The great number of ruined sites indicate that a heavy population once lived there, and agree with the large number of towns mentioned in the Bible and other ancient literature. Even the caves seem to have been used at times for living and other purposes. There were continual Philistine raids in the springtime to rob the threshing floors when the people were busy during the harvest treading the grain, winnowing it of chaff, and placing it in the garners. Such harvest scenes as those enacted 3,000 years ago are plentiful today within the same valleys and on the same plains.

Today there is peace in the Shephelah, with no thought of

82

marauding bands to carry away the golden harvest. But it has not always been so, for this territory more justly deserves the name of "The Hills of Conflict" than most any other in Palestine.

Those who have lived here in times past have been accustomed to war and invasion which have come at frequent intervals. Here Israel and the Philistines frequently met in conflict and fought their bitter and often decisive battles; here the Maccabeans were nurtured and breathed the air of conflict, meeting their Hellenistic enemies and overcoming them with inferior numbers. Here the British yeomanry under Allenby forced the Turco-German forces along through these narrow mountain defiles before they were well aware that the British would not be content to camp in the Plain of Philistia and Sharon below.

There are four valleys that descend through these hills through which the tides of war have surged during the centuries. They are the Valley of Aijalon, the Valley of Sorek, the Valley of Elah, and the Valley of Zephathah.

The Valley of Aijalon begins at the Plain of Sharon and rapidly ascends to the foot of the Central Mountain Range. Here the high walls of rock seem to forbid further passage, except where three gorges break through and ascend as narrow defiles up past the two Beth-horons to the plateau at Gibeon, five miles northwest of Jerusalem.

The Philistines came up this valley to get at Israel; and here the Maccabeans, the Greeks, the Romans, and the Crusaders fought some of their most noted battles. The narrow defiles proved an aid to the defenders, and defeat became so common here that military leaders came to shun the place or carefully study the terrain when they made a drive on the uplands of Palestine. General Allenby is a classic example, for he carefully studied the Bible, Josephus, and George Adam Smith before his final drive on the uplands of Judea.

The Valley of Aijalon will ever be memorable because of Joshua's experience there. When the long-drawn battle was turning to victory and time was getting short, lest darkness come on and limit the victory, the leader of the Lord's host called on Jehovah to stay the sun in its course—that the sun no longer whirl the earth about in the usual manner. God stayed the earth in its course, and since then men have been saying that if need be, God will do almost anything to help His people who will dare ask largely and trust Him implicitly.[5]

The Valley of Sorek lies south of Aijalon and at present is known as *Wady Surar.* As the second approach to the mountains of Judea, it springs away from the Plain of the Philistines near Ekron and Gezer and advances broadly through the hills of the Shephelah, narrowing as it approaches the Judean uplands a few miles west of Jerusalem. In its lower places it is one of the most fertile portions of the Shephelah.

It was up this valley that the Philistines sent the ark of the Lord on a cart drawn by lowing milch cows that, as if by divine compulsion, took the "straight way" from Ekron to Beth-shemesh where the people reaping in the fields saw the ark coming up the road, and went out to meet it.[6]

The Valley of Sorek will ever be associated with Samson the strong man. It was at *Zorah,* overlooking this valley, that his parents lived and worshipped God when an angel announced that a son would be given them, who should be dedicated to the Lord for the express purpose of "troubling the Philistines." After coming to manhood, he crossed and recrossed this valley time and again as he went down into the Philistine plain.

Today the valley is well covered with grainfields, possesses a number of thriving Jewish colonies, and has running directly through it the railway that connects Jaffa to Jerusalem.

The Valley of Elah is the third approach through the Shephelah to the Central Mountain Region of Judea. At Tell es-Safi, which is thought by some to be Gath, the native city of Goliath, the valley leaves the Plain of the Philistines and ascends eastward until it reaches the great watershed of Judea southwest of Bethlehem. This valley offered a fairly convenient pass for the Philistines, and they often endeavored to make use of it in their warfare against the Israelites.

84   The Valley of Elah will always be remembered as the scene where God proved that fearless faith in Him was not without reward. For it was here that David, the shepherd lad, met and

overcame Goliath, the giant, with a simple sling and a smooth stone and sent the Philistines through this very opening near Gath back to the gates of Ekron. In the streambed running through the center of this valley are thousands of stones—"round and smooth" like the five stones which David chose and placed in his scrip as he went out to meet Goliath.[7]

The Valley of Zephathah, now called *Wadi Zeita,* is the fourth and final approach through the Shephelah. This valley has its beginning just west of the fine old fortress of Beth-zur which guarded the highroad to Jerusalem. The pass through this beautiful valley vibrated to the tread of military men of Egypt, Babylon, and Europe, but perhaps the most famous and startling event of this valley took place when Nebuchadnezzar of Assyria captured Lachish in 701 B.C., and used it as a base of operation against Judea.

Also, there are two wadis which penetrate the Shephelah: Wadi Hesi and Wadi Sheriah.

Wadi Hesi rises in the mountains some six miles southwest of Hebron and finds its way to the sea between Gaza and Askelon. On this watercourse is located the important site of *Tell el Hesi;* and up this way was an important roadway leading into the highlands.

Wadi Sheriah rises far south of Debir (Kirjath Sepher), and after flowing some miles, it joins the more famous Wadi Ghazzeh, and then flows into the sea four miles south of Gaza.

It was inevitable that the people who fortified and held these four southern passes would control the highlands of central Canaan. It was likewise inevitable that the Shephelah, the immediate approach to these passes, would constitute disputed territory and a battlefield. The history of the region is a story of continual struggle gathering round the names of the Philistines, Hebrews, Greeks, Romans, and others who dared to invade the hill country of Judea or to descend from the highlands in formidable attacks on the plainsmen. To visualize these valleys is to better understand the wars which have been waged in this area from Joshua's time to Allenby's.

Six of the more famous cities of the Shephelah were Aijalon,

Zorah, Timnath, Gezer, Maresha, and Lachish. These cities are not inhabited now. Some have been excavated, and the others which have not are just mounds.

Aijalon is the town from which the Valley of Aijalon derives its name. Near here Joshua was able to complete the routing of the five kings because of the miraculous prolongation of daylight.

Zorah will ever be associated with the strange, strong man, Samson. Near here, out in the field, an angel talked with a wonderful woman, the wife of Manoah. Nearby is an ancient rock altar which could well be the one upon which Manoah offered a "meat offering," and "the angel of the Lord talked with Manoah, then ascended in the flame above the altar."[8] Here Samson was born, and here he gave the first indication of his great mission to liberate Israel from the yoke of the Philistines. After the tragic death of Samson at Gaza, his body was returned and buried here near Zorah. A two-room home, with walls constructed of solid stone, is now shown visitors as the "home of Samson."

The spies and raiders of the Danites started from Zorah when they went in search of a place to settle in another section of Palestine—and eventually settled permanently at Dan.[9]

Four miles southwest of Zorah, on the crest of the ridge opposite, are the ruins of *Timnath.* This is the home of the Philistine woman to whom Samson was married. While on his way to see his love one day, a lion roared at him from out of the thickets. Samson killed the lion with his own hands, and bees built in the lion's carcass and there stored their honey. On passing by later, Samson observed the unusual phenomena and formed the riddle, "Out of the eater come forth meat, and out of the strong come forth sweetness."[10]

Gezer, now called *Tell el Jazar,* commanded the entrance to the Valley of Aijalon, and was one of the older sites known in Palestine. Its name is said to mean "precipice," which seems suggestive of its isolated position high on a hill in the extreme northwestern section of the Shephelah.

Excavations revealed a well-built stone wall about 16 feet

thick surrounding the city. On the south stood a massive brick gateway. Within the very heart of the city there is a great tunnel about 200 feet long, with a vertical depth of 94 feet. Here along this descending stair-cased tunnel were smoke-stained niches wherein had set olive oil lamps to give light. At the bottom of the tunnel was a living spring that furnished a never-failing supply of water for the people both in time of peace and in time of siege. This tunnel was constructed about 2000 B.C. and abandoned about 1400 B.C.

The area around Gezer is quite fertile and well watered. On these hillsides immediately surrounding the city mound can be found literally hundreds of threshing floors where the people and their animals tread the grain and winnow it of chaff just as they have done for centuries.

Maresha, one mile south of Beit Jibrin, was the home of the prophet Micah, who said God would be compassionate and "cast all their sins into the depths of the sea."[11]

Lachish and Azekah were the last cities in Palestine to fall during the Babylonian conquest. Lachish is seven miles southwest of Beit Jibrin on the road from Gaza to Hebron. For long centuries it has been but a tell or mound known by the natives as *Tell Duweir.*

An excavation was carried on in the season of 1932-35 to try to trace the sources of the various foreign contacts which influenced the development of Palestinan culture. There is ample evidence of influence from Egypt.

Under the Jewish monarchy Lachish was not so important as a city, but continued to be one of the principal fortresses. It was enclosed by a double wall connected by a double gatehouse. However, the city came to a violent end, being twice destroyed by fire within a few years. These two destructions have been connected with the two invasions of Nebuchadnezzar in 597 and 586 B.C. Between the two destructions the fortifications seem to have been somewhat restored. After the final capture there seems to have been a governor's official residence here during the Persian period, for there are remains of such a structure. From this point Lachish disappears from history as shown by the excavation.

The tell, or mound, covering the ancient fortified city of Lachish along the road from Hebron to Gaza.

For the Bible student, however, the main interest lies not in its history as a fortress of Judah, but in objects found in excavations carried on here. One of these was a tall water vessel with writing in Phoenician or proto-Hebrew characters; also a blade of a Hyksos dagger with four pictographic characters suitable to the age of Hezekiah, and a clay seal bearing on its back the impression of the fibers of the papyrus document to which it must have been attached when found, although proof of identity is impossible. Of greater significance, however, are the "Lachish Letters" which were found.

Even though these excavations may not add much to our definite knowledge about Lachish, there is no doubt that they add life and color of detail to the books in the Bible.

*

The
Central Mountain
Region

*

CHAPTER **7**

The Beauty of Lebanon

*L*ebanon, the "White Mountain," is the most northern zone of the Central Mountain Region. The range is nearly 100 miles in length, from north to south, but usually no more than 15 to 20 miles in width. *Leban* means "white," and the name in this instance is derived from the gleaming white limestone rocks and its ramparts of perpetual snow that in the winter season makes it to appear like a great white ghost silhouetted against the horizon. During other seasons of the year there is snow in places, yet the mountain has miles of greenery and is marvelous for its massiveness and its sheer loveliness.

The Lebanon range is largely made up of long, broad, east-west ridges, broken by hundreds of hills which are eventually dwarfed into insignificance by the wind-swept summits along the divide, or by the great peaks which rise behind them. *Mount Sunnin* stands 8,557 feet in its majestic beauty in the high ranges northeast of Beirut—the pride and joy of all who live in this area. On farther north is *Kornet es Sandra,* which rises to an elevation of 11,032 feet above sea level, the highest peak of the entire range.

One cannot traverse this region from north to south without meeting constant obstacles in the way of rugged ridges to be climbed or gorges and turbulent rivers to be crossed. The only possible routes from end to end of this famous mountain range is along the Mediterranean coast or along the valley of Bekaa, east of the range.

To penetrate the Lebanons from the west or the east, one must walk or ride a donkey through deep valleys, by charming glens, and along turbulent streams which leap from limestone caves and roar along in their white swiftness, now under a natural bridge, and then to cascade from terrace to terrace on toward the sea.

The worth of the Lebanons cannot be better described than as "a great treasure-house of interest" in its history, geography, geology, botany, ethnology, and archaeology. Its lofty summits, its frightful chasms, its deep caverns and subterranean lakes, its magnificent fountains and cascades, its noble cedars, its vineyards; its orchards, walnut and olive groves; its ruined temples and nameless vestiges of hoary antiquity; its monasteries, churches, Druse chapels, and palaces; its picturesque villages; and the daily practices and beliefs of its people combine to make it a fruitful theme of study and an endless delight to the passing traveler and the most scholarly and patient explorer.[1]

In viewing Lebanon, crowned with its diadem of cedars, one becomes enraptured and delighted by the different tints of azure, which, shaded by the diversity of distance, blend together between sea and sky. He breathes a soft and balmy air, and the soul itself becomes subdued and filled with reverence before this land of ancient renown which God bequeathed to His chosen people when He divided the world among the nations. The land which Moses desired to see, but never entered; one which King Solomon knew intimately, and other Hebrew people visited frequently.

Its picturesque landscapes with their varied splendor always astonish visitors. The plains, the uplands, the valleys, and the mountains make the country look like a small universe.

The Bible, finding no more appropriate criterion of beauty than Lebanon, extols its perfumes, its flowers, its cedars, its meadows, and its beautiful views.[2] Its soft-flowing waters, green trees, plants, attractive shrubbery, and brilliant shades truly make it a revelry of beauty. Under a cloudless sky and a golden sun everything testifies to the terrific force of the Word of God. Peaks pierce the sky at a prodigious height; crests, bolder still, rise beyond and appear as though eternally on fire in the midst of the sun-struck snow. Below, in the deep valleys, flow the famous waters of ancient and celebrated rivers. Above these rivers tower masses of rock, some of which are sharp like titanic blades of stone, and others massive and round like gigantic cannonballs; and on yet higher is the perpetual whiteness of its ever melting, yet eternal, snows. The people who live here say that Lebanon bears winter on its head, spring on its shoulders, summer on its bosom, while autumn lies slumbering at its feet.

No city of any size is found in these mountains, yet there are Roman-built bridges which span streams, and there are more than 1,300 villages and rural towns which nestle along these valleys, cling to hillsides, or perch high on mountainous tablelands. Some live in the midst of this indescribable beauty, work their gardens, tend their orchards, and ply their simple trades, yet seldom sense the wealth which lies all about them. Others do realize the wonders of their country, for when they pray, they say, "Thank God for this beautiful land. It must be beautiful or folks wouldn't come so far to see it."[3]

92   The *Cedars of Lebanon,* which have adorned the mountains from time immemorial, have always been renowned in literature and history as the emblem of majesty, strength, and beauty. In

93

A few of the famed "Cedars of Lebanon" which are not nearly as plentiful as they once were.

size they are somewhat like our redwoods of California, but not so tall. Isaiah speaks of them as "the cedars of Lebanon that are high and lifted up, the glory of Lebanon." The Psalmist says that "the righteous shall grow like a cedar in Lebanon."[4]

In the course of his warning message to Pharaoh, Ezekiel uttered an allegorical dirge over the king of Assyria whom he compared to a cedar of Lebanon which had prospered until "no tree in the garden of God was like unto him in his beauty," but when his "heart was lifted up" in pride, God delivered him to the woodsman who came and laid his branches low (Ezek. 31:1-14).

In ancient times the Lebanon mountains, for 100 miles along their higher ranges, were covered with cedar forests whose trees were known to be suitable for carving, to be heavy with resin, to emit a fragrance, to take a high polish, to resist termites, and to be exceedingly durable. Kings and rulers and craftsmen and military men used them freely in shipbuilding, coffin construction, idol manufacture, siege engines, and the ceilings of temples and palaces in all the Middle East countries.

From about 2850 to 1350 B.C., Egypt got its supply of resinous woods from here, and with these they ceiled and adorned their famous temples. The Assyrians began making use of them about 1100 B.C., and shortly before 700, Sargon II made especially heavy demands on them. King David built himself a palace of cedar wood (2 Sam. 5:11). Solomon, Zerubbabel, and Herod used them to roof, ceil, and adorn their magnificent temples at Jerusalem. Nebuchadnezzar, the mighty monarch of Babylon, in an inscription dug from the libraries of that mighty city, says:

> At that time the place—my royal abode—I rebuilt in Babylon. Great cedars I brought from the beautiful forest of Lebanon to roof it. A great wall of mortar and brick I threw about them. . . . The great gates of both Imgur Bel and Ninitti Bel. . . . With burnt brick and brilliant blue glaze tile on which bells and serpents were engraved I made them skillfully. Great cedars for their covering with bronze. Those great gates I ornamented to the astonishment of men.[5]

94

Almost all the famous temples throughout the Near Eastern countries, including that of Diana of Ephesus, were ceiled with these cedars. Tiglath-pileser visited the Lebanons for the purpose of obtaining cedarwood to adorn the temple and palaces of Ashur (now called *Kalat Shergat*) in ancient Assyria. Alexander got the timber supply for his siege of Tyre in the Lebanons, and other generals of military might have used this area as their base of supply.

It was long supposed that the supply of timber from these forests was inexhaustible, but time has proven otherwise. Of their former magnificence all that now remains consists of a few groups, scattered at wide intervals over the mountains. In all these groups, with a single exception, the trees are comparatively young and of small size. The only grove of any size and age is the far-famed group of some 600 which are about 40 miles northeast of Beirut. They stand nearly 7,000 feet above the level of the sea, and 2,000 feet below the summits of Lebanon. Among these 600 trees, there are about 12 which are the remaining representatives of the ancient forest.

These time-honored trees grow to 100 to 120 feet in height. The trunks of the older trees are of enormous girth. Several are from 6 to 10 feet, and one is 42 feet in circumference measured a short distance above the ground, at which point it sends off five immense branches, each from 3 to 5 feet in diameter, thus, in reality, constituting five trees of immense size. This tree with its branches measures two or three hundred feet in circumference.

No certain estimate can be formed of the age of these trees, but the largest of them, known as the "Guardian," is reputed to be at least 2,000 years old—some say as much as 3,000. Certainly the oldest of these trees waved in their wild way when Christ was born at Bethlehem, when Rome declined, and when the Crusaders passed by to recover the tomb of Christ. For centuries they have stood as silent sentinels of the far-famed Lebanon, and a remnant of those "cedars of the Lord" which went into so many sacred edifices which are famous wherever the Bible and ancient history have been read. Long the symbol of peaceful life they are now the political emblem of the Republic of Lebanon. 95

The country of Lebanon is an ideal summer resort. The mountains are cool, and there is no rain between June and October. The sea breezes combined with the cool mountain atmosphere lend health and vigor which is surpassed by few other places on the globe. Tourists never tire of the ever-changing beauty of the scenery, the lusciousness of its fruits, the courtesy and hospitality of the people. No matter what village you visit, there is always someone to show you around.

It is little wonder that Lady Hester Stanhope, the niece of the great William Pitt, should become enamored of these gorgeous mountains. With her uncle gone, and Sir John Moore—Britain's most efficient military general, and the only one she ever loved—dying with her name as the last words on his lips, she packed up and traveled in Eastern lands to finally purchase a mansion on a mountaintop 12 miles northeast of Sidon. Here she added 25 rooms and spent a fortune on horses, guards, servants, and just living the last 20 years of her life; to finally die on June 23, 1839, and be buried on the hilltop midst the trees, the flowers, and the singing birds.

CHAPTER **8**

Upper Galilee

Upper Galilee begins with the Leontes River as its northern boundary line, and continues southward to an irregular line running from the north end of the Sea of Galilee by *Wady Maktul* leading up from the Plain of Gennesaret to the canyon just south of Safed, and thence westward to the Plain of Acre. It is actually a continuation of the Lebanon mountain chain, and is made up of a series of broad mountain plateaus which rise in elevation from 2,000 to 4,260 feet above sea level. The highest and most noticeable point is *Mount Jermuk,*

97

which is the principal landmark of the entire section—the highest point west of the Jordan.[1]

The numerous valleys and narrow passes of this highland territory are made fertile by a rich red loam soil, much of which has for centuries been protected and kept moist by a growth of entangled shrubbery. The rainfall here is heavier than elsewhere in Palestine, wells are numerous, the climate equitable, and the mountains well wooded with such trees as oak, pine, beach, carob, myrtle, bay, and maple. Here also are olive orchards, fruit trees of various kinds, and many grainfields which usually produce an abundant harvest. The wealth of olive trees made Galilee literally a country flowing with oil. "It is easier," says the Talmud, "to raise a legion of olives in Galilee than to bring up a child in Palestine."

The terrain of certain sections of Upper Galilee is marked by extinct craters, ancient basaltic dikes, and bubbling hot springs, all of which show unmistakable signs of former earthquakes and volcanic activity.

Though the ancient Galileans for the most part were a quiet, peaceful, simple, hill-country folk, they were proud of their country; and when liberty was challenged, they went forth lionhearted to fight for their homeland against the Roman oppressors. Josephus writes, "The Galileans are inured to war from their infancy . . . nor hath the country been ever destitute of men of courage or wanted a numerous set of them." Also, excavations have uncovered the ancient remains of great pillars and fine capitals, beautifully carved stones, ornamental decorations, and inscriptions, which indicate that they were a people who excelled in the building craft.[2]

Cities and villages have long dotted the Galilean hillsides. Here lay the "twenty cities" which Solomon gave Hiram in return for the cedars of Lebanon, which had been carried to Jerusalem for the purpose of ceiling Solomon's new palace and Temple.

At certain intervals through the past centuries, the country has been ravaged by earthquake and war. It was the vanguard in the fight against Rome and the battleground in the fight for the preservation of the ancient synagogues of that time with their

A shepherd with a flock of fat-tailed sheep in Upper Galilee

Jewish symbols and Hellenistic art forms. It was in Upper Galilee that the Jews showed such self-sacrifice for their culture, their country, and their homes. Almost every acre there is a reminder of those events.

After the fall of Jerusalem the bulk of the Jewish people concentrated in Galilee; and it became for many centuries onward, until the Arab conquest, the center of Jewish political and religious life. Principal among the ancient and present cities are the following: *Abel-beth-maachah, Safad, Meron, Gischala, Zebulun, Kedesh, Hazor, Rosh Pina, Metulla,* and *Kfar Gilaid.*

Abel-beth-maachah ("meadow of the house of oppression") was a city of importance in the extreme northern portion of Palestine, which played a rather important although somewhat tragic role in ancient Bible times. It was to this fortified city that Joab pursued Sheba, son of Bichri, and the "wise woman" tossed the rebel's head over the wall and saved the city (2 Sam. 20:14). It was taken by the Syrians under Ben-hadad (1 Kings 15:

20), and later by the Assyrians under Tiglath-pileser (2 Kings 15:29). In Roman times it was known as Abila. Today it is known as *Tell Abil,* and is a typical unexcavated city mound rising out boldly on an upland plain some six miles west of Dan, overlooking the Lake Huleh lowlands that stretch away to the southeast.

Safad, one of the four "holy cities" of the Jews, and supposedly the city to which Christ referred when He said, "A city that is set on a hill cannot be hid," proudly curls about the top of Mount Safad, 16 miles north of Tiberias and 3,400 feet above the Sea of Galilee.

Within the city are narrow streets, flights of steep steps, whitewashed houses with extended balconies, and synagogues on which appear mysterious Cabalistic signs. About the place are large olive plantations, fruitful vineyards, and the strangest mystical charms pervading the atmosphere—deep rooted in the past, yet ample to entertain the eye of the present. On a clear day, much of Upper and Lower Galilee and the Sea of Galilee may be seen from this tableland city.

In the glory days of the kingdoms of Israel and Judah it was called Tsafet, or Zefat, which means the "place of outlook." From it a beacon light was lighted announcing the rising of the new moon, which was first proclaimed in Jerusalem on the Mount of Olives and relayed from high point to high point until Safad's beacon served as a signal for northern Palestine.[3]

Safad excites an attitude of reverence in the hearts of the Jews; for it was the refuge of many ancient rabbis after the fall of Jerusalem and the bitter defeat of Bar Cochba at Bittier in A.D. 132; and as a scholar's retreat it became the seat of a great Talmudic school, a center of Judaic and Cabalistic lore. It is even probable that the celebrated *Midrash Ha Zohar,* the Book of Splendor, the Bible of the Kabala, attributed to Simon ben Yohai, was edited here by a Spanish rabbi who flourished about A.D. 160. It was also the residence of Joseph Caro, author of the *Ahulchan Aruch,* the last codification of the Jewish law; and his pupil, Rabbi Jacob Berov, who endeavored to reestablish Palestine as the center for rabbinical ordination.

In the 16th and 17th centuries, Safad became the center of

immigration from Spain and the rendezvous of the Jews for the study of Cabalist mysticism. Jewish poetry saw its revival when Alkabetz wrote the famous Sabbath Eve hymn, "Come, My Friend, to Meet the Bride." At this time the first printing press of all Asia was set up, and the first Hebrew book printed in Palestine.

In 1607, there was reputed to be in Safad 300 rabbis, 18 rabbinical colleges, and 21 synagogues. Because it housed this great rabbinical school, Safad earned for itself among the Jews the high distinction of being one of the four holy cities of Israel.

Here the Jewish mystics dreamed dreams, saw visions, and compiled the *Zohar,* in which it was stated that the Messiah would appear first in Upper Galilee. Isaac Luria stands out as the giant and genius of all these mystics, and the grandest figure of Safad legend, and his pupil, Rabbi Haim Vital, almost as famous. It was the mystics' dreaming which made possible the messianic movement that had its strange fulfillment in the Shabbathai Zevi, and which also bore fresh fruit in more recent years when the modern dream of the return to Palestine stirred the heart of Israel.

An earthquake occurred at Safad in 1765, in which most of the inhabitants were killed; but the town was resettled so that by the early 1800s it housed 4,000 Jews. Unfortunately another disastrous earthquake occurred in 1836 and once again took the lives of most of the community. Since this disaster the city fell from its proud Jewish pinnacle, and its schools and synagogues no longer had preeminence. However, it is now flourishing again under the new Israeli government and is known especially for its "artists' colony."

Meron, four miles northwest of Safad, is a small village located in a picturesque setting of fine groves of olive and fig trees. It is frequently mentioned in the Talmud and is revered by the Jews as one of their most sacred shrines, because it was here that the famous rabbis and celebrated Jewish sages of centuries past, who lived at Safad and elsewhere, were buried: Rabbi Simon ben Yohai, the one whose teachings inspired the Jewish revolt against the Romans; his son Rabbi Eleazar; Rabbi Jochanan Sanderlar, a distinguished disciple of Rabbi Akiba, who would accept no payment for his teaching but made a living by repairing the sandals of his students; and of Rabbis Hillel and Shamai, the two most celebrated scholars who were famous for their interpretation of the Law and their teaching of the Talmud. Even the prophet Obadiah is said to be buried here.[4]

Once a year, on the anniversary of the death of Rabbi Simon ben Yohai, vast crowds come in procession from Safad, carrying decorated scrolls of the law. They throng the way to the tomb of Simon and light festive fires into which silks, jewels, and other valuables are thrown as sacrifices. Hundreds of candles burn in front of the tomb while young and old in glad abandon dance in ecstasy their religious dances from sunset to dawn. At midnight the sound of prayer mingles with the sound of song, and the sound of song accompanies the stepping of the dance, and the stepping of the dance keeps in time with the blazing of the fires and the words

Rabbi Simon ben Yohai,
He will never die;
His name is glorified on high,
Rabbi Simon ben Yohai

rise to the star-laden sky from the lips of Jews who have come from every quarter of the globe to Meron of Galilee to give expression to that more intense longing for a communion with God by means of ecstasy.

Gischala, now called El Jish, is located five miles northwest of Safad. It was a prosperous city in the time of Christ and is thought by some to be the original home of Paul's parents. It was the native home of John of Gischala who tricked the Romans in A.D. 67. This was the last of the Galilean fortresses to hold out against the Romans. The army had surrounded the city and offered John protection for surrender, but he begged that they would recognize the sacredness of the Sabbath day and withdraw their army until the following day when terms could be formally concluded.

When Titus, in all good faith, withdrew his troops for the

night, John of Gischala and his band of Zealots marched out of the city under cover of darkness and made their way to Jerusalem. On Monday the Romans took the city without its leaders. At a later date Gischala was totally destroyed by an earthquake; not a house of any kind was left standing. However, the village has been partially rebuilt.

Zebulun, now called Neby Sebelan, is only a few miles southwest of Gischala and is wedged between the southern half of Naphtali and Asher.

Kedesh or *Kedesh-Naphtali* was one of the six cities of refuge in Old Testament times, the birthplace of Barak (Judg. 4:6), and the traditional burial place of Naphtali, Barak, Deborah, and Jael. The site of ancient Kedesh is now partially occupied by a small Arab village located on the end of a ridge overlooking the Kadesh plain. The ruins about the place are quite extensive, the most imposing of which are those of a structure called the Temple of the Sun.

Hazor is situated three miles south of Kedesh, at the head of one of the most rugged ascents in Palestine. It is in a strong position, occupying a full 200 acres on top of the mound. Once a royal town, but in recent times a rocky hillock honeycombed with broken cisterns, it is surrounded in places by broken walls and partially filled moats.

It was destroyed by Joshua during the great battle with the Canaanites but was rebuilt and became the capital of another Jabin, who long oppressed the northern tribes. He was finally overthrown in a crushing defeat in the great battle of Tabor, when Deborah and Barak led the Hebrews. Extensive excavations have been carried on at Hazor, since 1955, by Dr. Yigael Yadin. Ten city levels were found on the mound of the acropolis, one of which was identified as the "Solomonic level."

Rosh Pina, the "Mother of Colonies," is situated on a parcel of land at the foot of Mount Canaan, just a short distance east of Safad. It was founded in 1882 by about 50 Jewish families from Romania who walked or rode camels from Beirut to the site which had been purchased by Reb Davis. On seeing the rock and boulder-crowned area, they were overwhelmed by its grandeur and exclaimed, "The rock rejected by the builders became the cornerstone [Rosh Pina]" (Ps. 122:18). They made a covenant of peace with the Arabs and built with this verse reverberating in their ears.

In the following year they celebrated their first Harvest Festival and made a covenant between man and the soil by their first marriage. Unfortunately an Arab construction worker was accidentally killed by a shot fired in honor of the bride. After considerable compensation and intercession, peace was finally restored at a great "feast of forgiveness," and the next of kin renounced their right to avenge the death of their kinsman.

The settlers were often plagued by drought, malaria, mosquitos, pernicious illness, and death. They became discouraged and talked of abandoning the place and returning to Romania. But when the more courageous members had convened the settlers in the synagogue, one mother who had lost her only son cried: "Are you not ashamed to leave the graves of your beloved ones here and shamefully return to your 'airy-business' in Diaspora?" They reconsidered and took an oath on the Torah scroll not to abandon the colony, and to excommunicate the "traitors and cowards" who dared to do so.

Shortly thereafter Baron Edmund Rothschild took Rosh Pina under his wing and furnished money, new homes and courtyards, a large schoolhouse, a beautiful synagogue, and shelters for their livestock. The settlers piped water to their homes, planted vineyards and mulberry trees for cultivating silkworms, and built factories for silk manufacture. Other families came, and the colony has prospered ever since.

Metulla, the northernmost Jewish settlement, noted for its healthful and invigorating mountain air and excellent view of the upper Jordan Valley, is located west of Mount Hermon and the ruins of the ancient Jewish city of Dan.

104   It too was founded by Baron Rothschild in 1896. Its main industry is grain, and cattle, with vineyards, almonds, and fruit trees being added more recently.

Kfar Gilaid with its surrounding grainfields and its hillsides decked with various fruit trees appears as a blooming garden spot or oasis in the desolation of the surrounding country.

It was originally founded in 1917 as two separate colonies on land belonging to Baron Rothschild, but was eventually merged into one. The settlers were all former members of the famous organization, "The Guard," which rendered wonderful service to the Jewish settlements of Palestine in the days of the early colonization movement.

Upper Galilee is a pleasant land with good soil, many trees, an excellent climate, and reasonable rainfall. It has long had farms and villages inhabited by Moslems, Druzes, and Christian Arabs. This century has brought a number of Jewish settlements which have done very well with olives, grain, dairying, poultry raising, bee-keeping, fishponds, and other means of livelihood, yet the country is sparsely settled, and could well become the home of many other tens of thousands of industrious home seekers. The one thing needed here, and throughout the Holy Land, is PEACE.

CHAPTER **9**

Lower Galilee

Lower Galilee is situated just south of Upper Galilee and is north of the Plain of Armageddon and the Valley of Jezreel. To the west lies the Plain of Acre, while the Sea of Galilee makes up the eastern boundary.

This picturesque and beautiful country is largely composed of a series of low, long, parallel mountain ranges with broad plateaus broken by wooded glens; wide, fertile valleys; meandering brooks; and soft marshland. The rolling hills of Lower Galilee are not as rugged as those of Upper Galilee, and the valleys and plains are wider; and in season their fields of wheat and barley, with alternate stretches of fallow land, mark a checkerboard on the plains and along the lower reaches of the hills and mountains.

The soil in most of Lower Galilee is very fertile. Flowers of many varieties grow bountifully, and it is known for its great variety of fruits, melons, grain, and vegetables. There are forests of oak, orchards of olive and fig trees, and the evergreen cactus hedges which show off well against numerous white walls.

The villages in Lower Galilee are many, but its principal cities of historical interest are Nazareth, Sepphoris, Jotapata, Cana, Nain, and Endor.

Nazareth nestles within a circular vale and on the surrounding mountain slopes just above the Plain of Armageddon. It was never mentioned by name either in the Old Testament nor by Josephus, but it has a prominent place in the New Testament. Inwardly and silently the life of the Master, in His formative years, unfolded itself at Nazareth. Thirty out of the 33 years that He lived on the earth were here, and that life in those few years stamped the city with a sacredness which will last until the end of time.

It is sometimes said that Nazareth was an obscure place, but this is an inaccurate statement. The city, in Christ's day, was little more than a mile long and a half mile wide, and was almost completely shut in by surrounding hills. This provided seclusion, yet it was not an out-of-the-way place, for along the hilltops a few hundred yards east of the city there ran a much traveled branch road, and five miles east was the highway from Assyria to Egypt, over which went caravans of all kinds and men of every nation and tongue. As a young man Jesus could climb the high hill back of Nazareth and see the great Plain of Armageddon, Mount Carmel, the Mediterranean Sea, Mount Tabor, the Jezreel Valley, Gilboa, and the great international highway.

Jesus was a carpenter in Nazareth until that day He left the shop to enter His period of active ministry. Yet being a carpenter then meant some things different from now. Someone has suggested that the imagery of His teachings and His parables carry an atmosphere of the life of the soil—of nature and the farm such as you would expect to find in the country, rather than that of the carpenter shop. However, in those days—as in rural Palestine today—the carpenter made plows, yokes, and goads for field work, and made or mended carts, wagons, and chariots for the highways. These were made of wood, while most homes were made almost entirely of stone or of adobe brick and were constructed mostly by the masons.

As a carpenter, Jesus made yokes, and deep was the meaning of His words, "Take my yoke upon you, and learn of me . . . For my yoke is easy, and my burden is light" (Matt. 11:29-30). As a minister, Jesus Christ returned "in the power of the Spirit" into Galilee and taught in their synagogues. He came to Nazareth, where He had been brought up, and as usual went into the synagogue on the Sabbath day. It was there He read from the scroll of the prophet Isaiah the words:

> The Spirit of the Lord is upon me, because he hath anointed me to preach the gospel to the poor; he hath sent me to heal the brokenhearted, to preach deliverance to the captives, and recovering of sight to the blind, to set at liberty them that are bruised, to preach the acceptable year of the Lord (Luke 4:18-19).

When the people endeavored to stare Him out of countenance, He added, "This day is this scripture fulfilled in your ears." At that the people hustled Him out of the city and to the brow of the hill where they intended to throw Him headlong to His death. But He evaded them and left unnoticed. No record was ever kept as to the exact precipice, but a steep defile southeast is now called the Mount of Precipitation and is pointed out as the place where Christ's enemies had thought to end His career.

After Christ's time, there is little of importance on record about Nazareth until the time of Constantine, when the first Christian church was built there in A.D. 330. Then Nazareth became an object of great interest to which pilgrims flocked from all parts of the Christian world.

In Crusading times it became the seat of bishops, eight of whom are mentioned. In A.D. 1187 it was taken by Saladin, and his successors destroyed its churches, reducing it to an insignificant village. It was visited by Sir John Maundeville in A.D. 1332. In A.D. 1620 the Franciscans tried to establish themselves there, and in 1730 their first church, the Church of the Annunciation, was consecrated. Many Christians, chiefly Maronites, from Mount Lebanon began to make pilgrimages to it; and also Orthodox Christians from the Hauran in Transjordan.

Today Nazareth is a city of some 44,000 people, and as one passes along the narrow, yet attractive, streets, he hears the clang of hammers of the artisans who beat out brass and copper goods which lie on the ground both without and within the dark recesses of the shops. He may pause at the carpenter's shop where plows, yokes, tables, and stools are made, and the odor of sandalwood, wafted from the shops of curio makers, will remind one of the distant days when the Master was a woodworker in this selfsame place.

At the top of the principal Suke, the road turns abruptly to the left where the clothiers, the saddlers, and the drapers have their shops. The street is very attractive, and it is difficult to pass along it quickly without stopping to look, question, and purchase. The saddlers are particularly fascinating for, instead of plain brown leather, they deal in girths and reins of woven black, yellow and blue, and hung with woolen tassels.

Farther on, the grocery shops begin and the passerby has to push past trays of coffee beans and sugar and pink and white sweetmeats, big tins of paraffin, baskets of walnuts or almonds all crowding out of the shops onto the pavement, making the narrow street narrower still.

The chief water supply for the city of Nazareth has long been the Virgin's Fountain, which is the only living spring of water in or near the city. The women and girls fill their jars here morning and night. This sight, and the fountain itself, does much to give one a true picture of what occurred on many a day while Christ lived here in the long ago.

The houses in the main part of town are of gray limestone 109 and are crowded close together from the base to near the summit of the hill; these are interspersed with fig, tamarisk, and carob trees. Olive groves and green cactus hedges enliven the landscape and give the little mountain town a picturesque appearance which is not easily forgotten by anyone who has looked upon the place. Some of the numerous "holy places" here could be false, but Nazareth is real; and that being true, it is holy ground. The events that took place here have made it such. However, for those who desire to see what church leaders have to show in the way of traditional "holy places," there is a church building to mark each place.

First, in size and importance, is the *Church of the Annunciation* which is a new church (completed in 1966) which is said to be the largest Christian church in the Holy Land and one of the most holy shrines in the Christian world. Some regard it as the very cradle of Christianity. It is built over the site of a church which stood here from 1730 to 1955, and which itself was built over a Crusader foundation of the 12th century. The church stands on the site where, according to Christian tradition, the angel appeared before Mary to announce the birth of Jesus:

> The angel Gabriel was sent from God unto a city of Galilee, named Nazareth, to a virgin espoused to a man whose name was Joseph, of the house of David; and the virgin's name was Mary. And the angel came in unto her, and said, Hail, thou that art highly favoured, the Lord is with thee: blessed art thou among women. . . . Fear not, Mary: for thou hast found favour with God. And, behold, thou shalt conceive in thy womb, and bring forth a son, and shalt call his name JESUS. He shall be great, and shall be called the Son of the Highest . . . and of his kingdom there shall be no end *(Luke 1:26-28, 30-33).*

The Grotto of the Annunciation is in the basement, and the altar there is inscribed with the words: "Verbum caro hic factum est"—Here the Word was made flesh.

The Church of Joseph, or the Church of the Holy Family, is supposed to occupy the site of the home of Mary and Joseph, with Joseph's carpenter shop in the basement. In the basement the altar bears the inscription: "Hic erat subditus illis"—Here He became subject to them. Excavations have been carried on here for some time, but as yet no final proof has been brought forth that this was the site of the home and the shop in which the Great Carpenter lived and worked.

The Synagogue Church is located in a market lane, and the ancient church beside it is the one which, according to tradition, is the synagogue Jesus attended.

The Basilica of Jesus the Adolescent is a beautiful church on the mountain overlooking Nazareth from the west. Adjoining it is the seminary usually known as the "Boy's School." This is well worth seeing, and the view from the top of the hill is one of the finest in the Holy Land—a point of view from which Jesus must have feasted His eyes many times.

Kiryat Natsrat is the name of the new Jewish suburb built on the top of the hills which tower above the city on the northeast.

Sepphoris, three miles northwest of Nazareth, was the Roman capital of Galilee during Christ's time. Through Sepphoris ran one of the great high roads from the Mediterranean coast to Damascus. Tradition suggests that Sepphoris was the original home of the parents of Mary, mother of Jesus. At one time it was the headquarters of the Jewish Sanhedrin, and here the Romans crucified many a Jew while Jesus was a boy. Sepphoris is surrounded with olive trees, and about a mile to the south is Kustul Seffurieh, with the fine large springs, where the army of the Christians encamped before the battle of Hattin. The city now lies in ruins.

Jotapata, now called *Khurbet Jefat,* is a ruin five and one-half miles north of Sepphoris. It is thought to be the town which gave name to the Valley of Jiphthahel mentioned in Josh. 19:27, but its fame is bound up with Josephus, the famous Jewish historian. It was here that Josephus fortified himself and his army for his last stand against the Romans in A.D. 67. Water was then scarce but provisions were plentiful, and the city was on a high precipice only accessible from the north. Here it was protected by a high wall.

Vespasian, the Roman general, built a bank against the wall, but the defenders built the wall higher and poured down boiling oil on the Roman soldiers. Then the Romans built 50 strong towers near the walls, whence, out of reach of the boiling oil, they hurled stones and threw javelins. Jotapata held out 47 days; then, during a surprise attack at early dawn on the morning of July 1, A.D. 67, a huge battering ram made a breach in the wall, and the Romans poured in and took control of the strong city. The women were taken as slaves, 15,000 men were killed, and 2,000 were sent to help cut the canal of Corinth. Josephus and four companions jumped into a dry well and from thence went into an underground cavern. When they were discovered and asked to surrender with a promise that they would be spared, Josephus desired to do so, but his companions were unwilling. They formed a death pact, drew lots, and killed each other, till only Josephus and one companion were left. Then by mutual consent the two walked out and surrendered themselves to the Romans.

Assuming the role of a prophet, Josephus advised them that Vespasian would soon become the emperor of the Roman Empire. The Romans thereafter used Josephus as an advisor and historian in the Palestinian campaign. The hill on which Vespasian camped is half a mile to the north.

Cana lies about four miles northeast of Nazareth. It is the hometown of Nathanael, the disciple of Jesus, and has become famous as the place of the wedding feast where Christ performed His first miracle by turning water into wine for the guests. Cana is a large village with well-built houses, but with few special marks of antiquity. The place is known as *Kefar Kana* to all the people in this region. It stands amidst many pomegranate, orange, and olive trees, along with arbors of grapevine. Nearby is a spring which is called the "Source of Cana."

The town itself nestles among the stony hills as so frequently characterizes the hillside villages of Palestine. Cana has two churches, both claiming to be built upon the site of the marriage feast. One is Latin, the other Greek. The Latin church, however, is the older of the two. Each of the churches displays two large water jars, declaring them to be the identical waterpots Christ used at the wedding feast. One may walk along a narrow path leading by stone houses and mud hovels to the center of the village, which looks very prosperous. An ornate marble sarcophagus does duty as a water trough, and women can be seen filling their pitchers from its contents.

Nain, now called Nein, lies on the northwestern slope of Mount Moreh, overlooking the lovely expanse of the northern arm of the Plain of Esdraelon, out of which, just opposite, rises the majestic Mount Tabor.

Here our Lord restored the widow's son to life and thus proved himself Lord of life (Luke 7:11-15). The city of Nein is now a small village of about 20 huts on a rocky slope in the midst of extensive ruins. There is a small modern Latin chapel that lies in the midst of a Moslem population. Four miles to the east of Nein is the village of Endor.

Endor is obviously the Endor of the Old Testament, assigned to Manasseh, though lying without the borders of that tribe. It is mentioned also in connection with the victory of Deborah and Barak, but is chiefly known as the abode of the sorceress to whom King Saul made his way and consulted on the eve of the fatal battle of Gilboa. Demoralized and despairing, he skirted the enemy camp by night and heard his own doom foretold (1 Sam. 28:3-25). The name does not occur in the New Testament; but in the days of Eusebius and Jerome, Endor was still a large village four Roman miles south of Mount Tabor, corresponding to the present site. It was recognized in the time of the Crusades and is mentioned by Brocardus, but appears afterwards to have been again lost sight of, at least partially, until the 17th century.

The famous *mountains* of this section are: Mount Tabor, the Hill of Moreh, and the Mount of Beatitudes.

Mount Tabor, the finest and most beautiful of the mountains of Galilee, rises out from the Plain of Tabor to a height of 1,843 feet above sea level. It is located five miles southeast of Nazareth, and is in the triad of sacred mountains—Hermon, Tabor, and Carmel—so often referred to in Scripture (Ps. 89:12; Jer. 46:18). When the Psalmist exclaims: "Tabor and Hermon shall rejoice in thy name," he selected these two as the representatives of all the mountains of Palestine: Mount Tabor was the most graceful, and Mount Hermon the loftiest.

As a symbol of beauty, of grace, and of strength, Tabor

A patchwork of cultivated fields in Lower Galilee as seen from Mount Tabor.

carries its symmetrical outlines and proportions upward from its base to its crown. When viewed from the south, it appears like a huge sugarloaf or a hemisphere; but when seen from other directions, it has the appearance of an arched mound or dome—depending upon the direction from which it is viewed.

Its graceful slopes are dotted with trees, and its picturesque coves are grown over with groves of oak and other greenery where fallow deer may occasionally be seen. Into one of these coves Deborah and Barak rallied 10,000 men who, at the proper time, swept down upon Sisera and his Canaanite army and threw them into confused flight (Judg. 4:6-17). Here, on Mount Tabor, Zebah and Zalmunna, kings of Midian, killed Gideon's brothers (Judg. 8:18-21). Here, through the ages, many forces have struggled for possession of the mountain, and here on its summit many temples, forts, and churches have been built and destroyed.

In former years, access to the top was by thousands of steps cut into the steep slope, but now a narrow roadway ascends the

114

mountain in a series of hairpin curves. The summit is a half-mile-wide rounded cone crowned by the beautiful Franciscan Basilica of the Transfiguration, with its adjoining pilgrim hostel, the Greek Church of St. Elias, and many ancient ruins.

From the summit of Tabor (some stand on top of the high Crusader wall) a fine view is afforded—the eye taking in the snowy top of Mount Hermon, Safad, the Sea of Galilee, Mount Carmel, the Plain of Esdraelon, Gilboa, the Jordan Valley, and the land beyond the Jordan.[1] An early tradition placed the scene of Christ's transfiguration on Mount Tabor, and vast numbers of pilgrims have visited the place with this in mind. But the tradition has been suspected as a fourth-century convenience, seeing it does not agree with the account given in the Gospels, nor with the fact that it was permanently occupied by a Roman garrison during the time of Christ. Most all students of the Bible agree that the Transfiguration must have taken place on Mount Hermon, for the events before and after took place around the base of Hermon.[2]

Mount Moreh or the **Hill of Moreh** is more or less insignificant as to appearance, yet its prominence in location has caused it to play a conspicuous part in various events of history. Not that the mountain itself has often been utilized, but many incidents have taken place at various points about its base, and many armies have camped nearby. The villages of Shunem, Endor, and Nein nestle at its feet; on its crest is a Moslem *weli* to which the faithful make pilgrimages; and about its foothills a number of thriving colonies are now located.

This mountain has sometimes been called "Little Hermon" but is in no way to be confused with Mount Hermon. The strange designation began in the fourth century when it was difficult for the zealous pilgrims to visit the true Mount Hermon far away to the northeast; the accommodating monks found it desirable to show this as Mount Hermon. The identification was exceedingly unfortunate, for there is no authority whatsoever for calling it any other than Mount Moreh.

Belvoir, the famous Crusader castle-fortress, occupies one of the most picturesque scarps extending eastward from Mount

Moreh. It rises 1,400 feet above the Jordan Valley and is so situated that one standing on its heights may see the movements of men much of the way between Tiberias and Beth Shean. It commands a view of two highways ascending from the Jordan Valley westward into the interior: one by the Jezreel Valley and the other by way of the Tabor Valley.

In Roman times the fort of Agrippina stood here. In 1168, the Crusaders purchased the site and erected Belvoir, one of their famous castle-forts which held off strong Moslem forces until January, 1191, when the eastern tower was undermined and destroyed. Seeing the hopelessness of continuing the struggle, the Christian forces sued for peace and were permitted free passage to the city of Tyre. Belvoir was dismantled in 1241, and eventually an Arab village rose amid its ruins. However, it too was abandoned in 1948. In 1966-67, excavations were carried out at the site by M. Ben-Dor on behalf of the National Park Authority. Stables, storerooms, cisterns, a kitchen, a very fine hall with pillars, and capitals made of black basalt stood next to the church.

Kurn-Hattin, "The Horns of Hattin," four miles northwest of Tiberias, has been known to the world since the time of the Crusades as the **Mount of Beatitudes,** from which Christ delivered His matchless sermon as recorded in the Gospel of Matthew. No really authentic history confirms the Crusaders' conclusion, yet there is a fine natural amphitheater there, and no other mountain or peak in the vicinity answers to the Gospel description so well as this place; therefore with some the tradition has passed almost unchallenged.

At its eastern end is an elevated point or horn, rising about 100 feet above the plain; and at the southwestern end another rocky ridge almost as high. Between the two is a natural depression, which gives to the mountain at a distance the appearance of a huge saddle. The place is called "Horns of Hattin" because of this appearance. When viewed from the west, this place has the appearance of two great horns protruding in the air only a little way above the gradually rising land elevation, while on the north there is a very steep descent of 800 feet to another plain, which again terminates at the Sea of Galilee. The mount itself, with its twin heads, rises 1,038 feet above sea level.

The natural depression between the horns makes up a very natural amphitheater which would accommodate a few thousand people. Here, with its naturelike arrangement, the multitude were gathered eager to catch Christ's words and to receive His gifts.

Having spent the previous night in solitary prayer, Christ stood forth, amid the scenery of the mountains, with majesty on His brow, love in His heart, and truth on His tongue. Alluding

The "Horns of Hattin" looking east toward the upper end of the Sea of Galilee.

to the fowls of the air, He looked up, and, behold, they were hovering near Him at the moment of speaking. Referring to the grasses and lilies, they were flourishing at His feet and perfuming the breeze just as they do today. To the north, situated on the edge of a high hill, was the little town of Safad. His message was so wise and so divine that its sentences burned like fire in the human hearts. It was like a flood that swept everything before it. No one has endeavored to contest the simple statements or deride the sweet spirit in which this sermon was pronounced, or to render illogical the underlying basis of the whole. It easily rates as the greatest message ever spoken.

Therefore, it is not considered strange that many modern pilgrims have stood here and read: "Blessed are they which do hunger and thirst after righteousness"; "Let your light so shine"; "Love your enemies . . . pray for them which despitefully use you . . . that ye may be the children of your Father which is in heaven"; "Is not the life more than meat, and the body than raiment?"; "Seek ye first the kingdom of God."

Aside from its scriptural associations, Hattin is a historical center to which the terminal lines of the Crusades point. Here, in July, 1187, the Crusaders were marshalled under King Guy and the grand master of the Knights Templars, and were opposed by the Mohammedan forces under the gallant Saladin. Around the Horns of Hattin the battle raged until King Guy was taken prisoner, the grand master was slain, and the heroic knights either slain or made prisoners. The cross gave way to the crescent, the flower-embowered mountain was bathed with the blood of martyrs, and the might of the Crusaders was forever broken in Palestine.[3]

When on the summit of Hattin, all nature seems silent yet eloquent. Lying spread out like a carpet before one are fields of varied hues. On the north down the steep declines nestles the peaceful city of Hattin. On the northeast one sees the forbidding brow of the Robber Hill, and on beyond the northern part of the Sea of Galilee and on its western shore the beautiful Plain of Gennesaret.

At the present, Lower Galilee is undergoing intense settlement and development by the Jewish people. Agriculture, poultry, and cattle raising promise a great future for thousands of happy and industrious families.

CHAPTER **10**

The Plain of Armageddon

The Plain of Armageddon, frequently called *The Plain of Esdraelon,* or simply *The Emak,* is a vast inland basin—a great fertile plain in the midst of the land.

From the landward slopes of Mount Carmel near *Tell el Kassis* the plain rises gradually to the southeast and continues far into the curving cove at the foot of Mount Gilboa. On its northeast it continues to Mount Tabor. The Galilean mountains form a northern boundary, and the Samarian mountains bound the southern limits. The plain itself is from 5 to 14 miles wide, and approximately 22 miles long at its greatest length.

The word *Armageddon*, or *Harmageddon*, is the Greek form for "The Mountain of Megiddo," or "The Hill of Megiddo." Megiddo means a "place of troops," and the plain takes its name from the city of Megiddo which lies on a hill, guarding the entrance to the pass of Megiddo on the southwestern border of the plain.

The plain has an average altitude of 250 feet and is hollowed out slightly so that it catches the drainage from the surrounding chains of mountains. These mountains rise to a fair height on all sides and slope gradually away to the plain far below.

The *river Kishon* drains the Plain of Armageddon. It rises in the northern hills of Samaria—around the foothills of Gilboa and the Springs of Jenin—and flows northwestward through the Plain of Armageddon, and empties into the Mediterranean under the brow of Mount Carmel. It is a sluggish river in the summertime but often becomes a roaring and dangerous torrent during the winter. As a river, the Kishon is second only to the river Jordan in Palestine and has played a prominent part in the varied events of the plain.

At intervals for more than 30 centuries the plain has been

The vast plain of Armageddon (Esdraelon) as seen looking east from Mount Carmel.

used as a common battleground of nations. Being the middle ground between Asia and Africa, and stretching out for many miles, it has afforded ample terrain for chariots and horses and men to spread themselves. Therefore military men of many nations met here to fight their decisive battles and endeavor to settle their differences, until historians have regarded it as the world's classic battlefield.

Physically, the plain is like a vast stage set for peace or for war, with five natural openings or passes carefully arranged for men of peace or for armies to make their entries and their exits. At the western end is the *Pass of Kishon* through which the Kishon River breaks through low-lying hills to enter the sea in Haifa Bay; halfway along the southwestern side, Megiddo guards the *Pass of Megiddo,* through which comes the highway of the nations between the rich clime of Egypt and the populous nations of Asia; the *Pass of Jenin* at the southeastern corner accommodates the central highway from Judea and Samaria; the *Pass of Jezreel* leads from Arabia and the Jordan up by Bethshean through the Valley of Jezreel; and at the northeastern corner is the *Tabor Pass,* where the immemorial road from Damascus and Tiberias skirts around Mount Tabor and enters the plain.[1]

Long and impressive is the list of military conquerors who have entered through these passes and made battle on this historic plain. Names familiar in history, such as Thotmes III, Ramses II, Nebuchadnezzar, Sargon, Sennacharib, Pharaoh-Necho, Alexander the Great, Titus, Richard I, Saladin, Napoleon Bonaparte, and Allenby of the British Army are but a few of those who have entered into military engagements in this arena of war. Thus, the Assyrians, the Babylonians, the Persians, the Jews, the Egyptians, the Crusaders, the Arabs, the Turks, the French, as well as the British, and warriors from other nations have fought and had their fate to hang on engagements here.

No section of land on the face of the earth attracts more attention from biblical and prophetic students than does this plain. For the Jews it has held a place in their history since the origin of their race. It has demanded the attention of the Christian Church since the time of John and gathers climactic interest in the closing chapters of the Book of Revelation.[2]

The earliest battle fought by Israel on the plain of Megiddo was when Sisera, the captain of King Jabin's Canaanitish forces, came against Israel with 900 chariots of iron. Deborah and Barak rallied Israel in a wooded glen well up on the side of Mount Tabor, where they "watched till the lengthening line of the enemy's chariots drew out the western angle at Tell el Kassis and stretched opposite to them with Ta'anach and Megiddo behind them," then Israel gave them battle in a fierce highland charge, while God sent a heavy rainstorm, confusing and frustrating the invaders. The river Kishon filled to overflowing, the battlefield was turned into a sea of mud, and the chariots bogged to a standstill.[3]

Crazed with fear, their drivers and the accompanying infantry raced on foot westward for the Pass of Kishon at Tell el Kassis where the Kishon flows out to the Plain of Acre and to the Haifa Bay. Here the overflowing waters surged in swirling torrents through the pass and swept the proud Canaanites to their ruin. After this great victory, Deborah and Barak sang a song of thanksgiving unto God:

> They fought from heaven; the stars in their courses fought against Sisera.
> The river Kishon swept them away, the ancient river, the river Kishon. O my soul, march on with strength.[4]

One of Judah's sad, tragic battles was the one in which the good King Josiah went out very unwisely to stop Pharaoh-Necho of Egypt, and was slain at the Pass of Megiddo. In defeat and deep sorrow they returned with him in his chariot to Jerusalem and buried him in his own sepulchre. Then Jehoahaz was anointed king in his father's stead at the age of 23.

The British advance upon the plain by General Allenby in September, 1918, was one of the most skillfully planned of any battle ever to be fought in the Middle East. Allenby prepared by leading the enemy to believe that the main attack on them was to come from east of the Jordan—from the forces of Feisal and

Lawrence—and from the west bank of the Jordan, where in reality only a huge sham camp and a skeleton force was maintained. Allenby's surprise attack actually came from the Plain of Sharon directly through the Pass of Megiddo onto the plain. The enemy was thoroughly unprepared to receive an attack from this direction; therefore their forces crumpled up, the two German-Turkish armies were destroyed, thousands of prisoners taken, and Allenby's conquest virtually completed.

Generally the Plain of Armageddon or Esdraelon has been associated with thoughts of war, yet there have been periods of time—decades, even centuries—in which peace and prosperity has reigned; and during these times there have been peaceful pursuits, and through these passes and across this plain have come caravans and merchantmen, patriarchs and prophets, the master seeking the lost, and the prodigal son returning home from a far country.

The soil of the plain is largely composed of volcanic deposits that have poured into the plain for centuries. The subsoil is basaltic in nature. Together, through decomposition, these have given the plain a marvelous fertility. In the ancient past the rich plain was the breadbasket of northern Palestine, and a source of animal forage and food for the many caravans that passed by that way. The Midianites and other ancient peoples sometimes came and carried away its abundant harvests. An inscription on the wall of the Temple of Amon at Thebes tells how King Thotmes III, during the 15th century B.C., fought against Megiddo and carried away 924 chariots, 2,238 horses, and how he sent his army up to the Plain of Megiddo every year to cut grain necessary to keep the horses of his cavalry. On one of these expeditions he carried away 150,000 bushels.

At the close of the First World War the plain presented one of the poorest potentials of all places in Palestine. Then in 1921, the Jewish National Fund purchased the plain and made it their first big reclamation project. Swamps, marches, mosquitoes, and malaria were so prevalent that among the Arabs it was a common saying that a bird could not fly over it without becoming contaminated. Yet wise men knew that beneath all this noxious organic matter there was fertility. Men and women entered the plain with machines, with brawn, and with determination. They cut ditches, laid underground pipes, drained swamps, leveled land, harnessed springs, and planted trees until within a few years the marshes were gone, the mosquitoes killed, malaria stamped out, and the land restored to its normal productiveness.

Nahalal, the first settlement, was founded in 1921, and built in a circle—like a wagon wheel. In the center were such public buildings as the synagogue, the agricultural school, the communal center, warehouse, chicken runs, and dairy barns. Out from the central circle radiated 75 strips of land like slender slices of pie. Each strip of land contained 25 acres which was the home of a family who owned it as a corporate, independent, small holder. Members bought supplies and sold their products as a group, and helped each other in time of need. They marketed beef, milk, poultry, eggs, fruit, and vegetables.

125

The wagon-wheel arrangement of the Nahalal farming community on the Plain of Esdraelon.

Slowly but surely *Ginegar* and a dozen other colonies were laid out. Germans, Poles, Russians, and peoples from other lands filled the new settlements until today the Plain of Armageddon is dotted with colonies and villages and is crisscrossed with grainfields, gardens, vineyards, fruit orchards, and dairy farms which extend over most of the plain. Then there is the thriving city of *Afula*—crossroads for many ways. Water from the river Kishon, from 50 or more mountain springs, and from deep wells provide for considerable irrigation.

As seen from the heights, there are fields of wheat, barley, maize, millet, sesame, and fruit which form the checkerboard pattern on the plain and give it the appearance of being one of the most cultivated, fertile places in all the world. Varicolored strips of fallow ground break up the design made by these patchwork fields. The lower foothills on the outer edges of the plain are mottled by groves of fig and olive trees. In the northwest corner is the great Balfour Forest near the Jewish colony of Ginegar.

O Armageddon, what variables of human activity you have accommodated! On thy bosom great empires, races, and faiths have contended with each other, then marched on to judgment. Yet thy future is bound up with prosperous, peaceful settlements, and in the end, "the battle of that great day of God Almighty." As in John's vision, an angel "gathered them together into a place called . . . Armageddon . . . and there came a great voice out of heaven, from the throne, saying, It is done. And there were thunders, and lightnings, and a great earthquake, such as was not since men were upon the earth. . . . And every island fled away, and the mountains were not found" (Rev. 16:14-20).

CHAPTER **11**

The Valley of Jezreel

$\mathbf{T}$his narrow, yet exceedingly important valley is a beautiful, meadowlike expanse, from 2 to 3 miles wide and 11 miles long. It begins about a mile east of Afula, just northwest of ancient Jezreel, where there is a sudden fall of ground level eastwards, which visibly separates it from the Plain of Esdraelon or Armageddon. It breaks "as visibly as river from lake and has the slope and look of a current upon it." It passes below sea level about two miles from the Esdraelon plain; and with Mount Moreh on its left and Mount Gilboa on its right, it gently descends southeast for nine miles to Beth-Shan, where it falls over a ledge and 300 feet below merges with the Jordan Valley. Thus it separates Galilee from Samaria, and is a link between the Plain of Armageddon and the Jordan Valley.

It is also a transitory zone between the two in soils, climate, and living conditions. The valley is open throughout and offers a natural route for the high road from Damascus through this valley and over the great Plain of Armageddon, then on to Egypt.

Beautiful Jezreel Valley was the scene of considerable Bible history. It was intricately bound up with battles which often left its fertile acres strewn with war implements and soaked with blood. Here was fought the celebrated battle of Gideon and his 300 against the Midianites and their allies. At harvesttime the Midianites, along with other nomadic tribes, often made incursions through the Valley of the Jordan up to the Valley of Jezreel and on to the Plain of Armageddon. By sheer force of numbers, they took over the fields and reaped the harvest; they permitted their flocks and herds to trample down the fields; they plundered vineyards and gardens; and they seized cattle and robbed men and houses.

At a time when Israel had become morally weak by erecting altars to Baal on the high mountain peaks of the country, the foreign forces entered the country, encamped with headquarters at Shunem, and threatened all the land of Israel. In this midnight hour of Israel's hope, the Spirit of the Lord came upon Gideon. He blew a trumpet and collected a 32,000-man army at *Ain Harod* —a fine spring at the foot of the northern slope of Mount Gilboa. From the position of this spring, the vast host of the children of the east could be seen lying along the valley "like grasshoppers for multitude, and their camels were without number as the sands of the sea for multitude."

Most generals would have called for more soldiers, but, at God's word, Gideon called for less. Twice did he winnow his forces. Then when left with only 300 who had taken the water in their hands and lapped it as they went forward, he armed them with trumpets, pitchers, and a flaming torch within each pitcher. In the dark hours of that night, his valiant little army charged the

128

enemy hordes from three sides, blew their trumpets, broke their pitchers, shined their lights, and shouted, "The sword of the Lord, and of Gideon." The enemy went into a riot, fleeing headlong down the valley, and the world's military classic for night charges was in full force (Judg. 7:1-25).

Across this same valley went despondent Saul, king of Israel, to the witch of Endor. There on Mount Moreh's northern slopes a ghostly realism mocked his empty soul, not with a thrilling pancake story but a pronouncement of his own doom, and he

> rose up dumb and mighty—pale
> and terrible in blood stained mail,

and went back around the Mountain of Moreh and across the Valley of Jezreel to await the issues of the oncoming day, when

> Enthralled, past knowing cold or heat,
> or hearing thunder of the feet
> of armies,

his host was attacked on the rear flank, and he went down to an ignominious defeat and death on Gilboa's height. Soon the enemy came to strip the slain; and before the sun was set, King Saul's body hung on a wall at Beth-Shan.

This valley takes its name from the ancient city of Jezreel, which was situated on a low spur projecting westward from Mount Gilboa. Here at Jezreel was located the choice vineyard of Naboth which Ahab, the most unrestrained of all Israel's kings, lusted after until he lay upon his bed aflame with a fire of unsatisfied desire and would eat no bread. Jezebel, his doubly insidious, prophet-slaying wife, soothed him with the sinister promise, "I will give thee the vineyard of Naboth." Therefore, she hurriedly wrote letters in Ahab's name, sealed them with his signet, and said that Naboth had blasphemed God and the king. As phony witnesses she sent two men to testify at court who were "children of Belial," and then announced to the king, "Naboth is stoned, and is dead."

Ahab, while strolling in his stolen vineyard, was suddenly confronted by Elijah, and exclaimed, "Hast thou found me, O mine enemy?"

129

The Valley of Jezreel as seen from famed Mount Gilboa

Elijah's reply was, "Thou hast sold thyself to work evil in the sight of the Lord. . . . In the place where dogs licked the blood of Naboth shall dogs lick thy blood. . . . And the dogs shall eat Jezebel by the wall of Jezreel." All things spoken by the prophet came to pass—Jezebel's tragic end here in the city of Jezreel, overlooking the Valley of Jezreel.

The prophet Elisha oft made his circuit through this valley. And so it was that as he passed by, he turned into Shunem to eat bread. Here he was invited into the home of a good, kind Shunammite woman and her husband who made a little room on the wall and set there a bed, a table, a stool, and a candlestick that the prophet might freely pass in and out. Here was enacted the

tender scene when the prophet raised the dead son of his bene-
factress to life.

At the eastern entrance of the Valley of Jezreel, near its junc-
ture with the Jordan Valley, the historic city of *Beth-Shan* was
strategically located. It was perched on a high mound that made
it like a "toll keeper" on the much traveled route between
Damascus and Egypt. From its splendid position it dominated the
country for miles around. It was here, when after defeat by the
Philistines on Gilboa, the bodies of Saul and Jonathan were hung
high upon the walls until the men of Jabesh Gilead arose and
went all night and took them down and buried their burnt bones
at Jabesh Gilead (later they were reburied at Zelah, just west of
Rachel's tomb).

With the decline of the country, this fruitful valley became
lost to the outside world. Caravans of camels with tinkling bells
passed this way, but little notice was taken of them.

However, the Valley of Jezreel still lies there, overlain with
black, alluvial swamp soil, rich in organic components. It is now
given to the plowshare and is quiet from the forays of Midianites,
Philistines, and other marauders.

The little village of Shunem stands at the northwest portion
of the valley as of old, and many view it with thoughts of the
prophet Elisha and the "great woman" and her husband who
provided for "the man of God." Rich and prosperous kibbutz
colonies occupy the land today—Merhavya, Ein-Harod, Tel-
Yosef, Gide'ona, Geva, etc. Ain Harod, the fine, strong spring,
still flows from the enormous cave at the base of Gilboa. A youth
hostel stands on the banks of the spring whose waters go mostly
through underground channels to the surrounding colonies.
Only a small stream is now allowed to flow into its natural bed
known as the river Jalud which, since ancient times, has coursed
its way down the valley.

Far down the valley, on its south side, the fine mound of
Beth-Shan looms high on the horizon, and nearby is the Arab 131
village of Beisan which provides a splendid market for all kinds of
native needs.

CHAPTER 12

Samaria, Land of Places and Personalities

Samaria, sometimes referred to in the Old Testament as "Mount Ephraim," or as "the mountains of Samaria," is one of the most extensive as well as one of the most interesting of all the many sections of Palestine—interesting largely because of its places and people. Its northern boundary begins at the southeast foot of Mount Carmel and runs southeast along the southern edge of the Plain of Armageddon, then swinging northward includes Mount Gilboa and the adjacent mountains to the Jordan Valley. Its southern boundary begins with the Valley of Aijalon and runs eastward along a line just south of Bethel to the deep gorge of Michmash and thence to the Jordan Valley. It comprises an area of approximately 40 by 50 miles, which, for the land of Israel, is quite large. It was the true geographical center of Canaan, and in those early days was thickly wooded (Josh. 17:18).

Although it adjoins Judea geographically, the difference existing between the two is amazing. Whereas Judea is of rugged, arid terrain, and its mountains are almost impassable, Samaria is a land of beauty and symmetry. Its graceful mountains, fertile valleys, flowing fountains, flowering shrubs, trailing vines, and millions of wild flowers make it an exceedingly desirable land. The average elevation is 2,000 feet, with a few mountain heights as much as 3,000 feet. The topography is made up of a series of high ridges with intervening elevated valleys and plains. The land is easily accessible in the northern portion, but the southern half is bordered by precipitous banks and rugged wadies. The descent to the Jordan depression is very steep. In one place the drop is 2,800 feet in nine miles. On the western side the land has a gradual slope toward the maritime plain.

Agricultural potentialities are unusually fine due to the fertility of the land. Grapes, olives, pomegranates, plums, peaches, passion fruit, apricots, and nectarines are produced here in abundance. Pastures, shut in by the surrounding mountains, yield an abundance of grass; and the goats, sheep, and cattle are quite famous for the quantity and the quality of their milk and meat.

The land of Samaria has mountains and plains and city sites which are rich in historical setting—and made so by certain personalities. The more important of these places are: Shechem, Jacob's Well, Sychar, Joseph's Tomb, Joshua's Tomb, Mounts Ebal and Gerizim, Nablus, Tirzah, City of Samaria, Dothan, Jenin, Mount Gilboa, Megiddo, Shiloh, Ai, and Bethel.

Shechem, now identified with *Tell Balata,* is a mile and a half east of Nablus, between Mount Ebal and Mount Gerizim. It stood 133 guard over the crossroads here and was the religious and political center of Palestine during early Old Testament times. It is midway between Dan and Beersheba, and almost midway between the sea and the Jordan.

Shechem was the site of Abraham's first encampment in the Promised Land, and the place where he erected the first altar "unto the Lord, who appeared unto him" and renewed His covenant promise (Gen. 12:6-7). On returning from his 20-year sojourn in Haran, Jacob was kindly received by the people of Shechem who sold him land on which he and his servants dug a well. Here he received from the people their "strange gods . . . and their earrings" and buried them under an oak which was by Shechem (Gen. 35:1-4). Joseph came here in quest of his brothers, whom he later found at Dothan (Gen. 37:12-17). Joseph's body was brought from Egypt and buried at Shechem.

The Israelites, under the leadership of Joshua, were gathered here to reaffirm the covenant; and here long years afterwards, when Joshua was "old and stricken in age," he gathered all Israel and made his farewell address in which he uttered that ringing challenge, "Choose you this day whom ye will serve. . . . as for me and my house, we will serve the Lord." In reply the people said, "We will serve the Lord our God . . . and his voice will we obey." Then Joshua "made a covenant with the people and wrote these words in a book . . . and took a great stone and set it up there under an oak" (Josh. 24:14-26).

Shechem was one of the cities of refuge in the days of the judges.

Here at Shechem, after the death of Solomon, all Israel came together to make Rehoboam king, but his exorbitant demands for more taxes and greater service split the kingdom and sent him speeding in his chariot to Jerusalem, where thereafter he ruled over only 2 tribes. Jeroboam became king of the 10 northern tribes, rebuilt Shechem, and made it his court for a time, but later moved the capital to Tirzah.

The Assyrian invasions of 724-721 B.C. completely destroyed Shechem, but it was rebuilt by the Samaritans and became a prosperous city. Even a temple was built on Mount Gerizim, and the city became a rival to Jerusalem. John Hyrcanus brought about the final destruction of Shechem in 107 B.C., and along with it, thousands of Samaritans were put to death.

A team of archaeologists, under the direction of Dr. G. Ernest Wright, has excavated here for a number of seasons. Gates, walls, temples, and a wealth of pottery, coins, tools, and other smaller objects have been found, and considerable history has been confirmed—both secular and biblical.

Jacob's Well is one mile southeast of Shechem, on the high road from Jerusalem where it curves westward to enter the valley between Mount Gerizim and Mount Ebal. Situated on the ground purchased by Jacob "for an hundred pieces of money" from the sons of Hamor, the father of Shechem, this wayside well is one of the most authentic sites in all Bible lands (Gen. 33:18-19). Samaritans, Jews, Christians, and Mohammedans revere it as the very well which Jacob dug, and the one on whose curb Jesus sat when He talked to the woman of Samaria, who had come there to draw water.

Samaritan tradition dates back more than 23 centuries and was repeated by the Samaritan woman who said to Jesus, "Our father Jacob gave us the well" (John 4:12). Christian tradition dates from 333 when the Bordeaux Pilgrim visited the well, over which a small Christian church had just recently been built by Queen Helena. The Crusaders found the church in ruins and rebuilt it, but their church was destroyed during the 12th century. Its ruins, as a "heap of brown stones," lay for long years over the well.

In 1838, Dr. Robinson found the entrance to the well's mouth, measured the well, and found it to be 105 feet deep. In 1881, Dr. C. A. Barclay cleared away the mass of accumulated rubbish about the original mouth of the well and found that debris had fallen or been thrown into it until it measured only 67 feet deep.[1] Later the well was cleaned out to its bottom and found to be, in fact, 105 feet deep. But so many tourists, and others passing by, threw or pushed stones into it in order to hear how long it would take for a stone to splash in the water below, that it gradually filled again until it was only 75 feet deep.

In 1912, the Russian Orthodox church began building an

enormous basilica church around the well, but the work was stopped during the First World War. Later the place was purchased by the Greek Orthodox church, but it would require so much to complete the church that it has never been finished. Directly over the well is a small, richly adorned chapel, with walls covered with old paintings and icons, mostly depicting Jesus and the woman at the well.

The ancient well curb is many feet below the present level and shows deep grooves worn by the ropes by which the waterpots or waterskins were drawn up. The well measures 7 feet 6 inches in diameter. Its upper portion is lined with masonry, but the lower portion has been dug through solid stone. The water is cool, soft, and refreshing—much more palatable than the hard or "heavy" spring water that gushes from the limestone strata at Sychar. It is both a cistern and a spring—that is, it is fed both by infiltration through its sides and by an underground spring. Under present management, water is sold to tourists in small bottles and taken to most parts of the world. For those who desire it, the attending priest draws water for a drink and also lets down a steel platter with lighted candles so that one may see along the walls of the well down to the water level.

The associations of the well carry us back in the world's history to pastoral scenes, to patriarchal customs, and to the beginning of Jesus' ministry. By this wayside well He revealed His divine self to the perplexed Samaritan woman and spoke the profound truths: "They that worship [God] must worship him in spirit and in truth," and "Whosoever drinketh of the water that I shall give him shall never thirst; but the water that I shall give him shall be in him a well of water springing up into everlasting life" (John 4:24, 14). The sequel to it all was that the Samaritan woman accepted Christ and led many of the townspeople to know and accept Him, who in turn "besought him to tarry with them, and he abode there two days and many believed."

Sychar, the hometown of the woman who talked with Jesus at the well, is identified with the Arab village of Askar, which is about three-quarters of a mile north of the well. It lies at the foot of Mount Ebal and is built over the ruins of the ancient town of

Sychar. It has a spring, but the water is not as palatable as that in Jacob's well.

Joseph's Tomb. On a slight elevation about 400 yards northeast of Jacob's well is a walled-in, white-domed chapel tomb about 12 feet square. Inside the small chapel is a simple tomb about three feet high, and an inscription stating that in 1860 the place was restored by a British consul.

Here lie the embalmed, mortal remains of Joseph, whose character and faith in God were such that, when faced with fiery temptation, he said, "How can I do this great wickedness, and sin against God?" For his refusal to do wrong he went to prison, but God was with him, and soon he was called to the throne to be Egypt's prime minister.

At 110 years of age, he said to his kinsmen, "God will surely visit you, and ye shall carry up my bones from hence." "And the bones of Joseph, which the children of Israel brought up out of Egypt, buried they in Shechem, in a parcel of ground which Jacob bought of the sons of Hamor, the father of Shechem, for an hundred pieces of silver: and it became the inheritance of the children of Joseph" (Josh. 24:32).

This is one of the three places—along with the Cave of Machpelah at Hebron, and the Temple site at Jerusalem—that religious Jews claim is historically theirs by right of documented purchase.

Joshua's Tomb. Nine miles southwest of Shechem, in a rather rugged mountainous area, is Timnath Serah (now called Kefer Haris) where is located three domed tombs, which Jewish, Samaritan, Christian, and Moslem traditions say belong to Joshua, Caleb, and Nun. Other tombs, both here and in the Shechem area, are held sacred because they are said to belong to other old heroes of the Hebrew invasion.[2]

Ebal and *Gerizim,* twin mountains in the physical center of Samaria, are separated from each other by the beautiful Vale of Shechem. These mountains rise up on either side of the valley like lofty walls—Ebal on the northeast to a height of 3,044 feet, and Gerizim on the southwest to 2,870 feet above sea level.

From the slopes of these mountains the tribes of Israel assembled under Joshua, in fulfillment of Moses' command. On

Gerizim—the "Mount of Blessing"—stood the tribes of Simeon, Levi, Judah, Issachar, Joseph, and Benjamin. On Ebal—the "Mount of Cursing"—stood the tribes of Reuben, Gad, Asher, Zebulun, Dan, and Naphtali. In the midst of the valley separating the two mountains stood the ark of the covenant and the priests.

With the elders, officers, and judges arranged about the sacred symbol, and the vast multitudes covering the mountainsides and filling the plain below, the loud-voiced Levites turned their faces Gerizim-ward and uttered the blessings that would certainly visit the lives of those who lived righteously. Then, turning their faces Ebal-ward, they uttered the evil that was destined to descend upon those who transgressed the law. A tremendous AMEN! arose from the mighty congregation, 10-fold louder as it reverberated from Ebal to Gerizim and from Gerizim to Ebal. The scene was impressive and the effect upon the vast assembly was extremely wholesome.[3]

Jotham's parable of the trees was later spoken to the men of Shechem from a prominent ledge well up toward the top of Mount Gerizim. A certain ledge here is now popularly called "Jotham's pulpit" (Judg. 9:4-21).

Nablus, whose name comes from Neopolis, the "new city," is located between the mountains of Ebal and Gerizim, just southwest of the site of ancient Shechem. It was founded in A.D. 72 by the veterans of the armies of Vespasian and Titus. For a long time the inhabitants here were Romans, and from these was born, in the beginning of the second century, Justin Martyr, a philosopher, carefully trained in the schools of Greek philosophy. In his search for truth concerning God, he met an old man of venerable appearance who referred him to the apostles and prophets. He not only studied these but watched the Christians and decided they were not guessing at the truth, neither were they demonstrating divine things by reason, but were witnesses to the truth which they had themselves experienced.

138   Justin Martyr became a Christian and his knowledge widened, his love deepened, and his life was enlarged and intensified. The mirror of his soul became burnished, and his mind luminous and symmetrical. He devoted himself to the work of

teaching and writing in defense of the Christians and of their faith. When a wave of persecution of the Christians broke out under Antoninus, Justin felt the destiny of a people hung on what he did; therefore he made a contribution to his own generation and to the world's betterment by presenting to that emperor an admirable apology in the Christians' behalf, which had the desired effect. In A.D. 165, he defended the Christians to Marcus Aurelius, but for this he was rewarded with a martyr's crown.

After the Crusades in the Middle Ages, the population of Nablus became more and more Arabic. Today Nablus has a population of 45,000, of which there are some 44,000 Moslems, 750 Christians, and 250 Samaritans. These Samaritans live in a small colony to themselves and have a high priest and a synagogue, in which is the ancient Samaritan Pentateuch. Each high priest is required to keep a record of the chief events transpiring during his term of office, and these records reach far back into the past. Rev. Youhannah El Karey, a native Baptist missionary of Shechem, says he inquired as to whether there was any reference to Jesus Christ in those high-priestly records. He said that two such references had been discovered—one to the effect that Jesus Christ had come to their town and done many wonderful works, and another that He had been crucified in Jerusalem. Once each year the high priest leads his congregation up Mount Gerizim where they kill seven white lambs and observe the Feast of the Passover.

Many wealthy citizens have built their homes on the slopes of Mount Gerizim and Mount Ebal, and the place enjoys an atmosphere of prosperity. Fruit orchards, vegetable gardens, and olive groves have long characterized the environs of Nablus. The people sell fruit and prepare fruit juices for the markets, but the chief local industry is the manufacturing of an especially high grade olive-oil soap, which they export to various neighboring countries. Other modern industries are now adding to the prosperity of the area.

Tirzah, now identified with a large mound known as Tell el Farah, lies seven miles northeast of Nablus. At an indefinite time,

139

after the division of the monarchy, Jeroboam made it the capital of his kingdom (1 Kings 14:17), but after his death it suffered from many years of turbulent history. Omri besieged and captured the place in 884 B.C. and reigned there for six years before he moved his capital to Samaria.

Excavators have found four periods corresponding with the biblical history of Tirzah. Period I (that of level III in the tell) came to a sudden end about the time Omri captured the place. During the period of Omri the house plans included courtyards and were quite substantial. Each represented the house of an Israelite family. Large administration buildings were shown to have been begun but not completed. This the excavators thought represented the city at the time Omri abandoned the place and moved his capital to Samaria.

Samaria. After reigning at Tirzah for years, King Omri negotiated a deal with Shemer for a beautiful site eight miles northwest of Shechem. Here, on this well-rounded hill 400 feet above the surrounding valleys, he constructed his royal palace

The hill country of Samaria

and named it Samaria, after Shemer. Ahab, his son and successor, married beautiful, wordly, wicked Jezebel, and in selfish luxury constructed an ivory-veneered palace, and "reared up an altar for Baal in the house of Baal, which he had built in Samaria. And Ahab made a grove" (1 Kings 16:31-32).

During his lifetime—most of which was spent at or near Samaria—Ahab was "busy here and there" with things which crowded God from his life, but when he died in battle, his body was brought to Samaria where "one washed the chariot in the pool of Samaria; and the dogs licked up his blood . . . according to the word of the Lord" (2 Kings 22:34-38). Here Jehu slew all the seed of Ahab; destroyed the prophets, the priests, and the servants of Baal; and went to the house of Baal and brought forth the images and burned them publicly. The temple, also, was demolished and laid even with the ground (2 Kings 10:24-27).

The city of Samaria was destroyed and rebuilt time after time. In 724, Shalmaneser, king of Assyria, gathered his armies and came into Israel to collect tribute. The cities about the plain of Esdraelon surrendered, or the inhabitants fled to the capital. Hoshea prepared for a long siege with the hope of receiving help from Egypt, but for this he looked in vain. The siege of Samaria continued for two years—724 to 722 B.C.—under Shalmaneser V; then Sargon II, his successor, continued it for a short time.

At last Samaria's heights were stormed, King Hoshea was led away to spend the rest of his life in an Assyrian prison, and the people were deported to Assyria, where they were sent to various sections of the country to be absorbed by the people among whom they dwelt, or finally to journey to other lands.[4] Captives from other countries were settled in Samaria—these mingled with the Israelites left there, and afterwards made up those who became known as "Samaritans."

Alexander the Great destroyed the city of Samaria in 331, and again it was destroyed by John Hyrcanus in 108 B.C. It was rebuilt by the roman general Pompey in 63 B.C. Then, in 27 B.C., Emperor Augustus gave it to Herod the Great, who fortified the city, rebuilt it on a magnificent scale, and gave it the name of *Sebaste,* in honor of his patron, the Emperor Augustus. Herod built a palace, into which he brought his beautiful Mariamne, whom in jealousy he afterwards murdered, along with two of his sons. What a sordid, checkered past for a city which had been built on such a charming site. But for nearly 900 years it had been known as the center of idolatry. However, there was to be a better day with the coming of Jesus Christ.

Here Philip the evangelist preached Christ, "and the people with one accord gave heed unto those things which Philip spake . . . And there was great joy in that city." Even Simon the sorcerer "believed" and was baptized. Then came Peter and John who taught the people about the Holy Spirit, and "preached the gospel in many villages of the Samaritans" (Acts 8:25). Christianity continued in Sebaste (Samaria), for in the fourth century the city possessed a bishopric, and in 1187 the Crusaders built a cathedral there, the ruins of which now serve as a mosque.[5]

The city of Samaria has been excavated. Gates, walls, columned streets, foundations for palaces, temples, and other structures have been found which adequately confirm history as recorded in the Bible and other sources—even a collection of several thousand pieces of ivory of great variety and design. Some pieces were cut to receive color inlay, other pieces were overlaid with gold or inlaid with lapis lazuli. These, the excavators thought, were originally mortised into the throne, into beds, couches, tables, cabinets, and in the paneling of the walls and ceilings of the palace—all of which gave substance to the account in 1 Kings 22:39 which lists the ivory house as one of the great achievements of Ahab.

Jenin, the ancient En-Gannim (garden spring), lies on the southeast rim of the Plain of Armageddon, beside the pass from the Plain of Dothan. It has a strong spring which supplies all its domestic needs; then after watering vegetable gardens, fruit orchards, vineyards, olive groves, and a few palm trees, it passes on north and west to become one of the chief tributaries of the Kishon River. Josephus mentions it as being located on the border between Samaria and Galilee. Some believe Jenin to be the place where Jesus healed 10 lepers, one of whom was the Samaritan who returned to give thanks (Luke 17:11-19). Ancient *Ibleam,* identified with modern Belameh, lies about a mile to the south of Jenin.

Dothan, now known as *Tell Dothan,* is located 5 miles southwest of Jenin and 12 miles north of the ancient city of Samaria. It is an isolated city mound which rises 175 feet above the plain, and has 10 acres on top and 15 acres on the slopes. An Arab village is now on the southern slope of the mound. Dothan means "two wells," and here they are today on the plain south of the mound—about 100 yards apart. Flocks of sheep and goats and some cattle still come here for water.

It was here that Joseph, after passing through Shechem, found his brothers, who, while he was yet "afar off," said, "Behold, this dreamer cometh. . . . now . . . let us slay him . . . and we shall see what will become of his dreams." Eventually, they sold him for 20 pieces of silver to a passing caravan of Ishmaelites and Midianite merchantmen, who "brought Joseph into Egypt . . . and . . . sold him . . . unto Potiphar, an officer of Pharoah's, and captain of the guard" (see Gen. 37:12-36).

Here the king of Syria laid siege to the city in an attempt to seize the prophet Elisha. When Elisha's servant arose early, he saw the horses and chariots, and the great host, and cried out, "Alas, my master, how shall we do?" When Elisha had prayed, the Lord opened the eyes of the young man. "And, behold, the mountain was full of horses and chariots of fire round about" —far more than those that composed the Syrian army (see 2 Kings 6:8-23).

Excavations conducted here since the spring of 1953 by Dr. Joseph P. Free of Wheaton College have revealed 11 levels of successive occupations from Early Bronze (3000-2000 B.C.) to the Middle Iron Age (900-586 B.C.). Special attention was given to Middle Bronze level (2050-1550 B.C.), the city of Joseph's day, and the Middle Iron level (900-586 B.C.), the city of Elisha's day. In this latter level, 15 pieces of silver was found stored in a pottery box—evidently the savings of some individual who was obliged to leave them.

Megiddo. Leading northwest, up to the southeast foothills of Mount Carmel, is a 20-mile chain of very important Samaritan

143

hills—a veritable southwestern backdrop for the Plain of Esdrae-lon or Armageddon. In those hills and on the border of the plain there are now many modern Jewish colonies, but in ancient times there were four very important fortress towns—Jokneam, Megid-do, Taanach, and Ibleam. These dominated the four passes which connected the Plain of Sharon with the Plain of Armageddon.

Of these four, Megiddo guarded the famous Pass of Megid-do, through which ran the great highway or military artery which connected Egypt and Assyria. Thotmes III, king of Egypt, came this way in 1468 B.C. to conquer the kings of Canaan. King Solo-mon, in the 10th century B.C., made Megiddo a bulwark for the defense of the kingdom, using it chiefly as a chariot city of which excavations have revealed the remains of extensive stable com-plexes. In each stable, a central passage was flanked on each side by rows of pillars serving as supports for the roof and as hitching posts. Between the pillars were mangers. Each section of stables accommodated about 24 horses.

Pharaoh-Necho came through this pass in 610 B.C., on his way to aid the king of Assyria at the Battle of Carchemish. In his effort to stop him, the good King Joash lost his life (2 Chron. 35: 20-24). The armies of Alexander the Great passed here on the way to Egypt; Napoleon on his way to Acre; and General Allenby in pursuit of the Turco-German forces, whom he was driving from the Holy Land. This phase of his work was so significant that later he was knighted as Lord Allenby, Viscount of Megiddo.[6]

The Mountain of Gilboa. Just south of the Valley of Jezreel lies the farthest northeast portion of Samaria. It is a curving, bar-ren mountain ridge, 1,700 feet high and 10 miles long. Here, on Gilboa's height, was fought the fatal battle with the Philistines in which King Saul was disastrously defeated, and he and his sons were slain. On hearing of the tragedy, David's great soul was stirred to its depth, and he wrote that touching lament:

> The beauty of Israel is slain upon the high places: how are the mighty fallen: Tell it not in Gath, publish it not in the streets of Askelon: lest the daughters of the uncircumcised triumph . . .
> Ye mountains of Gilboa, let there be no dew, neither let

144

there be rain upon you, nor fields of offering: for there the shield of the mighty is vilely cast away, the shield of Saul, as though he had not been anointed with oil. . . .

Saul and Jonathan were lovely and pleasant in their lives, and in their death they were not divided: they were swifter than eagles, they were stronger than lions. . . .

How are the mighty fallen in the midst of the battle: O Jonathan, thou wast slain in thine high places.

I am distressed for thee, my brother Jonathan: Very pleasant hast thou been unto me: thy love to me was wonderful, passing the love of women.

How are the mighty fallen, and the weapons of war perished! *(2 Sam. 1:19-27)*.

Shiloh, where Israel first set up the Tabernacle sanctuary in the Holy Land, is situated on a low-lying hill in a secluded upland valley 10 miles south of Shechem. The place is now called Seilun, and the location fully agrees with that given in the Book of Judges which places it "on the north side of Bethel, on the east side of the highway that goeth up from Bethel to Shechem" (Judg. 21:19).

Here Joshua completed the division of the land among the tribes of Israel, and here the Tabernacle remained for more than 200 years.

Here Hannah prayed earnestly to God for a "man child," and vowed that he would be given "unto the Lord all the days of his life." Here Eli ministered as high priest, and here the child Samuel was dedicated to the Lord and grew up in the service of the sanctuary. Here "the Lord came, and stood, and called, Samuel, Samuel," and that fine lad answered, "Speak; for thy servant heareth" (see 1 Sam. 3:1-21).

Excavations were begun in 1922 by Dr. Schmidt, a Danish scholar. Among other things, he discovered the pottery remains and fragments of utensils used by the Israelites. The period of their occupation came to an end in the 11th century B.C. No traces of occupation of the site were found after the 9th century B.C.[7]

Bethel (Beth-el = house of God) is the place where Abraham built his second altar. It is where Jacob slept with a stone as his pillow and in his dream saw a ladder which reached from earth to heaven, and the angels of God ascending and descending. The Lord said, "I am the Lord God . . . the land whereon thou liest, to thee will I give it, and to thy seed . . . and in thee and in thy seed shall all the families of the earth be blessed." And Jacob said, "Surely the Lord is in this place . . . this is none other but the house of God, and this is the gate of heaven" (Gen. 28:10-17).

The legend of the old historians says that this stone on which the patriarch Jacob laid his head was brought to Spain, then transported to Ireland where Simon Brech was crowned on it about A.D. 700. It was then transferred from Ireland to Scotland and placed in the Abbey Church of Scone in A.D. 850, where the Scottish kings were crowned until 1296. At that time King Edward I carried it to England and placed it in Westminster Abbey where it was fixed under the seat of the coronation chair. It is called the "stone of Destiny" or "Scone Stone," and upon it all kings and queens of England have been crowned for almost 700 years.

Samuel came to Bethel once a year to judge the people (1 Sam. 7:16), and there was a school of prophets at Bethel when Elijah and Elisha were en route to Elijah's translation. On the return trip occurred the episode of the large crowd of young fellows who attempted to make sport of Jehovah's chosen prophetic leader. God challenged their rude and irreverent insults by permitting two she bears to come from the woods and maul 42 of those who had blatantly dishonored His chosen servant (2 Kings 2:23).

Jeroboam set up a golden calf and made an altar in Bethel, and "sacrificed unto the calf which he had made, and the priests cried, Let the people that sacrifice kiss the calf." By this altar stood Jeroboam, and his hand was withered and "the altar was rent" when he stretched forth his hand to seize the prophet of Judah who cried against the altar (see 1 Kings 12:28-33; 13:1-7). Here, later, came Amos, on one of the calf-cult's high days, and condemned the oppession of the poor, the perversion of justice, and the taking of bribes. He condemned their shams, cried against their substitutes, and declared, "The Lord stood upon a wall . . . with a plumbline in his hand" (Amos 7:7) and that "Bethel shall come to nought" (5:5). This prophecy was fulfilled; for, until the beginning of the 19th century, Bethel's site was unknown.

Baal-Hazor *(Tel Asur),* a mountain 3,334 feet high, nine miles northwest of Bethel, is where Absalom gave a dinner party and made his half brother Amnon drunk, then had him murdered in revenge for dishonoring his sister Tamar. The king's sons then mounted their mules and hurried back to Jerusalem, while Absalom fled to his mother's kinsmen in Geshur (Jedure) (2 Sam. 13:23-38).

Ai, the second place attacked by the incoming Israelites under Joshua, has usually been identified with Et Tell (the ruin), two miles east of Bethel. However, incomplete excavations there have thus far shown no definite traces of a city of Joshua's time. The biblical Ai could well have been little more than a temporary wooden fortification, manned by the men of Bethel and Ai, and such fragile strata as was left there could have been removed by erosion. Or, perhaps the Ai of biblical fame will be located elsewhere.

CHAPTER **13**

Judea, Land of Redemption

Blest land of Judea! thrice hallowed of song,
Where the holiest of memories pilgrim-like throng:
In the shade of thy palms, by the shores of thy sea,
On the hills of thy beauty, my heart is with thee.
—Whittier

Judea has ever been, and
148   always will be, regarded as the principal stronghold of Israel, the
home of her chief prophets, the site of her Temple, the sanctuary
of the Holy Land, and the soul of the Old and New Testament

world. Judea is the land of worship, of romance, and of tragedy; but beyond all, it is the land of redemption—God and man met in the Temple on Moriah; Jesus the Saviour was born in Bethlehem; He died and rose again for our sins in Jerusalem; and the Holy Spirit came to those who tarried in the Upper Room. The entire area is rich beyond other lands in hallowed memories and stirring sacred events.

Judea came to include all the lands originally assigned to Benjamin and Judah. It begins a few miles north of Jerusalem near Beeroth and Ramallah, and extends southward for about 50 miles to the region where the foothills of the Judean Mountains fade away into the plain a few miles north of Beersheba. The entire territory is only about 35 miles wide from the Shephelah to the Dead Sea—much *less* when the Wilderness of Judea is not considered. It is a rugged, mountain land with many valleys, and a few brooks here and there. Piled high in its very center is the great watershed which runs from north to south and drains the water eastward to the Jordan and westward to the Mediterranean. Along this watershed runs the high road from Nazareth to Beersheba.

The whole area of Judea possesses an average height of 2,500 feet above sea level. The greatest elevations of the range are in the vicinity of Hebron where a height of 3,340 feet is reached just north of the city. At Jerusalem the elevation reaches 2,585 feet; while Neby Sam'wil is 2,942 feet above sea level—the highest point in the environs of Jerusalem and northern Judea.

A great part of the eastern portion of Judea is desolate and stony with few trees and slight vegetation, while the western slope is hilly and stony; yet it receives more moisture, and the rocky, limestone composition of the hills is easily converted into soil. When terraced and cared for, they are beautiful beyond compare and produce olives, rich vineyards, and an abundance of deciduous fruits of most every kind. But when neglected, these hills become desolate.

During the winter season, Judea's valleys are turned into 149 rushing riverbeds as the water falls in sheets and rushes swiftly away to the Jordan Valley or to the Mediterranean Sea. Throughout this region one will find only six or eight perennial streams. Springs are very rare and true water-bearing wells are almost unknown. Covered cisterns, in which rainwater is collected and stored, supply man and beast during the long, dry, summer months. Added to this is the generous amount of dew which refreshes all living things from night to night.

The soft limestone formation has resulted in numerous caves and caverns. These have been used by the people for habitation and defense. They furnish an abode for the poor and, in summertime, protection from the heat. In time of danger the Isrealites hid themselves in the caves and dens. They were also used as cemeteries, for storage, and folds for flocks. Some caves were so important that they became historical landmarks.

One may stand on the height of Neby Sam'wil and survey a very large portion of Judea, and in some instances see even far beyond its confines. Thus Judea was a very small country—so small, in proportion to her enemies, that she could hope to exist only by the miraculous power of God. This is why almost every square mile of her territory, as well as every mountain and place, is associated with some important biblical event. The more important of these are: Hebron, Jerusalem, Ain Karim, Bethany, Bethlehem, Rachel's Tomb, Kish's Tomb, Solomon's Pools, Tekoah, Neby Sam'wil, Gibeon, Gibeah of Saul, Ramah, Ramallah, and Beeroth.

Hebron, one of the oldest cities in Palestine, will always be associated with Abraham, "the friend of God." Some 3,900 years ago Abraham pitched his tent in the Grove of Mamre, where now stands an ancient tree, which at least since the 16th century has been known as the Oak of Mamre (Gen. 13:18). Its short, gnarled trunk is over 30 feet in circumference; its twisted limbs are almost entirely bare of leaves and so weak that they have to be propped up by heavy iron beams; while around the ancient oak is a strong iron fence, designed to keep goats from nibbling the bark, and tourists from carrying away the whole tree piece-meal. It was here, while sitting in his tent door, that Abraham saw three men approaching him, and on offering them hospitality, found he was entertaining angels unawares (Gen. 18:1-33).

In the nearby fertile vale, 3,000 feet above the sea, lies Hebron, where Abraham settled after Lot had departed from him. Here Isaac was born; and here Abraham purchased the *Cave of Machpelah* in which he, Sarah, Isaac, Jacob, Rebecca, and Leah were buried. It was "out of the vale of Hebron" that Joseph was sent to deliver a message to his brethren. Here David reigned over Judah seven and a half years, until he was anointed king over all Israel; and here ungrateful Absalom raised the standard of rebellion against his royal father.

There are two ancient reservoirs in the south part of Hebron. The largest of these is 135 feet square and quite deep. It is thought that over this pool King David's young men hanged up the hands and feet of the murderers of Ishbosheth (2 Sam. 4:12).

The most interesting as well as the most conspicuous object in Hebron is the Cave of Machpelah, which Abraham bought from Ephron the Hittite for 400 shekels of silver. The object which looms large is in reality the "Great Mosque," a massive, castlelike structure 200 feet long, 115 feet wide, and 58 feet high, built over the cave. The building is very old, and the stones in the lower courses are beautiful and very large—one stone measures 24 feet in length, and another 38 feet long and 3½ feet high. These lower courses of masonry are marginally drafted after the style used in cutting stones during the time of Herod the Great, and Josephus mentions the beauty of the building in his day. Therefore, it is reasonably certain it was built by Herod. Arab tradition, however, insists that it dates back to King Solomon.

To reach the supposed burial place, you move up a long stone staircase beside the mosque, pass under a great arch, and enter a plain, many-sided hall. To one side, in a recess behind an iron grill, is a large, tomblike structure covered with costly embroidered tapestries, faded with age. This is the cenotaph of Abraham. Opposite, under a similar pall, is that of Sarah. To the southeast are the cenotaphs of Isaac and Rebecca, and to the northwest, Jacob and Leah. In each case the cenotaph is supposed to be directly over the actual tomb below the floor in 151 the cave.

The Cave of Machpelah is revered by the three great monotheistic religions—Jews, Christians, and Moslems—yet for generations the Moslems would not allow the Jews to ascend any farther than the seventh step on the stone steps beside the mosque. Above the fourth step to the left is a deep cleft in the wall, which many Jews believe to extend through the wall and to emerge into the burial chamber itself. Here, in this cleft, the Jewish pilgrims placed small notes with intimate requests which they hoped would be granted by the patriarchs. Nowadays multitudes of Jews come to Hebron, ascend the steps, and eagerly enter the cenotaph hall. Some merely stand in thoughtful reverence. Others touch the iron bars reverently, pray, and smile as though they were meeting someone they had once known well, and were seeing them again after a long, long time. No one is ever permitted to descend into the cavern beneath the floor, for fear of disturbing the rest of the saints.

Jerusalem, the city of the soul, the city where man's redemption was achieved, and the city that makes all men think of the Bible and of heaven, is located on a 1,000-acre plateau in the central Judean mountains.

Numerous significant events took place in Jerusalem, or outside its gray walls. The ones which had to do with our redemption are, of course, the more momentous. The magnificent Temple with all its deeply meaningful parts—beginning at the Beautiful Gate and climaxing with "the place of the mercy seat"—was the most revered. Here in the most holy place, God, in His Shekinah presence, met man in mercy and atonement as the high priest came with blood, once each year, representing the people. And just outside the city wall, Jesus Christ, the God-man, gave His life on the lone gray hill of Calvary to "put away sin by the sacrifice of himself"—the true Offering and Atonement of which every sacrifice in the Temple was only a type.

Illustrious lives have left their imprint on the Holy City—Melchizedek, Abraham, David, Solomon, Isaiah, Jeremiah, Nehemiah, Judas Maccabaeus, Gamaliel, and Jesus Christ in whose honor Jerusalem came to be called "The City of the Great King."

The story of the glorious city extends over a period of 4,000 years and is told in some detail in the author's 180-page book,

Jerusalem,[1] but the following chapter of this present volume gives a capsule study of this most famous of all cities. But first we will consider some of the other significant sites in the area.

Ain Karim, according to tradition, is the "City of Judah" two miles west of Jerusalem where John the Baptist was born to Elizabeth and Zacharias the priest. The traditional site of their home is covered by the convent and church of St. John, within which is a small circular chapel, or grotto, cut in the natural rock, to which you descend by seven steps. Over its entrance is written in Latin the first words of Zacharias' prophetic benediction, "Blessed be the Lord God of Israel." An inscription on a marble slab in the floor states that "here the forerunner of our Lord was born."

The paintings on the walls give many details of his eventful life—his birth, his teaching in the wilderness, his baptizing of Christ, and his tragic death. One picture, as an altar piece, depicts the virgin Mary's visit from Nazareth to her cousin Elizabeth.

Bethany, the quiet village where Mary, Martha, and Lazarus lived, is two miles east of Jerusalem, on the southeastern slope of the Mount of Olives. From the earliest ages the name and places here have had a peculiar charm for the Christian heart, because here in the quiet home of this good family, Jesus revealed so much of both the human and divine side of His unqiue nature. Here He taught of the many aspects of life, here He raised Lazarus from the dead, and from some spot overlooking Bethany He ascended "into heaven, and sat on the right hand of God."

Eusebius (265-340) is said to have seen the "tomb of Lazarus" at Bethany (Jerome, *Onomastikon*); it was shown to the Bordeaux Pilgrim in A.D. 333; and Paula visited it just after 400. Moslems and Christians have marked many sacred sites here, and Christians built churches over some of them in the sixth century and during the Crusades; but these churches and other markings of more or less certain sites are all gone now—even the highly endowed nunnery established by Melissinda, the queen of King Fulco.

153

The ruined tower shown as the remains of the "house of Simon the Leper" dates no further back than the Crusaders; and the "grave of Lazarus," reached by descending 22 slippery steps, has no certain marks of an ancient Jewish grave. Though there is little about the center of the village to impress the earnest Christian, yet it is when you move out in the serene landscape, among the pine and olive groves, and see the sheep grazing on the hillsides, that you are reminded of the dignity, sacredness, and undying interest which Christ imparted to the area. The Mount of Olives is in its proper relative position, and there can be no doubt about the correctness of the identification of Bethany.

Bethlehem, so familiar to all, lies six miles south of Jerusalem. It, along with Jerusalem, is one of the most famous cities known to man, and a focal point of pilgrimage for the entire world. Jacob knew it as "Ephratah" (the fruitful), and buried his beloved Rachel in its suburbs. Ruth gleaned in the nearby fields of Boaz and became the ancestress of David and of our Lord. David was born here and later was anointed to the kingship by the saintly Samuel. And here Jesus Christ the Messiah, the Saviour of the world, was born.

The name Bethlehem in Arabic means "House of Meat," and in Hebrew it means "House of Bread"—bread for the body, bread for the mind, bread for the emotions, and bread for the soul. At every Christmas the hearts of all Christendom are turned here, and old men rejoice with littel children over the Gift of gifts, the Bread of Life from heaven.

What sacred mystery surrounds Bethlehem, and what mighty influences for good have gone forth from this lovely place during the past centuries! Because man could not climb the long road to a faraway heaven, the God of love came down to man and was born of the virgin Mary in Bethlehem of Judea. Angels sang "Glory to God in the highest, and on earth peace, good will toward men." Shepherds came to see the young Child and returned to glorify and praise God, and wise men came from the east to worship Him and to present Him gifts: gold, frankin-cense, and myrrh.

Bethlehem was reverenced by Christians from the earliest times—especially the grotto of the manger where Christ was born. So devoutly was the place venerated during the early part of the second century that Emperor Hadrian (76-139), in his attempt to wipe out Christian worship, built over the place of the manger a temple and placed within it a statue of Adonis.

In A.D. 328, when Helena, the mother of Emperor Constantine, came to Bethlehem to erect a church over the place of Jesus' birth, the location presented little or no difficulty, for, ironically, the ruined temple of Adonis marked the place. With ample funds furnished by her emperor son, she completed and dedicated the Church of the Nativity in 332. The Pilgrim of Bordeaux, who came in 333, and many other pilgrims who came later, mention its beautiful interior ornamented with gold, silver, marble, mosaics, embroideries, and paintings. Emperor Justinian (527-565) rebuilt the church, and in the operations the floor level was raised, a stone pavement laid, and the colonnades reset.

The soldiers of Chosroes of Persia, who in the year 614 destroyed other churches in the Holy Land, spared the Church of the Nativity when they saw the mosaics of the wise men in Persian dress. Justinian's church stands today, but with many restorations carried out by the Crusaders in the 11th and 12th centuries. It is regarded as the oldest Christian church extant. In appearance it is like a citadel. The large original entrance has been closed down with masonry until now there is only a low opening, especially made in its present form about 1500, to prevent intruders on horseback from desecrating the church. Above this entry may still be seen the original pointed Crusaders' arch.

In 1934, Mr. William Harvey carried on limited excavations, and about 18 inches under the floor of the present church, he discovered portions of the mosaic floor of the original church built by Helena and Constantine. Some of these mosaic designs were of flowers, fruits, and birds; others were geometric in design. No religious scenes were used in these floor decorations since they would be trodden underfoot.

Three Christian faiths share rights in the large Nativity complex—Roman Catholic (Franciscan friars), Greek Orthodox,

155

and Armenian. Each has its own chapel and altars. The Protestants are allowed to sing carols and conduct a brief service on Christmas Eve in the open courtyard. Next to the basilica of the Church of the Nativity is the commodious Chapel of St. Catherine, from whence the Latin Mass is broadcast and televised on Christmas Eve.

Below the eastern end of the nave of the main basilica of the church, two stairways lead through bronze Crusader doors down into the "grotto of the Nativity," 20 feet below the floor level. This cavelike chapel room measures 12 by 40 feet, the marble walls are completely concealed by tapestries, and ornate lights hang from the ceiling. At the eastern end of the chapel is a small crypt, the marble floor of which is inlaid with a vermillion silver star, lighted by 16 silver lamps. A simple inscription in Latin announces the most stupendous event in all history: "Here Jesus Christ was born of the virgin Mary." Nearby is a manger which

156 The marble floor of the "Grotto of the Nativity" in Bethlehem. The inscription on the silver star reads: "Here Jesus Christ was born of the Virgin Mary."

completes the setting for the profound statement: "And she brought forth her firstborn son, and wrapped him in swaddling clothes, and laid him in a manger; because there was no room for them in the inn" (Luke 2:7). People of the most widely divergent temperaments and degrees of culture and stations of life have knelt devoutly at this shrine and lifted their hearts in unfeigned gratitude to God for this best Gift of His love.

From one end of the grotto a passage leads to several small, subterranean, chapellike caves. One contains the altar and cave of the Holy Innocents before which the Franciscan friars in their daily rounds sing the old hymn *"Salveta Flores Martyrum"*—"All Hail, Ye Little Martyr Flowers." This is in memory of the innocent children's martyrdom by Herod. The English rendering is as follows:[2]

> Hail! flowers of martyrs, whom, on the very threshold of life, the persecutor of Christ cut down, like tender rosebuds scattered by the wind. Hail! first victims for Christ, tender lambs offered to Him; with childlike innocence you play around His altar, with palms and crowns the sign of your martyrdom.

Close to the altar of the Holy Innocents is the *Chapel of St. Jerome,* which was once the study of this illustrious scholar. Here he spent 30 years (390-420) in prayer, fastings, and study, to finally complete his monumental work, the Vulgate, which was the Bible translated from the Hebrew and Greek into the Latin —the language of the Romans. This translation not only enriched the lives of the people, who previous to this time had only a scanty knowledge of the Word of God, but it was of inestimable value also to the Reformers and Protestant translators of the Bible.

In the fertile plain below about a mile east from Bethlehem on a green slope is a group of ruins and a grotto surrounded by olive trees, where the angel of the Lord is said to have appeared to the shepherds with the glad tidings of great joy. Over those fields the heavenly host sung the first Christmas carol which was to resound through all ages in all lands of Christendom:

> *Glory to God in the highest,*
> *And on earth peace, good will toward men.*

Today Bethlehem is one of the world's most popular tourist centers. Some 20,000 people live here, of whom about one-half are Christians. At Christmastime they very graciously receive the world as their guests. However, an unknown poet has well said:

> *Though Christ a thousand times*
> *In Bethlehem be born,*
> *If He's not born in thee,*
> *Thy hope is all forlorn.*

Rachel's Tomb. Beside the high road that runs through the center of Palestine, less than a mile from the city of Bethlehem, is Rachel's tomb. Beautiful Rachel, with whom Jacob fell in love at first sight at the Padan Aram well, and for whom he served a double seven years ("they seemed unto him but a few days, for the love he had for her"). The romance had continued for more than a quarter of a century. Joseph had been born, and they had gone many places together. But as their caravan journeyed on the high road "from Bethel; and there was but a little way to come to Bethlehem, Rachel travailed . . . and the midwife said unto her, Fear not; thou shalt have this son also." And as her soul

Entrance to Rachel's tomb near Bethlehem

was departing, she called his name Ben-o-ni, but his father called him Benjamin, "the son of my right hand." And Jacob buried her there "on the way to Bethlehem . . . and set a pillar upon her grave" (Gen. 35:19-20).

The tomb has undergone many changes in the course of generations. Origen (A.D. 185-254), an early Church Father, first mentions the tomb. Jerome described it as a pyramid of 12 stones representing the 12 sons of Jacob. In the 12th century the Crusaders erected over it a domed room 24 feet square. In the 15th century the Moslems reconditioned the building and constructed a modern masonry-cenotaph over the site.

In 1841, Sir M. Montefiore purchased the grounds and monument for the Jewish community, added an adjoining prayer vestibule, and reconditioned the entire structure with its white dome and quiet reception or prayer room. In the middle of the burial room is the large concrete cenotaph, painted in battleship gray—no name, not an ornament, nor a carving. On Fridays and holidays the Jews come in large numbers to quietly revere the place, to pray, or, led by a young rabbi, chant the prophet Jeremiah's lovely lament: "A voice was heard in Rama, lamentation and bitter weeping: Rachel weeping for her children and would not be comforted, because they were not."

A motherly woman may stretch out her arms, embrace a corner of the gray cenotaph, and passionately kiss it again and again. The group may move around the tomb, touching, kissing, stroking its cold surface with affectionate hands, until all have made the full circuit. Then, with eyes shining, they file out into the sunlight.

At *Zelah,* about a half mile west of Rachel's tomb, on a low hilltop near a large and beautiful grove of olive trees is located the family burial **tomb of Kish,** where Saul and Jonathan are buried. At David's command, the bones of Saul and Jonathan were brought from Jabesh-gilead and buried here in the family sepulchre of Kish, Saul's father (2 Sam. 21:12-14).

The Pools of Solomon. Three miles south of Bethlehem, near the head of the Valley of Urtas, are three large reservoirs known as the "Pools of Solomon." They are chiefly hewn out of the native rock and partly built of squared stones. The pools are about 150 feet apart, and the bottom of each is higher than the top of the one below it. They are strengthened by buttresses and connected by well-cut channels. The upper pool is 380 by 229 feet, and is 25 feet deep; the middle pool is 423 by 230 feet, and is 39 feet deep; while the lower pool is 582 by 207 feet, and is 50 feet deep. To enable the pools to be cleaned and water to be drawn when not full, there are flights of steps inside the lower end of each. They show signs of having been repaired, and at least partially lined with cement from time to time.[3]

These reservoirs are supplied by surface drainage from the nearby hills, by *Ain Saleh* (a splendid spring flowing from an enclosed rock chamber known as the place Solomon referred to as "a spring shut up, a fountain sealed"), and by three other smaller springs. Below the lower pool is an ancient, rock-laid aqueduct leading to Jerusalem about eight miles away and 82 feet lower. A second aqueduct leads toward Herodium, east of Bethlehem, where Herod had a palace. The village of Urtas lies near the bottom of the valley, about a mile east of the pools.

The entire area of luxuriant verdure fits very well into the setting of ancient Etam where King Solomon is said to have made a paradise of pleasure—"planted vineyards, made gardens and orchards, and planted trees of all kinds of fruits . . . and made pools of water to water the wood that bringeth forth trees" (Eccles. 2:5-6). Josephus amplifies the account by telling us that Solomon clothed himself in white, and in a gold-lined chariot drove to his fine gardens at Etam each morning.[4]

The Romans made use of these pools, along with the *Ain Arroub* springs farther south. Their aqueduct connected the two water sources as it trailed around the hills to finally enter the Great Sea under the Temple area at Jerusalem. It is quite possible that the Roman reservoirs were enlargements and restorations of the pools originally prepared by Solomon.

The Palestine government, following World War I, repaired the pools and installed a large pumping station below the lower pool. A pipeline from the springs of Ain Arroub leads to the pools, and all the water is now pumped on to Jerusalem.

Tekoah is the home of Amos the herdsman prophet who, at the call of God, arose up and went to Bethel where he preached plain yet profound truth for all men for all time. It was also the home of "the wise woman" whom Joab employed to induce King David, by a parable, to recall Absalom from banishment (2 Sam. 14:1-22).

Tekoah was the eastern outpost of Judah, five miles southeast of Bethlehem and 10 miles south of Jerusalem. It was on the dividing line between the desert and the arable land. To its east was the Wilderness of Judea, and to its west the lands which lay along the high road which led through Hebron, Bethlehem, and Jerusalem.

Being located on the perilous caravan route from En-Gedi to Judah, and situated on an elevated plateau, it was the signal-station where the trumpet was blown and the fire signals set up in time of potential danger ("blow the trumpet in Tekoa, and set up a signal of fire"). Well did these warning signals work for Jehoshaphat when Edom, Moab, and Ammon was observed marching around En-Gedi up toward Tekoah. Then Jehoshaphat called the people to prayer, and was advised by the prophet Jahaziel, the son of Zechariah, "Ye shall not need to fight in this battle . . . the Lord will be with you." The following day Israel only sang while the Lord brought consternation and defeat to the enemy armies in the narrow pass east of Tekoah, and the place was called "The Valley of Berachah" (2 Chron. 20:1-26).

Neby Sam'wil is a conical hill, 2,942 feet above sea level, five miles northwest of Jerusalem. It is the most conspicuous promontory in northern Judea, and believed by Edward Robinson, G. A. Smith, and W. F. Albright to be the *Mizpeh* of Benjamin. (Others think Mizpeh should be identified with Tell en-Nasbeh, eight miles north of Jerusalem.) Popular tradition has long designated it as the burial place of the prophet Samuel, and during the Middle Ages the Jews gathered in large numbers to hold solemn celebrations at the shrine—although the records state that Samuel was buried at Ramah (1 Sam. 25:1).

161

The Crusaders called the place Mount Joy, because from the top of this mount they had their first glimpse of the Holy City.

The summit is crowned by a dilapidated mosque, once a Christian church, within which is shown a comparatively modern Moslem tomb as the tomb of Samuel. One of the most extensive and interesting views in all Palestine is obtained from the top of the mosque's minaret.[5]

Gibeon, one mile northwest of Neby Sam'wil, is the home of the ancient Gibeonites who tricked Joshua and the incoming Israelites into making a perpetual league with them, and the place where the Tabernacle was set up after the slaughter of the priests by Saul. Here also the Lord appeared to Solomon in a dream by night, and asked, "What shall I give thee?" and Solomon answered, "Give . . . thy servant an understanding heart to judge thy people, that I may discern between good and bad" (1 Kings 3:9). The area has been excavated by Dr. Pritchard.

Gibeah of Saul is perched on the summit of a lofty, limestone hill, on the east side of the highway, three miles north of Jerusalem. The Arabs call it *Tell el-Ful* (Hill of Beans), but in reality it was King Saul's royal palace and citadel where young David came to console the king with sweet strains of harmony from his harp, and to hold high friendship with Prince Jonathan. Excavations have revealed that Saul's well-constructed, two-story fortress-palace measured about 115 by 170 feet, or nearly 20,000 square feet for each of the two floors. His audience room where he contracted state affairs, and where David probably played his harp, "barely equaled the modest modern living room, 14 by 23 feet." Wine, oil, and grain jars showed that the basement rooms were stored with food. The 2,758-foot hilltop is now crowned with the abandoned shell of a new palace, which was begun for King Hussein.

Ramah, the native home, official residence, and burial place of Samuel the prophet, was located north of Jerusalem in the midst of that most interesting cluster of towns including Gibeah, Gibeon, Mizpeh, Beeroth, and Bethel, yet no one is certain of its exact location. Seven different places have been suggested.

162   After many years of study and research, the present writer has come to believe we are justified in considering Ramah and Ramallah as one and the same place.

Ramah is derived from the Hebrew and means "the height"; *Ramallah* is derived from the Arabic and means "the height of God." Ramallah is 2,930 feet above sea level, the highest and finest eminence in this area (aside from Neby Sam'wil, which is somewhat to the west). Ramallah overlooks the entire region and therefore the government broadcasting station is now located there.

Samuel is described as living by a very important hilltop, or high and holy place where he had built an altar, to which the people came to worship God. It was customary for them to wait for him to ascend the hill and pronounce a blessing before they partook of solemn feasts. Around this high portion of Ramah, in the center of town, there prevailed a profound sacredness, and many wonderful things took place there. Samuel was one of the most godly men history has known, and Ramah plus Samuel was the epitome of sacredness—the focus of spirituality for those times. After Samuel had anointed Saul, he said, "Thou shalt come to the hill of God . . . and the Spirit of the Lord shall come upon thee, and thou shalt prophesy with them, and shall be turned unto another man" (1 Sam. 10:5-6). As a judge, Samuel went year by year on a circuit to Bethel, Ramah, Mizpeh, and Gilgal. Then he would come back to his home at Ramah.

Ramallah, along with Bethlehem, has long been known as one of the cleanest, safest, and finest small cities of the Holy Land. It is now an educational and commercial center of some 25,000 people—the largest city between Nablus and Jerusalem. It is a Christian city—largely Protestant because of the splendid Quaker college located there.

The splendid springs at Ramallah are not only adequate for all local needs, but water is piped from there to Beitin (Beth-el) and to Der Dibwan, prosperous Arab villages to the northeast.[6]

Beeroth, now called *Bireh,* lies just across the highway eastward from Ramallah. It derives its name from the copious springs at the southwestern corner of the town, where some 13,000 inhabitants, all Moslems, now live. These springs serve the same purpose as the village well, where in the morning hours the women gather for gossip, then fill their waterpots and gracefully

163

bear them away for the day's water supply. They gathered here after this fashion 2,000 to 3,000 years ago. I first saw them gather here in 1926, and purchased a choice "dowry coin" from one of them—a Maria Theresa coin minted in 1780.

Because of this splendid watering place, ancient Beeroth was the customary resting place of pilgrim bands on their return from the great feasts at Jerusalem, for it was a short day's journey from the Holy City. Tradition has it that Joseph and Mary first missed their 12-year-old Jesus here, and tracing their steps backward, found Him "in the temple, sitting in the midst of the doctors [teachers], both hearing them and asking them questions" (Luke 2:41-46).

CHAPTER **14**

The City of Jerusalem

Jerusalem, whose history reaches back some 4,000 years, and whose name awakens more mystery and sacred memories to more people than any other place on earth, has been called "The City of Peace," or "The City of the Great King." Others think of it as "The City of God," "The City of the Soul," or as "The City of the Book." It is located on a 1,000-acre plateau, next to Gihon Spring in the central Judean mountains. It slightly slants toward the southeast and is encircled by the Kedron and Hinnom valleys. A lesser valley known as "the

Tyropoeon" drains central Jerusalem and divides the "Lower City" from the "Upper City." In Jesus' day this valley was spanned by broad and beautiful bridges supported by immense arches, but in the intervening centuries it has been largely filled up.

Jerusalem has long been surrounded by gray stone walls, varying in height from 30 to 80 feet, and in length from two to five miles. Only remnants of its ancient walls remain. These lie below the present ground level, or form the foundation for later walls. The present walls were built by Suleiman I, "The Magnificent," from 1538 to 1542, and are pierced by eight well-known gates —Jaffa Gate, the New Gate, Damascus Gate, Herod's Gate, St. Stephen's Gate, the Golden Gate, Dung Gate, and Zion's Gate. There are a number of minor gates which are closed.

Within those walls are five famous hills—Mount Ophel, Mount Moriah, Mount Zion, the Northwestern Hill, and Bezetha. Three temples were built on Mount Moriah—Solomon's Temple, Zerubbabel's Temple, and Herod's Temple. The temple area covered 35 acres. The deeply cloistered and colonnaded Outer Court was for the people—among them Gentiles from many lands. The Inner Court had at its center the magnificent Temple proper. On Mount Zion, on the Day of Pentecost, the Holy Spirit came to purify, empower, and guide individuals and the Church.

Modern Moriah, called "the Temple Mount," now has the Dome of the Rock, a Moslem shrine, with its fine grain marble, its beautiful blue Persian tile, its ornate Arabesque script, and its golden dome—altogether, one of the world's finest architectural masterpieces in detail, color, and contour. Directly underneath the dome lies the rough and partially tooled sacred rock in all its massiveness—a huge ledge of gray limestone 57 feet long and 43 feet wide, which is unquestionably the summit of Mount Moriah, where once stood the temples of Solomon, Zerubbabel, and Herod.

Directly south, against the southern wall of the Temple area, is the richly carpeted Mosque of *El Aksa,* Islam's holiest shrine after Mecca and Medina, where worshippers kneel for prayer in the direction of Mecca.

Solomon's Stables, a vaulted structure of 12 parallel rows of

The Western Wall or Wailing Wall in Jerusalem

aisles 200 feet long with 88 supporting columns, lies *under* the southeast corner of the Temple area. Apparently these were built by Herod, since most of the stones are of the Herodian pattern. Portions of the basic structure could have been built by Solomon. They were reconditioned and used by the Crusaders. Some of the rings to which they tethered their horses still exist.

West from these "stables" are *ancient underground water reservoirs* now in use. One known as the Great Sea has an estimated capacity of 2 million gallons. The water for these reservoirs comes from Solomon's Pools, seven miles away.

Solomon's Quarries are stone quarries which extend some 700 feet beneath the northern section of the Old City. Markings

167

in the side and end walls show the very shapes of large building stones which were removed. Throughout the quarries are small rock shelves on which the ancients placed earthen lamps that gave light to the laborers.

The **Wailing Wall,** which the Jewish people prefer to call "The Western Wall," is a part of the retaining wall bordering the outer court of Herod's Temple—a grand architectural fragment whose proximity to the Temple sanctuary has made it an object of veneration and Jewish pilgrimage since soon after the destruction of the Temple more than 1,900 years ago. Many of the carefully marginal-drafted stones in the five lower courses of this wall are so old and so strikingly beautiful that they are regarded as some of the world's finest and most venerable stones.

But the tens of thousands who frequent this wall each week come not to worship an ancient architectural relic, but to pray in deep earnestness and devotion to Almighty God. Their prayers are as varied as human needs and desires. Some write their prayer petitions on a slip of paper and insert them into cracks in the wall. Sometime ago Moshe Dayan wrote his personal prayer and placed it in the wall. It read simply, "Shalom"—Peace. How appropriate, for the Scripture enjoins men to "pray for the peace of Jerusalem."

The **Citadel,** or "Tower of David," is the oldest and most impressive of Jerusalem's ancient buildings. It is located immediately south of Jaffa Gate, and is usually the first of the ancient buildings to be seen by a visitor or pilgrim to the Holy City.

In 24 B.C. Herod the Great built his beautiful palace adjoining this site on the south, and as a means of protection erected three huge towers which he dedicated to Phasael, his brother; Meriamne, his wife; and Hippicus, a friend. When Titus razed the city in A.D. 70, he was impressed by the size of these towers and left them standing as a protection for the legion left to garrison the place. Later destructions took away two of the towers, and much of the third. What we see today is the base of the Phasael

168 Tower and reused stones from the other structures. The major portion of the remains which belonged to Herod's palace, and the towers, are buried beneath a mass of rubble more than 30

Looking over the northern wall into the old city of Jerusalem at the Damascus Gate.

feet deep. Some stones here are earlier than Herod's time; others are much later. We do not know if King David ever had a tower here.

The building, as we now know it, was rebuilt and remodeled by the Crusaders in the 14th century, by the Turks in the 16th century, and more recently by the British in 1929, at a cost of some $30,000.

The *place where Jesus Christ was crucified* has deeply concerned Christians from the earliest times. The apostles and thousands of others knew the place quite well. Then, in A.D. 70, the dark holocaust came with the destruction of Jerusalem by Titus. The people were killed or led away into slavery, and for some 60 years the Holy City lay in ruins. When it began again to be rebuilt, it was under a pagan regime, and neither Jews nor Christians were allowed to enter the city. When the Christians finally returned, none knew the place of the Crucifixion.

Helena, the mother of Emperor Constantine, came to Jeru-

The Garden of Gethsemane looking across to the city wall and the Eastern or Golden Gate.

salem in 326, and by the aid of Eusebius, bishop of Caesarea, and Macarius, bishop of Jerusalem, searched for the place where Christ was crucified and buried. Eventually they decided on the place where now stands the Church of the Holy Sepulchre. Few if any sites of the world have been regarded with such awe and treated with such reverence.

Others, in more recent times, have settled on a three-acre gray hill, just a few hundred feet outside Damascus Gate, as the probable Golgotha or Mount Calvary. It rises some 50 feet above the surrounding terrain and on its side toward the city bears a "certain fantastic likeness" to a human skull. Nearby is a garden and a tomb which is called "The Garden Tomb."

"The tomb is without ornamentation or ostentation, and for all that is the more impressive. No one worships the place, and it is to be hoped none ever will, but many notable Easter services have been conducted here." Among the speakers have been Dwight L. Moody, Dewitt Talmage, and Billy Graham. Thousands gather here from the many countries of the earth and in a small measure feel the force and simplicity of the angel's words: "Come, see the place where the Lord lay."

Other places of interest outside the walls of Jerusalem are: The Hill of Evil Counsel; The Potter's Field; Gihon Spring (the Virgin's Fountain); En-rogel (Job's Well); the Village of Siloam; the Mount of Offense; the Mount of Olives; the Garden of Gethsemane; the Chapel of St. Stephen; Jeremiah's Grotto; and "the Tomb of the Kings."

Jerusalem is rapidly becoming a great metropolitan city— composed of Ancient Jerusalem, the major portion of which is surrounded by walls and largely Arab in population; New Jerusalem, the Jewish city; and East Jerusalem, which is largely made up of Arabs. The last two sections mentioned are being rapidly filled with high-rise buildings which tend to obscure the skyline of the Holy City as it has been known for the past centuries. Yet more and more people come here to live, and about a half million tourists visit the city each year.

CHAPTER 15

The Wilderness of Judea

The Wilderness of Judea has long been known as the badlands of Palestine—"the Scapegoat Wilderness" into which the scapegoat was led "by the hand of a fit man," after the iniquities of the people had been confessed and put upon his head. It lies between Judea and the Dead Sea. Its northern boundary line is *Wadi Kelt,* and it reaches southward to the Negeb. It is some 15 miles wide and 50 miles long.

172 This "wilderness" is a dry, parched, eroded land, full of white, steep, rugged ridges, and is savagely cut from west to east

by hundreds of deep, torturous ravines and canyons which descend abruptly toward the Jordan Valley and the Dead Sea. The hills are largely made up of soft, chalky marl and other limestone compositions, and are bald and smooth and white, without a tint of green, other than soon after the scanty rainfall of the brief rainy season. At other times there is a startling desolation and an oppressive heat—almost like an oven. Occasionally there is flying dust which, when driven by the wind, sweeps the wilderness in blinding fury.

Its great gorges are black and yawning, and its precipices so steep as to make one shudder. All about there is barrenness, chaos, emptiness, isolation, and unfriendliness. These wild wastelands are so dry and sterile and unproductive that one cannot hope to produce any crop. Yet a few plants of retem, some thorns, a bit of grass, and a few flowers do grow here for a brief

173

Typical view of the rugged Wilderness of Judea

time after the winter rains. Also there are a few pleasant days during the year. David in his younger years occasionally grazed his flocks here, and in modern times three Bedouin tribes claim jurisdiction, each in their respective areas. Many groups of people have lived at certain places in this desert from time to time so that the Judean Wilderness becomes a place of singular interest. The places which for one reason or another have fascinated men and caused them to use them or to live here are *Wadi Kelt,* the *Mount of Temptation,* the *Jericho Road, Cave of Adullam, Herodium, Mar Saba, Masada, En-Gedi, Qumran,* and certain cave areas.

Wadi Kelt, through which flows the traditional "Brook Cherith," is a deep, wild ravine which forms the northern boundary of the wilderness. It rises six miles northeast of Jerusalem (where at first it is called Wadi Farah), and flows eastward for some 10 miles until it enters the Jericho plain. It is fed by three strong springs—*Ain Farah, Ain Fowar,* and *Ain el Kelt*—which ordinarily would make it a perennial stream, only that the water from Ain Farah is pumped back to Jerusalem, and an aqueduct conducts the water from the other two springs down to the Jordan plain for irrigation.

In its lower reaches, where it deepens to almost unthinkable depths, it is known as "The Valley of the Shadow of Death" made famous by David's Shepherd Psalm. Also, it is thought to correspond with the "Brook Cherith" of 1 Kings 17:3-5, where Elijah drank of the brook and was fed by the ravens. Here, its sheer walls of rock, sometimes only 12 to 20 feet apart, rise to as much as 200-300 feet and make it practically inaccessible to other than the hardiest of men. Built high upon the wild cliff, where a cavern was said to have been Elijah's lodging place, is the Greek Orthodox Monastery of St. George, where for 1,600 years have come thousands of monks to meditate and pray.

Some years ago, when the British ruled and there was peace in Palestine, the writer went through this "Valley of the Shadow of Death," armed with no more than a camera. We lunched at beautiful *Ain el Kelt* and began our descent of the valley. For the first half mile grass covered the sloping hillsides and shepherds pastured their flocks. Then passing down over a precipice, the valley grew deeper and wilder. In places it was only as wide as the stream bed. We had read of ravens, wild dogs, wolves, and hyenas being here, but on our trip we encountered only one wild dog who charged three times. Our defense was with stones which we drove at him with sufficient accuracy that he finally went away and bothered us no more. Near the lower end of the gorge we met up with two shepherd boys who were leading their flocks home as the shadows were deepening in the Valley of the Shadow of Death.

Mount Quarantana, the traditional *mount of Christ's temptation,* with its cells, its chapels, and a ruined church on its peak, towers up nearly 1,000 feet some two miles west of Jericho. "He was there in the wilderness forty days, tempted of Satan, and was with the wild beasts; and the angels ministered unto him" (Mark 1:13).

What appointments are here indicated, for when Jesus had finished His 40-day fast and was "afterward hungered," the angels "ministered unto him," and not far away was Wadi Kelt (Brook Cherith), where when Elijah was hungry, he was fed by the ravens. Ravens and angels spreading a feast! Surely the Lord can "make a feast in the wilderness."

The Jericho Road spans the distance between Jerusalem and Jericho—about 13 miles. It is the only real road which runs through this wild, wilderness land. Four ancient Roman milestones and numerous ancient land markings indicate that the Turkish road of 50 years ago, and in some places the present road, takes much the same course as the ancient Roman road on which "a certain man went down from Jerusalem to Jericho, and fell among thieves, which stripped him of his raiment, and wounded him, and departed, leaving him half dead." A priest and a Levite passed him by, heedless of his hurt. But a certain Samaritan, "as he journeyed, came where he was; and when he saw him, he had compassion on him, and went to him, and bound up his wounds, pouring in oil and wine, and set him on his own beast, and brought him to an inn, and took care of him" (Luke 10:30-34).

Multitudes of happy pilgrims journeyed over this road to

175

Jerusalem to break the unleavened bread at the festival of the Passover, and Jesus was the Center of attraction on certain of those occasions. At one point are the supposed ruins of the Good Samaritan Inn, and at another is the Apostles' Well. The United States furnished funds for construction of the present modern road.

The Cave of Adullam, which gave refuge to David and his followers when fleeing King Saul's jealous opposition, has for many centuries been identified with a large, impressive cliffside cave in the Wilderness of Judea, four miles southeast of Bethlehem. Located in the rough ravine of *Wadi Khureitun* with its rugged, precipitous sides several hundred feet deep, and the cavern's partially obscured entrance nearly 200 feet up on the rock wall of the canyon, there is a strange seclusion and wildness about the place.

It would seem all but impossible to reach the entrance. But a huge boulder has fallen from above and lodged within a few feet of the opening, so if by strenuous effort you gain a footing on the boulder, a wild leap will land you within the rather crudely chiseled doorway.[1]

You then enter a narrow, low passage leading to a small cave, from which a winding gallery leads to the great cave—a natural grotto 120 feet long by 40 feet wide and 40 to 50 feet high. It is probably the largest natural cave room in Palestine. Numbers of passages—one about 100 feet long—branch out in all directions, often leading to other fair-sized rooms, some of which are partially artificial. Through some of these caverns there are steep descents into a lower series of rooms, and from these there branch out still other caverns and rooms—some as much as 600 feet from the entrance. Parts of the cave have never been investigated.

Nearby is a copious spring of cold, fresh water, falling quietly into a small, rock-hewn basin—sufficient to supply the needs of David's 400 followers. The place matches well the details of the scriptural account.

Herodium, "The Mountain of Paradise," is a 600-foot high, cone-shaped hill standing out boldly on the plain three miles southeast of Bethlehem, and one mile north of the Cave of Adullam. It may have been the Beth-haccerem or "Beacon Mountain" of Old Testament times, from whence "fire signals" were sent, but in known history it is connected with Herod the Great. Desiring a country estate for his own pleasure, and having ample funds at his command, he raised the hill still higher, then on the very top he erected a massively fortified castle and a luxurious royal palace of great strength and splendor. The only way of access to this top level was by way of a superb stairway of hewn stone.

At the foot of the hill and on the surrounding plain, Herod laid out a beautiful town in Roman style, including a palace for himself and beautiful homes for his friends. The place was ornamented with trees and beautiful gardens. To insure an adequate water supply, he had an aqueduct constructed from the spring at Etam (near Solomon's Pools) to a central fountain at Herodium. From here it was channeled to various buildings and to the gardens. When all was complete and in operation, the natives called it "Jebel Fereidis" ("Mountain of the Little Paradise"). Herod used it as a quiet place of enjoyment with his friends and as his base when he took off on expeditions for hunting partridge, ibex, and other game in the wilderness. Herodium was also a signal light station where communication could be received from or sent to the Mount of Olives, Masada, Machaerus, and Alexandrium, north of Jericho.

The Christians frequently call it "Frank Mountain," from a 15th-century tradition that it was defended by the Crusaders for a long time against the Saracens, after the loss of Jerusalem. Recently it has been made into a national park.

Mar Saba Monastery is one of the strangest and most extraordinary places it is possible to dream about. Certainly you can hardly believe your eyes when you view it in reality. Partly hewn in the rock and partly built on strongly buttressed ledges, it rises up tier upon tier and tower upon tower from the south cliffs of the blasted and desolate *Wadi n-Nar* ("Valley of Fire"), which is the channel down which the Kedron flows to the Dead

Sea. No other place in the world is more weirdly situated, and no other place in the Judean Wilderness is more shrouded with mystery than this monastery of Mar Saba, located at sea level, four miles east of Bethlehem. From one outlook on the wall it is 590 feet down to the bed of the Valley of Fire.

St. Saba, a native of Cappadocia, who was famed for his sanctity, his learning, and his power to work miracles, penetrated this desert and became fascinated with the idea of founding a monastery in this wild gorge. In A.D. 483, at the age of 44, his dream was fulfilled when he gathered around him hundreds of deeply religious men under the rule of St. Basil, and began the construction of *Mar Saba* as a Greek monastery by authority of the patriarch of Jerusalem.

The foundations for the structure were and have ever been a marvel of engineering, for the stone ledges and the pinnacled piers and pilasters seem as one. The many towers, terraces, balconies, courtyards, chapels, shrines, rock-hewn cells, rooms, iron rails, and winding stairs all cling to and blend with the gray cliffside like a huge and intricately built swallow's nest.

In addition to its multiplicity of accommodations for monastic living and practices, it has an ornately decorated chapel with its stalls, walls, screen, and chancel gorgeous with gilding and paintings.

Mar Saba's library is reputed to contain rare manuscript treasures, but only such men as Curzon and Tischendorf have been permitted to examine them. Curzon reported seeing about 1,000 manuscripts, several of which were of great interest— among them a copy of the first eight books of the Old Testament, and a copy of Homer's *Iliad*.

It is said that at one time more than 3,000 monks and hermits lived at this monastery and in surrounding areas. Now there are only a few.

The entrance by which travelers are received is marked by a
178 large tower with dilapidated battlements. Here, at a small, iron-barred door, travelers must present their credentials and be carefully scrutinized before admission. No ladies are admitted, but

for their reception the tower outside is provided where they are supplied with simple fare and a night's lodging.

Masada, a majestic 23-acre flat-topped mesa, two and one-half miles off the west shore of the Dead Sea, is one of the world's most startling natural fortifications. Shaped like a great ship 2,000 feet long and 1,000 feet wide in the middle and tapering to narrow promontories at the northern and southern tips, its sides are composed of almost sheer rock cliffs which rise 1,000 feet above the barren wilderness of Judea, and 1,300 feet above the

Looking down on the fortress of Masada showing the three-tiered palace of Herod clinging to the northern slope.

waters of the Dead Sea. Stark, forbidding, and almost inaccessible, it was chosen by Herod the Great, in 37 B.C., as a site for his wilderness palace and fortress—a place of retreat and refuge in case of possible attack by Cleopatra of Egypt, by his own subjects, or by armies from the desert.

He encircled the entire top of the plateau with a great white wall 4,250 feet long, 20 feet high, and 13 feet wide. It had three gates and 38 towers. As his residence, he erected the "Western Palace," which was a very large and wonderfully fine place with throne room, living and reception quarters, luxurious baths, colored mosaic floors, and sumptuous apartments. About his palace, and at other places on the mesa, where colonnaded porticos, cloisters, walkways, cisterns, groves, gardens, and storerooms for both arms and provisions sufficient to supply 10,000 men for many years—"And thus was the citadel fortified by nature and the hands of men."

Later, to make his retreat doubly secure, more pleasant, and more impressive, he moved the sphere of his architectural activities to Masada's northern precipice, and there erected his three-tiered "hanging palace"—the architectural wonder of the ancient world. On the upper terrace were four spacious and highly decorated apartment rooms with a semicircular court extending out to the very edge of the cliff. The middle terrace, 60 feet below, was a circular pavilion and a colonnade. The lowest terrace was an elaborate apartment with its rooms and baths built on a 54-foot square, surrounded by a double colonnade. The wall frescoes were of imitation marble and precious stones. Inner staircases connected the three terraces.

But Herod was never to use Masada, except for possibly a few vacation trips. After his death, in 4 B.C., a Roman garrison was stationed at Masada, and this occupation continued until A.D. 66, when a large-scale Jewish revolt broke out all over the land. At this time the Jews made a lightning raid on Masada, destroyed the Roman garrison, and took charge of the plateau with its 180 fortifications and palace complex. As fighting continued throughout Palestine, many more zealous Jews came to Masada and strengthened the Jewish garrison.

After the fall of Jerusalem to Titus, in A.D. 70, the Jews gathered their remnants and prepared to stage their last desperate resistance at Masada. Titus' deputy general, Flavius Silva, came there in the autumn of 72 and laid siege to Masada, which was then defended by Eleazar ben Yair, the leader of the Zealots.

For long months they defended themselves in their natural fortress. But the Romans erected a huge ramp or causeway on the western side over which they could reach the rim of the plateau. At its head they built siege towers, catapults, and battering rams, and in the end attacked with flaming torches. Then, when the Jews could resist no more, Eleazar made a speech in which he set forth the horrors of the fate that awaited them as prisoners to the Romans, and begged them to kill themselves rather than submit. The garrison consented.

Embracing their loved ones, with sword and dagger they dealt the fatal blows. Personal treasures were collected in piles and burned. Finally they chose 10 men by lot to slay all the rest. When these 10 had done the deed, they in turn cast lots among themselves to determine who should kill his 9 companions and afterwards slay himself. Thus, in silence so the enemy should suspect nothing, one of the most touching tragedies in the annals of human history took place.[2]

The next day, April 15, A.D. 73, when the Romans at last got into the fortress they had besieged so long, they found two women and five children who had concealed themselves, and a mass of 960 dead bodies. An awful silence took the place of the clamor they had expected. Masada! O Masada of the Wilderness![3]

Yigael Yadin and a very large number of volunteers excavated Masada in two campaigns, one of seven months and one of four. In the Western Palace they found the throne room, reception halls, bedrooms, bathrooms, service quarters, and storage rooms in which were hundreds of broken storage jars containing remnants of food. Many of the jars bore labels describing their contents in Aramaic or Hebrew. In some of the Zealots' rooms they found domestic utensils, mats, shoes, and clothing.

Many bronze and silver coins were found, including "great

hoards" of silver shekels inscribed "Jerusalem the Holy—Shekel of Israel." Beneath the floor of the synagogue were found two biblical scrolls—parts of Ezekiel and Deuteronomy.

Today hardy souls may take the three-mile "serpent's trail" to the top; others not caring for the extreme exertion may now go up in an electric cable car. On the top of Masada, Jewish soldiers are initiated into the Israeli Army with the significant words, "It shall not happen again."

En-Gedi (Ain Jidy—"The Fountain of the Kid") is a small oasis halfway along the west shores of the Dead Sea. Here, almost 500 feet above the sea, an immense spring of warm water leaps from the base of a towering rock cliff and splashes from terrace to terrace down to a small but very fertile plain, half a mile broad and a mile in length.

As early as the reign of Solomon, En-Gedi was one of the richest areas in Palestine. Here were vineyards, date palms, camphire, gum arabic, myrrh, sugarcane, melons, and many other edible fruits, spices, perfumes, and plants that made up one of the world's famed garden spots. Josephus suggests that balsam saplings were among the presents brought to Solomon by the queen of Sheba. Apparently the cultivation of balsam was begun here by the king.

Above and around the fountains are lofty cliffs, deep ravines, and a wild desolation called "the wilderness of En-gedi," which one could not well overrate as a place of refuge. There are numerous natural and artificial caves and sepulchers in the area, some of which sheltered David and his followers when they dwelt here for some time in the "strongholds at En-gedi" (1 Sam. 23:2). Solomon exclaimed, "My beloved is to me as a cluster of camphire in the vineyards of En-gedi" (Song of Sol. 1:14). En-Gedi continued, with varying fortunes, until its destruction in the Arab invasion of the seventh century. Since than it has lain in ruins until recently a pioneering group of young people from Israel have planted a thriving colony here.

Khirbet Qumran, bordering the northwest shore of the Dead Sea, is where, about the year 150 B.C., the Essenes removed

182

themselves "from the evils and wrongs which surge up in cities," and built their own colony.

Here for almost two centuries they lived quiet and extremely simple lives and "devoted themselves to agriculture and other peaceful arts." Among their arts was copying the Scriptures and other sacred scrolls. They were so deeply imbued with a spiritual ideal that they lived in anticipation of the kingdom of God.

Finally, Rome came about A.D. 68 and destroyed or dispersed the Essenes, leaving only the ruins of their city. But before destruction came, they had hidden thousands of sacred scrolls in nearby caves. These were discovered in 1947 to 1956, and constitute the greatest archaeological discovery of modern times.

Oh, the wilderness! This Judean Wilderness! What thoughts it all conjures up! On its border have lived mighty men of God —Amos, Jeremiah, and John the Baptist. And in its wild wastelands Jesus, the Son of God, fasted, was tempted, said no to the devil, and angels ministered to Him. Here Herod built a "little paradise" at Herodium and at Masada, the mightiest fortress and palace of the Near East. And here the Essenes lived and left thousands of copies of the Bible for modern men.

CHAPTER **16**

The Negeb, or Southland

The Negeb, or dry southland, is that large, inverted land triangle with its base on an east-west line just north of Beer-sheba, and its apex at Elath on the Red Sea. In many respects the Negeb (or Negev) is a highland plateau made up of sandy plains, rolling hills, small fertile wadies, craters, and fantastically shaped mountains which rise here and there in irregular disorder. All of its annual rainfall of five to eight inches comes between December and March. During spring months the atmosphere is fresh and clear, the flowers bloom, and one hears

184

the whistling of the quail, the song of the lark, and the warbling of smaller birds. At other seasons much of the land assumes the features of a desert—dry, wadi-cut, and sand blown.

In ancient times the Negeb was one of the fertile and fascinating sections of Palestine—one to which the Hebrew patriarchs went and spent much of their lives. Here they dug wells, erected altars, called on the name of the Lord, planted groves, tilled the land, and reared their families. Over these swelling hills and within these valleys their flocks and herds roved by the thousands.

It was in the desert lands of this southwestern Negeb that Hagar wandered with her son Ishmael when driven from Abraham's tent encampment.

From here Abraham journeyed with Isaac to Mount Moriah, to offer him up there in sacrifice. During the lifetime of Samuel, his sons were made judges, lived at Beersheba, and judged the Israelites who lived in this southland of Palestine.

Elijah, when fleeing from the fury of Queen Jezebel, came to Beersheba and, leaving his servant, went a day's journey southward into the wilder portions of the Negeb. There he "sat down under a juniper tree" and asked the Lord to let him die. This juniper tree, known as *Retem,* is a species of the broom-plant and is still the largest and most conspicuous shrub of these deserts, providing the traveling Arab with shelter from the wind at night and from the sun by day.

More advanced forms of civilization in the Negeb began with the Nabateans, an Arab people of the first century before Christ. The pressure of large, dynamic populations was so great in the Edom area that thousands were forced to seek sustenance and shelter in these less-favored lands, where other large civilizations less trained in the arts of life must have miserably perished because of a lack of knowledge of how to conserve the natural water supplies. But here the Nabateans not only survived, but built up a civilization that evoked the admiration of all who saw or heard of their exploits. They conserved rainwater by a system 185 of dams and cisterns, and a network of cut channels along which they directed runoff water from the hills, built towns along the caravan routes, "worked out the refinements of soil and water management" so that there was ample provision for agricultural pursuits as well as for domestic purposes.[1]

When the Roman conquerors took over, just previous to and during the early Christian period, this district underwent further and more extensive development. They dug wells, built reservoirs, and constructed aqueducts to lead water for long distances to irrigate lands which would otherwise have lain fallow. They erected public buildings, established garrisons, and built a civilization that will always impress those who see these lands and gain a fair acquaintance of the climate and history of the country.

Civilization in the Negeb reached its peak under the Byzantines who succeeded the Romans. Taking over the entire Roman development, they further improved the country by constructing stone walls for terracing and conserving the soil. They built vast rock cisterns and immense dams for conserving the water. The peak of this civilization was under Emperor Justinian during the sixth century A.D. During this time the Negeb developed a population of around 100,000 people who enjoyed improved roads and a flourishing trade. Then, in the seventh century, the Arabs took over in the Negeb, and civilization gradually dwindled, to finally suffer its deathblow under Turkish misrule.

With the passing of the centuries the face of the land changed. The reservoirs and other water controls were permitted to be destroyed, the rock terraces to deteriorate, and the soil to wash away by seasonal rains. Sand-blown deserts replaced a notable civilization. Only here and there vestiges of destroyed cities, remnants of ruined reservoirs, and fragments of sculptured stone remained to tell the tale of the glorious past.

With the beginning of this century the once fertile parts of the country were largely made up of fields of sand and crumbling ruins over which lizards glided by day and jackals crept with the coming of twilight, while hoot owls broke in upon the deathlike stillness of the night. A few scattered Bedouin tribes encamped here and there in their black, sackcloth-of-hair tents, grazed their sheep, goats, horses, and camels wherever they could find water

A typical Jewish kibbutz (colony) in the Negeb

and sufficient herbage, and clung to their ancestral modes of life.[2]

In 1942, a committee of experts from the Land and Afforestation Department of the Jewish National Fund explored the Negeb and carried out tests to ascertain its water resources, weather, soil, and flora. Of the 2,375,000 acres comprising the area, they advised that 400,000 acres were suitable for cultivation and another 400,000 suitable for reforestation. In 1943, therefore, the Jews established three experimental settlements south of Beersheba—at Revivim, Gevulot, and Beit Eshel. These served as the "agricultural bridgeheads" of the Negeb. One night in October of 1946, after the Yom Kippur fast, convoys of secretly loaded trucks went rumbling into the Negeb, and by daylight next morning 1,000 veteran settlers had set up 11 new settlements, each complete with prefabricated wooden huts, including stockades and watchtowers. Ever afterwards the activities of that night were known as "Operation Negev."

By 1948, there were 26 settlements in the Negeb. Then with the coming of statehood, and the large influx of immigrants looking for living space, the Israeli authorities were obliged to further open the way for large-scale settlement in this great southland. Planning for the Negeb was no longer on the piecemeal order but as a part of a concerted, all-embracing effort to bring as much of the area as possible back to fertility and usefulness. Almost every week a new settlement sprang up.

By 1959, these efforts to reclaim the Negeb were further aided by Prof. Michael Even-Ari, professor of botany at the Hebrew University. He and a team of Israeli botanists and agrarian experts took the lead in endeavoring to follow the farming patterns of the ancient Nabateans in constructing fields; building systems of dams, cisterns, and canals; growing the same crops by the same methods. They were thus using the same water conservation and irrigation techniques used in past ages, all of which proved practical, indeed.

188   Furthermore, in their conquest of the Negeb, the Jews laid a 108-inch pipeline which brought water from the northwest shore of the Sea of Galilee across Lower Galilee, and along the Plain of

Sharon to the Negeb—160 miles—to aid them in the irrigation of the land. A second water pipeline was laid from the headwaters of the Zerkon River at Antipatris.

Armies and crews of khaki-clad young men and women, along with others who were not so young, then moved into the Negeb. Working under the instruction of these experts, they made surveys, operated bulldozers, built houses, bored wells, dug ditches, laid pipelines, constructed huge stone catchments, planted trees, put in forage crops, arranged gardens, planted grain, and cultivated the rolling plains. Within two years, over 1 million tamerisk, eucalyptus, and other trees were planted in the forest areas, and tree shelter belts (or windbreaks) were planted in crisscrossing rows for a total length of about 500 miles.

A strange romance grew up about converting desert lands into homes—one of the world's most exciting battles between man and nature. Soon there were nearly 50 towns and settlements in the Negeb, and the work of creating new settlements, arranging new farms for new families, building schools for Bedouins and Jews, locating chemicals, and restoring the wastes of the great southland went forward with a pioneering zeal that was without parallel in modern history. The 18 tribes and sub-tribes of Bedouin Arabs—numbering in all some 15,000—were, as far as is possible, given title to certain areas of the land and gradually came to lead more settled lives.

The story of the founding of each of the colonies and the growth of some into fair-sized cities is absorbing and sometimes heartrending. We briefly recount the fortunes of four of the places: *Beersheba, Dimona, Sede Boker,* and *Avdat.*

Beersheba, the true capital of the Negeb, and the famous center of patriarchal life, signifies "the Well of the Oath," for here Abraham dug a well and gave seven ewe lambs to Abimelech in token of an oath of covenant between them. He then "called the place Beersheba," planted a grove, and "called on the name of the Lord, the everlasting God." Here Abraham received the strange yet deeply meaningful command to sacrifice his son 189 Isaac, and from here journeyed to the land of Moriah in unquestioned faith and obedience to the divine direction.

(Above) A view of a portion of the Bedouin market at Beersheba. (Below) The author bargains with a Bedouin in the Beersheba market for a string of miniature camels.

Here Isaac built an altar and "called upon the name of the Lord," and his servants digged a well. To Beersheba Rebecca came as a bride, and here their children were born. Here Esau forfeited his birthright, and Jacob obtained by fraud the coveted blessing (Gen. 25:34). And Jacob "went out from Beersheba, and went toward Haran."

To the Beersheba sanctuary Jacob came once more, when an old man, on his way to Egypt, and here God spoke to him in a vision of the night and dispelled all his fears, promising to bring him up again to the land after that his son Joseph "should have put his hand upon his eyes" (Gen. 46:1-4).

A strange sacredness pervades the atmosphere about these ancient ruins and about the ancient wells which are yet in use. Tradition says two of them are the very wells which the patriarchs and their servants dug. In this case tradition could very well be right. These wells are circular, and the larger one is 12½ feet in diameter and about 45 feet deep. The old stone curb, deeply grooved by the ropes of many centuries, has now been replaced by a newer well-mouth somewhat higher up. Yet, until recent years, many herds of camels, cattle, and sheep drank here daily from stone and cement troughs.

Present Beersheba gradually grew up two miles west of the wells but had a population of only 2,000 when General Allenby's forces captured it in the summer of 1917 and left a neat military cemetery at the edge of the town. The place had small growth, however, until the Jews took over in 1948. It then became the true capital of the Negeb, as it mushroomed into a frontier city of 85,000.

It is amazing to see modern Beersheba, with its attractive residences; its modern hotels; its schools, hospitals, shops, museums, industrial areas; its many blocks of apartment buildings; and its university of 550 students. Perhaps most colorful of all is its Thursday morning Bedouin Market, when the tribes of the nearby areas come to sell their camel colts, lambs, goats, young donkeys, chickens, turkeys, copper and silver ware, fine needle work; and to buy cloth, flour, rice, coffee, sugar, and other basic needs. Their clothing, their manners and customs,

191

and their unhurried bargaining in buying and selling make your dreams suddenly have relation to reality. Bible characters take on flesh and blood and live before your very eyes—especially when you see camels, goats, and sheep being watered from ancient wells, women wearing long black veils, men dressed in sweeping robes, and white kaffiyehs—much as they did in Abraham's day.

Dimona, a colony 20 miles southeast of Beersheba, was started in 1955, when a small group of immigrants pitched their tents, laid out a townsite, began to build simple wooden homes, and went forward with the construction of water, sewer, and electric light systems.

In time a textile plant and an atomic reactor were built. Then other immigrants came and sturdy stone houses became the vogue. Fortune further favored the Dimona settlers when the phosphate mines opened at Oron, a few miles south, in the Big Crater. Many substantial dormitories arose to serve the commuting workers, until today the population of Dimona stands at around 24,000 and bids fair to increase.

Sede Boker (Field of the Rancher), 30 miles south of Beersheba, was established in 1952 by a group of 16 young men and 3 young women whose aim was to raise sheep and cattle. From the very first year they prospered, yet suffered a tragedy when one of the girls was murdered by Arab marauders.

In 1954, Prime Minister David Ben-Gurion brought great encouragement to the colony when he went into temporary retirement and with his wife, Paula, not only built their permanent home here, but sponsored the construction of the Sede Boker Institute of Negev Studies—a sort of University of the Desert. Its complex of buildings houses a regional high school, a teachers' training college, and an institute for special seminars on desert farming, architecture, and general living. During its 25 years the colony has inaugurated a splendid water system and successfully developed fields, gardens, orchards, and pastures to meet their needs. During the summer season they operate a roadside stall where fresh grapes, plums, apples, and peaches, neatly packed in plastic bags, are sold to grateful travelers.

192

Avdat, or Abde, eight miles south of Sede Boker, offers a

An aerial view of the excavated ruins of the ancient Nabatean city of Avdat in the Negeb.

flavor of the ancient. Perched high on a flattened hilltop are the restored ruins of a small, acropolislike city with its graceful Corinthian columns rising in the clear desert air, and its houses tumbling down the sides. The place was founded by the Nabateans in the third century B.C., and for 1,000 years continued with varying fortunes under the Nabateans, the Romans, and the Byzantines.

It fell to the Arabs without resistance during their conquest of the Negeb in A.D. 634, and gradually declined until the 10th century, when it was abandoned for another 1,000 years. The network of ruined dams, cisterns, and hillside channels attest the engineering abilities of the Nabateans 2,000 years ago, and serve as models for modern engineering. Extensive excavation and large-scale restorations began in 1959, under Professor Even-Ari of the Hebrew University, and are now completed. The ancient dam has been rebuilt, the run-off water system revived, a roadside cafe brought into service, and a small museum that displays statuettes, pottery, and inscriptions of the people who lived there during those long yesteryears.

CHAPTER **17**

Sinai, Land of Revelation

The Peninsula of Mount Sinai," says Dean Stanley, "is, geographically and geologically, one of the most remarkable districts on the face of the earth. It combines the three grand features of earthly scenery—the sea, the desert, and the mountains. It occupies also a position central to three countries, distinguished for their history and geography among all other nations of the world—Egypt, Arabia, and Palestine. It has been the scene of a history as unique as its situation; by which the fate of the three nations which surround

195

it have been decided and through them the fate of the whole world."[1]

In form, the Sinai Peninsula is somewhat like a great inverted land triangle, which lies between the two arms of the Red Sea known as the Gulf of Suez and the Gulf of Aqaba, and between the Suez Canal and the Negeb. Its irregular baseline along the north is some 150 miles, and it measures about 240 miles to its southern point. When seen from high in the air, or as a three-dimensional map, it has the appearance of a huge stony heart—a 20,000-square-mile mass of sand, sandstone, limestone, and granite mountains broken up into very irregular and fantastic forms.

At its baseline, along the Mediterranean coastal belt, it is barren and sandy with long stretches of 200-feet-high sand dunes, interspersed here and there with salt marshes and well-watered oases with their picturesque groves of date palms. Here passes one of the most ancient roadways in the world: the "Way of the Sea," which for millenniums has served as a link between the two great empires of Egypt in Africa and Assyria-Babylonia in Asia. In olden times it was known locally as "The Way of the Land of the Philistines" (Exod. 13:17), and Moses was told not to bring the children of Israel by that route when they left Egypt because of the warlike tribes they would meet around the Gaza district.

Through the ages, caravans of merchants have crossed this way in time of peace, and colorful armies in time of war—the Pharaohs, Alexander, Napoleon. The British Expeditionary Forces improved the roadway and brought a railway and a water line through here in 1917 on their way to Gaza. Some felt the prophecy of Isaiah was beginning to be realized: "In that day there shall be a highway out of Egypt to Assyria" (Isa. 19:23).

At the center of the peninsula is the great *Plateau of the Tih*, which rises to a height of 4,000 feet above the sea and consists of a vast plain, broken in places with mountain ranges, and drained toward the north in slightly depressed stream beds, or "seils." These converge on the so-called "River of Egypt," or Wadi El Arish. Over this arid tableland runs a roadway from Elath to Suez. On this road is Nakhl, a famous watering place for caravans of all kinds. To the west of Nakhl is Mitla Pass which has figured prominently in recent Arab-Israeli wars.[2]

In the south central portion of the peninsula is a striking group of peaks—Mount Serbal, Mount Katherine, Mount Shomer, and Mount Sinai, of which 7,363-foot Mount Sinai (known through the centuries by the natives as *Jebel Musa,* or Mount Moses) holds chief attraction. On its surface here, the whole face of nature is wild and rugged and naked—appearing like the "Alps unclothed." Yet the very nakedness of the peaks imparts to the scene a grandeur, a solitude, and a beauty peculiarly its own.

Straight from the miraculous crossing of the Red Sea at Suez, past the copper and turquoise mining center at Serabit el Khadim, came Moses leading the vast concourse of Israelites along with the "mixed multitude," and encamped them before Mount Sinai on a long, broad plain since known as "the Plain of the Tribes." Having a previously arranged appointment for an encounter with God, Moses went up where "the glory of the Lord covered the top of the mountain like devouring fire." On the third day there were thunders and lightnings, and a thick cloud upon the mountain. A trumpet sounded long, and waxed louder and louder.

And God spake all these words, saying,

I am the Lord thy God . . . Thou shalt have no other gods before me.

Thou shalt not make unto thee any graven image, or any likeness of any thing . . .

Thou shalt not take the name of the Lord thy God in vain . . .

Remember the sabbath day, to keep it holy. . . .

Honor thy father and thy mother . . .

Thou shalt not kill.

Thou shalt not commit adultery.

Thou shalt not steal.

Thou shalt not bear false witness . . .

Thou shalt not covet *(Exod. 20:1-4, 7-8, 12-17).*

197

And "he gave unto Moses, when he had made an end of communing with him on Mount Sinai, two tablets of testimony, tablets of stone, written with the finger of God . . . the words of the covenant, the ten commandments" (Exod. 31:18; 34:28).

How simple, yet how profound! What depth of wisdom—the Creator and Governor of the moral universe giving to man righteous laws. These were to be his guidelines to help him discern the structure of the moral universe, to keep him in the good way, and to guard him from the consequences of evil. No wonder these laws of Sinai have become the "cornerstone of all morality," the basis for the laws of all good governments, the very pillars of respectable society.

The Monastery of St. Katharine at the foot of Mount Sinai where the famous Codex Sinaiticus was found in 1844.

It was here at Sinai that the people brought in their gifts, and the craftsmen constructed the Tabernacle exactly as God had laid down the plans. Here, too, many centuries later, God spoke to Elijah with a "still small voice" that was stronger than wind, earthquake, or fire (see 1 Kings 19:4-18). In a vale, at the foot of Mount Sinai, is the *St. Catherine Monastery,* a Greek Orthodox institution, built here in the desert solitudes by Emperor Justinian in A.D. 527. Its massive walls and square, squat design give it the appearance of a fort, yet when within, one readily gains the impression of a treasure house of decorative art and of gruesome antiquity. Its banner-hung church, its many cells, its 50 guest rooms, its library of precious manuscripts, its crude cymbals which call to prayer, and its charnel house where the bones of those who have served here before are laid out in rows—from skulls to skeletal feet. In one instance the skeleton of an abbot, in full clerical dress, watches over his lifeless flock. Over the monastery the standard of the Lamb and the Cross is on its highest towers, and with the proper credentials one will find a whole-hearted welcome here, along with frugal fare.

Kadesh-barnea, the place next in importance to Mount Sinai, was for the children of Israel "eleven days' journey" northward, on the northeast border of the peninsula. And so it is today, for just 50 miles southwest of Beersheba, in a lush little valley, near a branch of the River of Egypt, is "the powerful spring" of *Ain el Qudeirat* which flows all year; and the oasis which it creates tends to remind one of how, in a small way, the Garden of Eden must have looked. Within this area are two more splendid springs: *Ain Qudeis* and *Ain Qoseimeh.*

Ain el Qudeirat is the strongest of the springs, and is generally regarded as the original Kadesh-barnea. The other springs, with their oases, are nearby—*Ain Qudeis* five miles to the southeast, and *Ain Qoseimeh* some two miles to the west. The Israelites would have made use of the whole group of springs with their oases and extensive pasturelands, for it would have required much water and land to sustain so great a throng of people. The topographical requirements of the biblical narrative are well suited to this area.

Many men have searched for Kadesh-barnea—John Rowland, H. C. Trumbull, C. Leonard Woolley, T. E. Lawrence, Jonathan Cape, Nelson Glueck, Y. Aharoni, and others—and all have concluded that here in this area is to be found the historic spot where the Israelites encamped during much of their sojourn in the wilderness. It was from here that Moses sent the 12 men to spy out the land; here Miriam, Moses' sister, died and was buried; and from here Moses sent a delegation in vain to the king of Edom, asking permission to pass through the territory of Edom on their way to Canaan.

199

Many armies, expeditions, and caravans have crossed and recrossed Sinai, yet the people who live in these parts seem to remember but the one. Their mountains, valleys, springs, and places of encampment are named after Moses, Aaron, and Jethro, and you will not talk to them long until they will speak very reverently, respectfully, and enthusiastically of the children of Israel as though just last year they had passed through.

Sinai "is no ordinary land of broken plains and naked ranges, and scanty water" and copper, and silver, and turquoise, and oil. "God walked abroad in it and divine purpose was made manifest there of old. It has always been . . . a sanctuary of revelation and reformation, with the spirit of the Holy pervading the very atmosphere."[3]

*

The Jordan Rift Valley

*

CHAPTER 18

The Beka'a, or Valley of Lebanon

Lying between the Lebanon and Anti-Lebanon mountain ranges is the broad rift valley which is known in the Bible as "the valley of Mizpeh," or simply as "the valley of Lebanon" (Josh. 11:8, 17). Ancient writers knew it as "the Entrance of Hamath" or as the Coele-Syria (Hollow Syria), while in modern times it is usually known as the Beka'a (the valley).

The valley is 205 miles long, from 3 to 10 miles wide, and is drained by two well-known rivers—the Litany and the Orontes. The *Litani* rises just north of Baalbek and flows southward to a

A vineyard in the Valley of Lebanon, with the Lebanon mountains rising behind.

point just west of the headwaters of the Jordan, where it turns sharply to the west and passes through the Lebanons by a narrow gorge, and finally discharges its waters into the Mediterranean five miles north of Tyre. The *Orontes* river rises just north of the sources of the Litany, and flows due north through the great plain within and beyond the Lebanons, for a distance of about 130 miles; then, like the Litany, it turns sharply to the west and pours its flood of waters into the sea.

This beautiful and exceedingly fertile valley lies at an average of 3,000 feet above sea level and at one point attains an elevation of about 4,000 feet. In the winter it is sometimes covered with snow, but in the springtime its great fields of plowed earth, of flowers, and of ripening grain coupled with its lush orchards present a pattern of rich reds, browns, greens, and yellows which, in the south, spreads out for more than 70 miles between the two mountain ranges.

On entering the valley, one may think of it as a secluded mountain retreat, but such is far from the case. For, from time immemorial, there has run through it the far-famed highway which links Mesopotamia with Egypt. Over this route and

203

through this valley have passed numberless caravans, many military expeditions, and multitudes who have gone on state errands and missionary enterprises. Abraham passed this way as he "came into Canaan"; Eliezer went to Mesopotamia and returned through the valley when on his mission to obtain a wife for Isaac. Jacob passed along this way in going to Padan Aram where he married beautiful Rachel, and returned by the selfsame road some 21 years later.

The cities of this valley which played a large part in the sacred and secular history of the ancient world were Hamath, Riblah, and Baalbek. Imposing mounds stand today to attest the importance of the first two of these cities, and the impressive ruins of Baalbek bring forth the admiration of all who see them.

Hamath was on the Orontes River, near the northern entrance into the Land of Promise—thus "the entrance of Hamath" (Num. 34:8). Its king sent presents to David when he defeated the king of Zobah (2 Sam. 8:6), and it was frequently mentioned in the Bible as Israel's ideal northern border. Dan, however, was actually the north limit most of the time. It was only at brief intervals, under David, Solomon, and Jeroboam that the country about Hamath was subject to Israel.

Riblah, now called Ribleh, is located on the Orontes, 35 miles north of Baalbek, where the old caravan route from the coast intersects the main highway, then passes on eastward to Palmyra (Tadmore). Being so strategically located from a military point of view, and being so near the vast forests of the cedars of Lebanon which were essential for building machines of war, the military leaders of Babylonia and Egypt used Riblah as a camping ground, a base of supplies, or center of operations while carrying on war in Syria and Palestine.

While encamped here with his army, just previous to the battle of Carchemish, Pharaoh-Necho deposed Jehoahaz of Judah and put him "in bonds" (606 B.C.). After Necho's withering defeat at Carchemish, he took the Judean king back to Egypt where he died (2 Kings 23:32-34). When the Babylonian army made a breakthrough in the siege of Jerusalem in 586 B.C., King Zedekiah and all his men of war fled out of the city by night.

204

But the Chaldeans' [Babylonian] army pursued after them, and overtook Zedekiah in the plain of Jericho: and when they had taken him, they brought him up to Nebuchadnezzar king of Babylon to Riblah in the land of Hamath, where he gave judgment upon him. Then the king of Babylon slew the sons of Zedekiah in Riblah before his eyes: also the king of Babylon slew all the nobles of Judah. Moreover he put out Zedekiah's eyes, and bound him with chains, to carry him to Babylon (Jer. 39:5-7).

Baalbek, the "City of the Sun," is situated at an altitude nearly 4,000 feet above sea level, and is the most ideal spot in the entire valley, or as it is generally regarded, one of the grand spots of the world. Here the climate is ideal, the soil excellent; and clear, cool, spring water breaks forth at various places in or near the city. During much of the year the trees put forth their shade and fruit, flowers bloom, and a variety of birds sing their sweetest lays. Thus, from time immemorial Baalbek, with its natural advantages, has been a miniature earthly paradise to which people from far and near have resorted.

The tradition persists that Baalbek was one of King Solomon's summer resorts, that it was the "Baalath" which he built as a center of commerce on the caravan route to Mesopotamia, and that here he built the magnificent "house of the forest of Lebanon" (1 Kings 7:2-5). It could well have been, for in Solomon's day it was a place of beauty, and a place that for natural advantages outranked all other places in this section of the country.

However, the present magnificent ruins of the temple of Jupiter and the temple of Bacchus, as we now know them, were begun by the Roman Emperor Antoninus Pius (A.D. 138-61) and continued by Septimus Severus and other rulers down to Caracalla (A.D. 211-17). As a center of sun worship, Baalbek acquired renown as the seat of an oracle and was visited by leading rulers and prominent people from far and near. Under Constantine the temples became Christian churches, but when captured by the Arabs in the seventh century, they were turned into fortresses and served as such during the Middle Ages. In 1664 and again in 1795, these buildings were shaken by violent earthquakes, from which they never recovered.

This 1,500-ton building stone, 70 feet long and 14 by 13 feet on the end, apparently never reached its destination in the building of the city of Baalbek.

Some of the enormous blocks of stone used in the construction of the Temple of the Sun (Jupiter) measured 60 feet long by 12 thick, and its 54 columns, of which 6 are still standing, were 72 feet high and 22 feet in circumference. In a quarry, just a half mile south of the Acropolis of Baalbek, lies a block of stone said to be the largest in the world. It is 70 feet long, 14 feet high, and 13 feet wide. Its weight is estimated to be about 1,500 tons. However, at one end it is not entirely loose from the quarry.

A great chain of inland cities—Antioch, Aleppo, Homs, Hama, and Baalbek—occupy the valley today, and enjoy a prosperous civilization which is all but unique.

CHAPTER 19

The Rise of the Jordan

The Jordan, most famous of all rivers, finds its origin in the vast reservoir of snow and ice which perpetually covers the summit of Mount Hermon. This melts and sinks down through secret caverns to form subterranean springs which come to the surface in the lower foothills of the mountain. These abound all about Hermon, but at four places on its west and south, springs converge and break forth in the form of powerful fountains, each a river almost full grown from the beginning of its course. The four are found at Hasbani,

Dan, Banias, and Nahr Bareighit. These constitute the main sources of the Jordan River.

1. *The Springs of Hasbani* are the first, the highest, and the most remote source of the Jordan. They are located in the western foothills of Mount Hermon, 1,700 feet above sea level, and a half mile northwest of the village of Hasbani. Coddled here in the hills and watched over by great Hermon, where olive and oleander thrive and wild flowers bloom in profusion, there are some 20 crystal clear fountains which, with a low, gurgling sound, flow upward, in artesian style, from a small islandlike area next to a steep and rugged, yet beautiful, limestone cliff. The water from these fountains flows in all directions immediately after boiling up from the earth, but they soon settle into a beautiful pool. From there they gracefully flow over a moss-grown dam of strongly stratified rock some 30 feet wide and 5 feet thick, and start southward on their 115-mile trip to the Dead Sea.

At first the stream takes the name of Hasbani, as if it were too small to be called the Jordan. In winter and spring, however, the

208

The Springs of Hasbani, the first and most remote source of the Jordan River.

stream is rather strong and sometimes boisterous as it meanders through a picturesque country, passing villages, turning mills, and is finally joined by other tributaries.

2. At the city mound of ancient *Dan* is the *Fountain of the Leddan,* which is the second and *largest* source of the Jordan River. This place was first known as *Laish,* where lived a small colony of people from Sidon. Their manner of life was quiet and carefree, and they felt secure in this place where "there was no want of any thing that is in the earth" (Judg. 18:7, 10). But all this was changed when the tribe of Danites charged them on a dark night, scaled the walls, set the city on fire, and destroyed the inhabitants (Judg. 18:27). The city was then rebuilt and called Dan after the father of the conquering tribe. Ever after it marked the northern boundary of Palestine, which gave rise to the proverbial expression "From Dan to Beersheba." Here King Jeroboam built a temple and set up in its shrine one of his golden calves as an idol-god to be worshipped by the Israelites who lived in the northern portions of his kingdom. The place is now known as *Tell el-Kadi,* the "Mound of the Judge." Jacob, when in prophetic mood on his deathbed, said, "Dan shall judge his people"; and to the Arab, the place where Dan dwelt will ever be the "Mound of the Judge."

The city mound is now without inhabitants but is a most interesting site. It rises from 30 to 80 feet above the plain and is nearly 1,000 feet long and over 700 feet wide. In places the uneven summit has many trees such as acacias, oaks, poplars, wild figs, and wild olives. At the southwest corner of the mound a pair of exceedingly large trees, one an oak, the other a terebinth, mark the traditional site of the sacred area, where may have stood the golden calf. One of the trees measures 19 and the other 21 feet in circumference. These shade the tomb of an unknown Mohammedan saint and are hung with small strips of cloth—each rag representing the prayers of a pilgrim who has journeyed and prayed there.

Dense jungles of bush and briars, as well as ruins of bygone civilizations, cover portions of the mound. A few small garden patches grow where water can be had from a small spring which flows from the jungle of reeds and bushes well up on the mound. Underneath the surface of the mound many objects of antiquity lie hidden, awaiting the spade of the archaeologist.

The main Fountain of the Leddan rises under the western shoulder of the city mound. Fresh from the deep caverns of towering Mount Hermon, these waters come bubbling and whirling out from under a screen of wild figs and vines, forming a pool of pale, clear blue, 100 feet in diameter. Out of this bubbling basin the newborn river rushes, foaming down the hillside through lines of oleanders, flowering bushes, and overhanging willows toward the plain. This is the largest of all the fountains of Palestine and is considered to be the largest in the world. It is 500 feet above sea level and its immense volume of water entitles it to be regarded as the *chief source of the Jordan.*

3. The third and most impressive source of the Jordan is the **Springs of Banias,** at the village of Banias, three miles southeast of Dan. Here, directly under the southern base of Mount Hermon, 1,000 feet above sea level, is a 100-foot cliff of ruddy limestone with niches and shrines and inscriptions carved on its face. At the bottom of this rock cliff is a dark cave whose mouth is partly filled with loose stones; and over these stones a foaming "full-born river" flows out and glides southward through a luxuriant, cavelike depression where a pastoral paradise is formed of towering oaks, trembling poplars, splendid sycamore, gray green olives, wild figs, trailing vines, drooping maidenhair fern, and myriads of wild flowers.

It is little wonder that through the centuries people, creeds, nations, and religions have longed to have a village, a shrine, or a city here at Banias, for it is one of the world's outstanding beauty spots. It has about it a strange mystery that has always cast its spell over the imaginations of men. Here the Phoenicians established the idolatrous worship of Baal and revelled in their splendid possessions until Joshua drove them out. The Canaanites dedicated the place to Baal-gad, to whom they paid their reverence in the presence of the gushing waters. For the Greeks, no finer or more ideal place could be found for the abode of Pan, the flute-playing god of the hills and woodlands, of the shepherds and hunters. Therefore they built a shrine to Pan and called the place Paneas. There the rites of Pan and all the nymphs were celebrated. A Greek inscription carved in the face of the cliff still exists, declaring, "Pan and his nymphs haunt this place."

When Rome conquered the territory, Herod the Great built here on the shelf rock above the cave a beautiful white marble temple in honor of Emperor Augustus Ceasar. Herod's son Philip made the city more beautiful and named it Caesarea Philippi to distinguish it from the coast city of Caesarea. Subsequently it went by various names, but eventually came again to be called Paneas. Arab inability to pronounce the letter *p* caused them to call it Banias.

It was here at Caesarea Philippi in this "paradise of nature" that Jesus withdrew with His disciples for quiet rest, and asked of them, "Whom do you say that I am?" And here, where so many had vainly worshiped Baal, Pan, and Baal-gad, the stalwart Simon Peter made the great declaration, "Thou art the Christ, the Son of the living God" (Matt. 16:13-16).

On a lofty mountain spur, 1,500 feet above the springs and village of Banias, stands the great and mighty castle known as "The Castle of Subeibeh." It was originally built either by the Phoenicians or the Romans, and rebuilt in turn by the Crusaders, the Arabs, and the Turks. Deep valleys defend this fine, old, ruined castle on its north and south; while on its west, at the end of the spur, is a deep, rock-cut ditch or moat, which makes it inaccessible. Only from the east can it be approached, and then one is obliged to pass along a narrow and difficult path and over a bridge entirely open to the view of the defending garrison.

The castle is surrounded by walls 10 feet thick and in some places nearly 100 feet high, with numerous round towers, built with identical blocks of stone two feet square. The interior of the fortress is an uneven area of four or five acres, dotted here and there by houses, cisterns, huge walls, and wide courtyards. At the eastern side of the castle area and 150 feet above it stands the citadel with a great wall and moat of its own, so that, as Josephus said, the garrison could retire into the citadel and make

211

a protracted defense even after the main castle had been taken by an enemy.

Within the castle are numerous subterranean rooms, vaults, and passageways. At the western end is a stairway cut in the rock, descending at an angle of 45 or 50 degrees. Popular belief regards this stairway as extending down to the fountain of Banias, but it may only lead to subterranean reservoirs for water. This great old castle commanded the highway leading from the Jordan Valley to the Plain of Damascus. It was so strongly built, so strategically located, and so well defended that it has been rightly called "the Gibraltar of Palestine."[1]

The waters of Banias, after passing through the parklike verdure about the village of Banias, soon veer southwest and hurry on to meet and converge with the river Leddan some six miles from Dan. Then, as one, the waters of Dan and Banias move on to meet and merge with waters from Hasbani.

4. *Nahr Bareighit,* the fourth and westernmost source of the Jordan, is the small mountain stream which rises as a strong spring in the "Meadow of Ijon"—the Ijon of the Scriptures, and the most northern possession of the tribe of Naphtali (1 Kings 15:20). Through the middle of this beautiful valley, five miles long and two miles wide, this gentle stream meanders. As it approaches the southern end (not far from the Jewish colony of Metullah), it deepens its bed and passes through the ridge by a remarkably deep and narrow chasm and, in the form of waterfalls, pitches over the precipice and moves along to join the river Hasbani about three-quarters of a mile above the point where the Hasbani joins the junction of the Leddan and Banias streams. The confluence of these four perennial streams form the Jordan, which travels sluggishly through what was once dense papyrus growths and enters the now greatly reduced Lake Huleh.

CHAPTER 20

The Grand Huleh Basin

The Grand Huleh Basin is located between the southern foothills of Mount Hermon and the Bridge of Jacob's Daughters. It is 5 miles wide and some 15 to 20 miles long from north to south. From time immemorial it has been known for its broad, fertile, grazing plains in the north; its amazing variety of its plant life and all but impenetrable papyrus marshes in the south central; and its small but unusual lake, known as the Waters of Merom, or Lake Huleh, in the south. It is the first and highest of the three lakes in the Jordan Rift Valley. Into this lake pours the waters of the Jordan, which later run into the Sea of Galilee, and later still into the Dead Sea about 1,300 feet below sea level.

It was here, by the Waters of Merom, that Jabin, king of Hazor, and the combined military forces of the north "came and pitched together to fight against Israel." The Lord said unto Joshua, "Be not afraid because of them: for to morrow about this time will I deliver them up all slain before Israel," and so it happened. "Joshua turned back and took Hazor: for Hazor was the head of all those kingdoms" (Josh. 11:5-11).

The soil of the upper plain of this basin is deep, loose, and in places sandy, and is well watered. In ancient times the city of Dan stood on a low hill near the head of the plain. But for long centuries the area has been sparsely occupied by seminomadic tribes whose chief occupation was the raising of cattle, principally water buffalo. These large, black creatures could well be the "behemoths" of the Bible. In large herds they graze this plain during the early morning hours, and during the heat of the day lie in the water "among the willows of the brook" with their mouths "all turned upstream" on a level with the surface, as if, like Job's behemoth, "he trusteth that he can draw up Jordan into his mouth" (Job 40:15-23).

The Marshland is the center area of some 10 to 15,000 acres of wet sediment land immediately north of Lake Huleh, which has been built up as century after century the Jordan has crept sluggishly into the lake. The dense masses of growth here are cane, bush, water lily, and the papryus plant (of which paper was first made). These have formed an almost impenetrable jungle where crows form rookeries, rear their young, and from which they come and go in droves that number in the hundreds and even thousands. In these jungles wild boars, panthers, wolves, jackals, foxes, and many other animals and birds, great and small, hide away at certain seasons of the year and make the place an ideal rendezvous for hunters. Here, during his earlier years, came Herod the Great to hunt the game swarming in the papyrus thickets, and to distinguish himself with his javelin-throwing.

Lake Huleh, known in the Bible as the "Waters of Merom," lies 12 miles south of Dan, and is seven feet above sea level. Originally it was about 3 miles wide and 4 miles long—little more than an enlargement of the Jordan which flows into it on the north

214

A Jewish shepherd boy in the lush Huleh Basin

and out of it on the south. The lake has long been blessed with an abundance of fish of many kinds, and was an ideal refuge for waterfowl. Some of the birds were permanent residents, while tens of thousands of others were migrants on their way between northern Europe and tropical Africa. Therefore, in the spring and late autumn the lower end of the lake was almost completely covered with ducks, geese, cranes, brants, bitterns, storks, pelicans, and other forms of bird life. Dragonflies hummed over the lake, and kingfishers swooped down for fish. The lake was of little use to man but offered seclusion for wildlife.

When Israel became a state in 1948, one of her first thoughts was to reclaim the Huleh Basin. The Jewish National Fund purchased the land, and in 1950, the work began. During these years a dramatic transformation has been taking place. The channel of the Jordan River below Lake Huleh has been broadened and deepened, and the two large channels passing through the marshland above have been widened, deepened, and so directed as to meet in a V form in the center of what was Lake Huleh. Drainage canals have been dug to drain the waters from the swamps into the new river channels. The size of the lake itself has been reduced, so that it is now little more than a fish pond, through it is still a bird refuge. Some 18,000 to 20,000 acres of the marshland and lake area have been drained sufficiently dry to be leveled, plowed, and cultivated. In the very area where until not long ago the malaria-carrying mosquito, the black buffalo, and the wild boar reigned supreme, scores of new settlements have now been established. The rich, black soil is said to be capable of producing food for 100,000 people. Malaria, the curse of marshlands, has almost altogether disappeared since the importation of topminnows—native American fish that live chiefly on mosquito eggs.

The principal crops which are proving suitable to this area are cotton, sugarcane, wheat, sorghum, ground nuts, tulip bulbs, feed crops, and mixed vegetables. Sugarcane thrives in many parts of Israel, but the cost of water has limited its planting. Here in this water-surplus area its production promises to be a genuine boon to the country. Vegetables grown here ripen early and are among the finest. Tulip bulbs mature in one season, rather than in two or three, and the Dutch pay well for the service. Rice does well here, and some is grown, although the government discourages its cultivation because it is conducive to mosquito breeding. Carp ponds abound in the region. Also in a section of Huleh's marshland, there are 3,750 acres of peat land —one of the richest peat deposits in the world. As this is exploited, it will be used to enrich worn-out soils in other parts of the country.

The climate in the Huleh Valley is fairly mild with an average annual temperature of 68° F. The direction of the winds in the summer are generally from perpetually snow-covered Mount Hermon in the north. During the rest of the year the directions vary. There are an average of 100 cloudy days during the year, of which about half are rainy days. During the rest of the year the skies are "a canopy of clear blue."

Reclaiming the Huleh area from decay and disease and making it bountiful for Jew and Arab has been styled "the crowning achievement" of the Jewish National Fund. Now the area is being called "The Huleh Plain," in Upper Galilee.

About two miles below the lake site, the river is crossed by an ancient bridge, built of black basalt, which the Arabs call *Jisr-Benat-Yacob* (Bridge of the Daughters of Jacob). The name often puzzles travelers and archaeologists, but probably derives from an early but mistaken tradition that Jacob and his family crossed the Jordan here on his return from Padan Aram. However, the crossing is of ancient origin, for at the eastern end of the bridge is a ruined khan, and the remains of an old road paved with basaltic blocks, which goes on toward Damascus. In all probability Saul of Tarsus crossed the Jordan here as he journeyed to Damascus and his rendezvous with the Lord.

Down a narrow depression, fringed with willow and oleander, the Jordan descends at the rate of 90 feet per mile for 9 miles, through wild and beautiful scenery until it reaches the Sea of 217 Galilee, where it is hushed to rest for a time in the bosom of this quiet and beautiful sea.

CHAPTER 21

The Beautiful Sea of Galilee

The Sea of Galilee lies 682 feet below sea level, in the upper portion of the great Jordan Rift Valley. It is shaped somewhat like a pear and is 13 miles long and 6½ miles wide. Its water is clear and sweet, and varies in depth from 60 to 156 feet. Through it runs the Jordan River—entering in at the northeast corner and flowing out at the southwestern end. Around most of the 50-mile shoreline of the sea there is a broad, pebbly beach, mingled with a generous sprinkling of small, conical-shaped shells. For almost 3 miles, from

218

Magdala northward, the beach is almost entirely made up of these white shells.

About the sea there are hot mineral springs, the strongest and most famous being the three which are located a mile south of Tiberias. Herod the Great, Cleopatra, Herod Antipas, and many other historical characters are said to have taken health baths here. Today it is the center of a much patronized health resort. Close by is the white-domed tomb of Rabbi Meir.

The waters of this sea are a deep blue, its atmosphere is invigorating, and the whole environment speaks peace—except for an occasional storm that sweeps down through the great gorge, lashing the surface of the lake into white-capped waves.

About this sea, the myrrh-scented hills rise easily and slope away in such a fashion as to impress the beholder with the elegance of the setting so appropriately provided by nature. The fertile acres of the far-famed, crescentlike plain of Gennesaret favor mankind with a "garden that has no end." Here in the springtime the birds sing their sweetest lays, the flowers bloom in wild profusion, while out over the sea the glistening white sails gracefully hoisted above the sailing vessels carry the fishermen or the travelers to their desired havens. Of all places in the whole world this, more than any other, lends itself to quiet, peaceful rest.

It was about the shell-strewn beaches of this lake that Jesus walked when His voice fell upon the ears and restless souls of many of those disciples who were to make up the apostolic group. For the most part they were simple fishermen who netted the fish of this beautiful sea. That tender voice and those striking words, "Follow me, and I will make you fishers of men," first heard about blue Galilee, challenged their attention, quieted their fears, enchanted their souls, and empowered their lives until they cared only to follow Him with an undying devotion. Some, like Him who called them, were to go to a cross; some, to be dragged to their deaths through the streets; some, to the arena where they would be done to death by wild beasts. But go where they would, experience what they might, His voice, first audible in Galilee, could not be forgotten nor confused with other voices.

> *"Follow me," I heard Him cry;*
> *I saw the stalwart men;*
> *I read the answer in each eye,*
> *Such as had never been.*

It was on the hills and mountains about this sea that Jesus spent nights of prayer, taught the multitudes, and pointed out the most profound lessons known to man. Here He healed the sick, unstopped deaf ears, cast out unclean spirits, raised the dead, and set the captives free. Here 19 of His 32 parables were spoken, and 25 of His 33 recorded miracles were performed. Here He challenged the attention of man as none other has challenged him; unfolded the plan whereby sinful souls might become the children of the Most High; and pointed the way to the celestial gathering place.

These waters He loved and controlled at will. Upon them

220

Looking across the northern end of the Sea of Galilee from the vicinity of Tiberias.

He walked. At His command the wild winds were subdued and boisterous waves became calm. "What manner of man is this that even the wind and the sea obey him?" asked His disciples when they perceived how familiarly He directed these waters.

The sight of this lovely Lake of Galilee, sleeping in its "deep blue beauty" amidst its beautiful plains and ringlet of low-lying mountains, enchants the beholder and produces a devotional fascination that no tongue can tell and no pen can describe. Here the Christian senses the fragrance of the Christ life and becomes more fully absorbed in the spiritualities of the past than at any other place in the world. Away to the north towers Mount Hermon, hoary and high, standing as a silent sentinel guarding the majestic scene—the most sacred and the most famous sea known to men.

The rabbis of old used to say that after God had made the seven seas, He made the Sea of Galilee for His own particular pleasure. In Leslie Savage Clark's inquisitive lines is the same thought, "Of all the seas in the East and West, did God, perhaps, love Galilee the best?"

When Christ was in Galilee, nine cities formed an impressive and almost continuous circuit about the shores of the sea. They were Tiberias, Magdala, Capernaum, Chorazin, Bethsaida, Gergesa, Gamala, Hippos, and Taricheae. And one could stand on some eminent point and at a glance see them all—the entire theater of His Galilean ministry. How indelibly it fixes itself upon the mind of the one who has seen it—the sea, the shore, the hills, and the sites of the cities where He lived and taught and drew from common things His lessons that have changed the thinking of much of mankind, and transformed the lives of millions.

Tiberias is situated on a sloping plain about midway up the west shore. Herod Antipas (the son of Herod the Great) surveyed the walls and began construction of the place as the capital of his Galilean province when Jesus was 21 years of age, and completed it when the Master was 27. Herod named the city in honor of the emperor Tiberius.

221

For more than two miles the city arose along the lake front behind a low, strong seawall. There were temples, palaces, theaters, amphitheaters, baths; a forum, a praetorium, a racecourse, a strong citadel, and many elegant houses. Then to please the Jews, he built a large and beautiful synagogue. They eyed the city narrowly, however, and the stricter Jews chose not to live in it, since portions of the place were built over the site of an ancient cemetery. Besides, many of its luxurious buildings were adorned with costly works of art which they considered "idols." Christ went near the city many times, but we have no record of His ever entering it, unless it was involved in His having preached "in all the cities round about."

Jewish attitude was changed, however, following the revolt led by Bar Kochba and the final destruction of Jerusalem in A.D. 132. Tradition says that Simon ben Yohai, the supposed author of the Zohar, bathed in the hot springs in the southern suburbs of the city and was cured of a sickness which he had acquired while hiding away from the Romans. Out of gratitude he declared Tiberias a fit city for the habitation of the Jews.

In due time the chief rabbis moved to Tiberias, where they produced the Mishnah, reestablished the Sanhedrin, and completed the Palestinian Talmud. They not only made Tiberias a center of language and literature, but one of the four sacred cities of Palestine, the other three being Jerusalem, Hebron, and Safad. In time, several Jewish rabbis and scholars, whose tombs are venerated, were said to have been buried in this vicinity. Among them were Maimonides (1135-1204), the Spanish Jewish rabbi, theologian, philosopher, commentator, and one-time physician to Saladin.

Tiberias is now a modern Jewish city, a "caldron of cultures in which new Western ways and old Oriental ones mix comfortably and colorfully." Its streets are lined with bulging markets, its avenues with gleaming hotels, and its hills with elegant homes. In its midst, as a chief landmark, stands the old Scottish mission, which has been dispensing the gospel and medical care to all classes of people for more than 50 years.

222   *Magdala* and the Plain of Gennesaret. The former home of Mary Magdalene was a seaside village three miles north of Tiberias, at the southern end of the beautiful Plain of Gennesaret.

The name Migdal-el meant "The Tower of God." All who have gone there during the past century have spoken of it as a ruined and unattractive, mud-and-stone village whose rock tower was rent asunder by a deep chasm. Yet romantic indeed must have been its situation in Christ's day, with palms and balsams, fruits and flowers around it, the blue lake in front, the precipitous Wad el Hamam (Valley of Doves) behind, and beside it the fertile Plain of Gennesaret with its extensive fields of fruits, flowers, vegetables, grain, and groves flourishing everywhere. Josephus called it "the ambition of nature where there is not a plant that does not flourish there." Near Magdala a Jewish colony has been built, and the Jews are responsible for restoring to the plain its original gardenlike quality.

At *Tabgha,* northward along the shore there is a grove; three clear, cool streams; some pools; the remains of an ancient mill; and beloved Father Tepper with his tiny hospital and comfortable hospice. Here, in the mosaic floor of a fourth-century Byzantine church, is pictured the story of the miracle of the loaves and fishes—a basket of bread set between two fish (though the actual miracle probably took place near Bethsaida, several miles east). Nearby is depicted peacocks, storks, ducks, and geese, along with gaily colored birds perched on lotus flowers.[1]

Above Tabgha, on the traditional site of the Sermon on the Mount, is a church, a monastery, and the Mount of Beatitudes hospice. The view of the Sea of Galilee from here is one of the best and the biblical scenes as vivid as one could desire.

Capernaum is identified with the ruins of Tell Hum, five miles northeast of Magdala and three miles west of where the Jordan River enters the sea. It was once the commercial metropolis of all northern Palestine, and was the hometown of Simon Peter, James, and John, and of Matthew, the customs official who "rose up and left all" to follow the Man of Galilee. And more wonderful yet, it was the adopted home of Jesus, who "on the Sabbath day entered into the synagogue and taught" (Mark 1:21). The partly restored ruins of a magnificent successor to this original synagogue, built sometime later (presumably during the second century A.D.), can be seen at Capernaum today. The walls

were decorated with lovely friezes depicting palms, vines and grapes, acanthus leaves, pomegranates, and garlands. Cut in the marble floor and elsewhere are the traditional symbols such as the seven-branched candlestick, the six-pointed Star of David, and a shofar, or ram's horn. An Aramaic inscription scratched on a limestone pillar reads: "HLPW, the son of Zebidah, the son of Johanan, made this column. May blessing be his." "Those names," says Dr. Glueck, "correspond roughly to the New Testament Alphaeus, Zebedee, and John, mentioned, by an interesting coincidence, in the list of Jesus' disciples and their families" (Mark 3:17-18).[2]

Here, in those days, ran the great highway of nations—the Roman road known as the "Way of the Sea." It ran down from Damascus and across the Lower Galilean hills, dipping down to the lakeside at Capernaum on the way across Armageddon to the maritime plains and Egypt. Here at Capernaum the Romans maintained a military garrison, and the government operated one of the largest and most important custom houses for collecting import duties on vast volumes of incoming merchandise. Matthew sat at customs here and was widely known as a government official.

Along this artery of trade and travel came merchants, diplomats, scholars, and camel-men who passed from Persia and Mesopotamia to the Nile Valley and Africa. Rich crops of grain, nuts, and fruit were grown locally; sheep, goats, and camels were raised; important fishing companies operated boats and nets, and men worked with them about the sea.

A variety of industries such as had to do with metals, leather, dyeing, weaving, and fish processing were carried on here. In the marketplaces buying and bartering were brisk and went on almost continuously. The population of Capernaum was the largest of all cities beside the sea, and for variety was representative of various cross sections of life.

In this weltering mass of mankind—Greek, Jew, and Roman—sat Matthew in the customs house, and here came Christ to speak as man never spoke, and work as no man ever worked. Here on these beaches, and elsewhere about these shores of

225

Ruins of a second-century synagogue built at Capernaum

Galilee, Christ, the Saviour and the greatest Teacher of all time, spoke to the people many times—at least once from a flat-bottomed boat that was "thrust out a little from the land, lest the multitude should throng him." On an eminent point not far away He gave the Sermon on the Mount, in which He imparted to man the secret of a happy life. Little wonder that this sermon has been called "the greatest thing ever spoken," for in it was divine wisdom transcending everything which had gone before or was to come afterward.

Bethsaida, the "Fisherman's Village," was located some three and a half miles from Capernaum, on the east side of the Jordan, near the point where it enters the Sea of Galilee. Bethsaida was built somewhat like Paneas, having had the same architect. Josephus says: "When Philip . . . had built Paneas . . . at the fountains of Jordan, he named it Caesarea. He also advanced the village Bethsaida, situated at the lake of Gennesaret, unto the dignity of a city, both by the number of inhabitants it contained, and its other grandeur, and called it by the name of Julius, the same name with Caesar's [Augustus] daughter."[3] It was to Bethsaida that Jesus withdrew upon hearing of the beheading of John the Baptist by Herod Antipas. Near Bethsaida is the desert place where Christ fed the 5,000 (Luke 9:10-17).

Today the Sea of Galilee has pleasant shores fairly well lined with the greenery of gardens, fruit orchards, eucalyptus, and palms. There are some good hotels, many Christian hospices, and a score of Jewish colonies adjacent to the sea—some directly on its shores. To the south of the lake is *Degania,* founded in 1909 by Russian pioneers. It is now a well established kibbutz with large trees, massive barns, gardens, orchards, groves of date palm, and well tended fields. Degania B, a more recently founded colony, "exudes a fresh-built flavor" along with colorful gardens, semitropical plants, and towering palm trees.[4]

The colony of *Nof Ginossar,* on the plain of Genessaret, has a 64-room, air-conditioned guest house with a quiet, unhurried atmosphere and a second-floor dining room with a fine view of the Sea of Galilee and the colorful orange and banana groves.[5]

En Gev is a Jewish colony across the sea from Tiberias, on a small peninsula between the Golan Heights and the lakefront. It is a green and pleasant place, with fishing boats, vineyards, groves of bananas and dates, and a seaside cafe where you may purchase a platter of St. Peter's fish with chips and salad and eat either inside the modern, air-conditioned restaurant or outside on the patio on the lakefront. Out there you can throw a piece of bread into the water and see schools of fish by the hundreds put on impressive spectacles.[6]

The Sea of Galilee supports a thriving fishing industry, excursion boats sail across its waters, and those with maladies bathe in its celebrated mineral springs. Literally millions of pilgrims visit the scenes of Christ's ministry, stroll along the shores of this sea, sense the lingering atmosphere of the sacred past, and with Longfellow say:

> And Him evermore I behold
> Walking in Galilee,
> Through cornfields waving gold,
> In hamlet, in wood, and in wold,
> By the shores of the Beautiful Sea.
>
> He toucheth the sightless eyes;
> Before Him the demons flee;
> To the dead He saith: Arise!
> To the living: Follow Me!
>
> And that voice still soundeth on
> From the centuries that are gone,
> To the centuries that shall be.

CHAPTER **22**

The Jordan River and Its Rift Valley

T here is no river in the world like the Jordan—none so remarkable in its physical geography, none so wonderful in its historic memories, none so hallowed in its associations, none so revered by millions whether they have seen it or not. Yet it is not a large river and is quite paradoxical in its nature. It rises in Mount Hermon—the highest mountain in Palestine—and after a short run of only about 150 air miles, it ends in the Dead Sea—1,292 feet below sea level—the lowest body of water in the world.

The river has never been navigable, has never been a water-way of commerce, has never had a prominent city on its banks. Nor has it possessed a factory, a foundry, or even a fishery of any importance. Yet it is so strangely and so vitally connected with so much of the march of civilization and with so many divine events that it has a fame among civilized nations not accorded any other river on earth. "Surely," says Magregor, "the Jordan is by far the most wonderful stream on the face of the earth, and the memories of its history will not be forgotten in Heaven."[1]

229

The Jordan River winds its way down the great rift valley, actually travel-ling more than 200 miles to cover the 65 miles from the Sea of Galilee to the Dead Sea.

The way of the river, from beginning to end, is through the Great Rift Valley, which is the greatest earth fracture and the deepest rift valley known. The most unusual portion of this rift is between the Sea of Galilee and the Dead Sea. Here it is known as the *Ghor,* or "sunken valley." Just south of the Sea of Galilee the valley is only 4 miles wide, while in the vicinity of Jericho it is 14 miles wide. Everywhere it is wholly below the level of the sea, yet on both sides the mountains rise up to elevations from 2,000 to 3,500 feet.

Within this Ghor is the *Zor,* which is a basin or inner gorge lying from 100 to 150 feet lower than the main valley, and is from 600 feet to two miles wide. Then within the Zor is the 90- to 200-foot-wide channel or bed in which runs the river itself.

From a small bay in the southern extremity of the Sea of Galilee, the Jordan makes its exit, running westward for about a mile; then, making a sharp curve to the south, it hurries along on its serpentine course to the Dead Sea. From sea to sea the river would measure only 65 miles in a straight line, but as it descends on its countless meanderings through the Zor valley, it actually travels more than 200 miles. When it leaves Galilee, the river moves in a deep, gorgelike channel 50 to 100 feet wide. Along its way, it varies in width from 60 to 240 feet and is usually from 4 to 12 feet deep. Where it enters the Dead Sea, it is 540 feet wide and about 3 feet deep.[2]

There are many quite high waterfalls on the Jordan, and more than 100 rapids, 29 of which are quite dangerous. South of the Sea of Galilee the Palestine survey party found and tabulated about 40 fording places, the most of which are available for passage only in summer and early autumn. Others have counted as many as 57 fords. These differences are explained by the fact that during the annual overflow of Jordan, some of these crossings may be changed or even washed away or afterwards left as part of an oxbow where the river has changed its course. During Roman times, and since, there have been eight or more bridges, four of which span the Jordan today.

The Zor begins about eight miles south of the Sea of Galilee and is often rimmed in by an irregular line of eroded gray marl cliffs 100 to 150 feet high. The floor of the Zor is usually covered with an almost impenetrable jungle of oleanders, willows, poplars, lofty cane, tangled bushes, creeping vines, and fernlike tamarisk. Here, in this junglelike growth, lurks the jackal, the wild boar, the hyena, and other forms of wildlife. Once the lion was here, but none have been seen since the time of the Crusades. A great many birds remain here the year around, while literally millions of the migratory variety—ducks, geese, brants, cranes, etc.—come and go with the seasons, on their way from the continent of Asia to Africa, or the reverse. At these seasons they sometimes spread out over the fields in such numbers that farmers' families have to drive them away by various means such as white flags on poles.

In the springtime, when the rains are heavy and the snows melt on Mount Hermon, the Jordan then overflows its slippery banks and spreads out over the Zor basin, driving the wild beasts from their lairs in the jungle, and making the river in some places more than two miles wide and very deep. In the Bible the Chronicler spoke of the Jordan "when it had overflown all his banks" (1 Chron. 12:15). Jeremiah said, "He shall come up like a lion from the swelling of Jordan" (Jer. 12:5). The children of Israel crossed the Jordan in the time of overflowing—the difficult, if not impossible, time—that they might "know that the living God" was among them (Josh. 3:10, 14).

There are many tributaries that enter the Jordan, the most of which are small; but there are four which are perennial and fairly large and quite important. Two of these enter from the east and two from the west. The two which enter from the east are the *Yarmuk* and the *Jabbok*. The two which enter from the west are the *Nahr Jalud* and the *Wadi Farah*.

The **Yarmuk River** was never mentioned in the Bible, even though it is almost as large as the Jordan. It drains the great Hauran Basin and is fed by a number of streams coming from southern Bashan and northern Gilead. It enters the Jordan five miles below Galilee, where the waters of both rivers flow into a large and beautiful lakelike reservoir over whose dam the water plunges some 90 feet. This reservoir feeds the Palestine Electric Corporation plant, which for many years produced electric power sufficient to serve the needs of most of Palestine. (This extensive plant has since been partially destroyed by acts of war.) The used but unconsumed waters of both rivers reach the main bed of the Jordan through a new channel. Since the mid-1960s water has been diverted from the Yarmuk River into the East Ghor Canal, which irrigates the north half of the east (Jordanian) side of the valley where live some 64,000 farmers and animal herders.

Some seven or eight miles below the power plant, the **Nahr Jalud** (river Jalud) flows into the Jordan from the west. This small and little-known river has its principal source two miles east of Jezreel, in the large spring of *Ain Jalud* (now called *Ain Harod*). It begins at a wide-mouth cave just under the northern cliffs of Mount Gilboa. At first it flows into a large pool, then makes its way down the Valley of Jezreel, past Beth-shan, and empties into the Jordan River just below the ancient ford which is now called *Abar'ah*. Here the men of Jabesh Gilead crossed when "they went all night" to take the bodies of Saul and Jonathan from the walls of Beth-shan.

The **river Jabbok** (now called *Zerka*) enters the Jordan Valley from the east, just below Succoth (now called *Tell Deir'alla*), where Jacob settled for a time after his night of wrestling with the angel of the Lord. Farther down, well within the rich bottom land of the Zor, and 20 miles above Jericho, the Jabbok empties its waters into the Jordan just above the small but impressive mound of Tell el-Damieh, the ancient city of Adam. About a mile west of Tell el-Damieh there are the remains of a Roman bridge and a new bridge over which passes the highway from Samaria to Gilead.

It was here at Adam (Adamah), that the waters were held back while 20 miles below this point Joshua and the Israelites crossed the Jordan on dry land. It being in the time of harvest when the "Jordan overfloweth all his banks . . . the waters which came down from above stood and rose up upon an heap" (Josh. 3:15-16). The water not only covered the entire Zor from bank to bank, but reached some 12 miles upstream, from Adam as far as the fortress of Zaretan.

An Arab historian states that about A.D. 1265 an earthquake caused a landslide of the chalky marl cliffs in this area which blocked the flow of the Jordan for some hours. A somewhat similar phenomenon took place during the severe earthquake of 1927. These two occurrences have caused some to assert that the Israelites chanced upon just such an occasion which enabled them to cross the Jordan dry-shod.

After examining this area, Dr. Nelson Glueck restates the historic fact "that landslides have at times blocked the normal channel of the Jordan, forcing it to chart a new course." As one who knows the Bible and the Jordan, Glueck then very wisely states that "the first contact of Israel with the Jordan had in it the elements of a miracle" which caused the river to "remain strangely entwined with their subsequent history." And so it is that an unusual phenomenon such as a severe earthquake may block the "normal channel" of the Jordan, but the blocking of the river for the Israelites to cross could and did have in it "the element of a miracle," seeing they crossed at the time of harvest when the river was in flood. At such a time, a cave-in of these high marl embankments would have had little effect.

This entire district hummed with industrial activity during the middle of the 10th century before Christ, when Hiram, Solomon's "master coppersmith," formed earthen molds "in the clay ground between Succoth and Zarthan" (1 Kings 7:46). Day after day, the long caravans of donkeys filed down into the valley from the eastern hills, bringing partly "roasted" copper and iron ore mined in the Arabah and the Ajlun areas, and charcoal from the forest of Gilead. Solomon and Hiram, with the aid of their workmen, turned out many extremely beautiful gold and copper objects such as the altar, the table, the pillars, the pots and pans, the candlesticks, the pomegranates, and many other things which furnished and adorned the new Temple of the Lord at Jerusalem (1 Kings 7:46; 2 Chron. 4:17).[3]

About two miles immediately west of Damieh Bridge is *Kurn Sur'tabeh,* a sharp, conical peak which rises more than 2,000 feet above the valley floor, and commands a view of much of the length of the Jordan Valley. A mass of ruins on its summit is a vivid reminder of the towering fortress of Alexandrium, built here by the Hasmonaeans and later rebuilt by Herod the Great to guard the road coming down from Neapolis (Shechem) and the Wadi Farah. The Talmud suggests that it was for a long time used as an observatory, on which beacon fires were kindled to announce the appearance of the new moon.

The **Wadi Farah,** which rises north of Mount Ebal and in the area of the ancient cities of Thebes and Tirzah, hurries down the eastern declivities of Samaria and, passing below Hurn Sur'tabeh, enters the Jordan River some four miles below Adam. Somewhere in this area Naaman dipped seven times, at the word of Elisha, and was cured of his leprosy.

Flowing on for some 16 miles, through fascinating desert landscapes often formed of ashen-gray marl buttes, mesas, and plateaus, the Jordan reaches Nimrin ford, which is usually called "the upper ford." Nearby is a ruined site, called *Tell Nimrin,* whose name is derived from Beth-Nimrah, the more ancient city site located almost a mile eastward. The Septuagint calls it Beth-abra (the house of the ford), which leads many to believe this to be the "Beth-abara beyond Jordan," where John proclaimed the coming of the Messiah King and His kingdom, preached repentance, and baptized thousands. It is where Jesus was baptized and later preached, "and many believed on him there" (John 1:28; 10:40, 42). This place is the scene of the annual immersion of many pilgrims from many parts of the world today.

The main thoroughfare from Jericho to Gilead has been by the way of this ford; therefore we may safely say that it has afforded passage for famous people from time immemorial—probably for the majority of the biblical characters who crossed the lower Jordan.

Just below the ford, on the site of an old wooden bridge which the Turks destroyed, the British military authorities constructed a substantial steel bridge in 1919, and named it Allenby Bridge. It is 1,200 feet below sea level, and until recent years was known as "the lowest bridge in the world." (Now, however, the Abdullah Bridge spans the Jordan just about a mile above the Dead Sea and so rates that unusual honor.)

Just below the Allenby Bridge there is a waterfall, after which the distinctive features of the Jordan rapidly change. Its channel widens, its banks flatten out, the undergrowth along its edge becomes less dense, and its waters flow more smoothly.

About four or five miles farther down is the "lower ford," known as the Pilgrims Bathing Place. This, according to the Greek church, is the traditional site of the baptism of our Lord. Since the sixth century thousands of pilgrims have visited Jerusalem every spring during Holy Week and have come down to this place on Monday after Easter to immerse themselves, in the belief that they are at the very place where Christ was baptized. In this they could possibly be mistaken, yet it was one of the "fords toward Moab" which Ehud took when he delivered Israel from the oppression of the Moabites (Judg. 3:28), and it was almost certainly the crossing place of Naomi and Ruth on their journey to Bethlehem (Ruth 1).

From the "lower ford," the Jordan moves along for four miles on the last lap of its journey. After an unparalleled descent of some 3,000 feet in its course of 150 miles, it emerges from its unique channel and quietly flows into the deep and lifeless Dead Sea.

CHAPTER 23

The Plain of Jericho

The Plain of Jericho, often likened to "a garden in the wilderness," or even "a little paradise in the desert," lies between the river Jordan and the Judean mountains. It is 5 miles wide by 18 miles long and lies 700 to 900 feet below sea level. It is famed for its climate, its fertility, and its semitropical luxuriance. Sheltered as it is from cold winds and

236 stormy weather, and having balsam and palm groves and almost every manner of fruits and flowers, it has long been known as the ideal country in which to winter. These favorable features

have been made possible because of the presence of four strong springs, and a number of wadis or streambeds which at the proper season carry considerable water.

Wadi Kelt (identified with the Valley of Achor) is fed by two large springs higher up, and the other streambeds come from the mountains on the northwest which run with considerable water during the rainy season. By the ancient mound of Jericho is *Elisha's Fountain* that pours forth a strong, wide stream which furnished drinking water for ancient Jericho. It now is used to irrigate several square miles of the plain extending eastward toward the Jordan. Four miles northwest of ancient Jericho are three springs known as the springs of *Ain-ed Duk*. Below the springs is a beautiful waterfall which, in medieval times, turned sugar mills. After propelling the mills, the water was conveyed to the plain by a network of aqueducts and canals.

— **Jericho,** once "The City of Palm Trees," was a Canaanite town of considerable importance. It was the first city taken by the children of Israel as they entered the Promised Land. Joshua laid a curse of most unusual nature upon the man who should rebuild the city, saying: "Cursed be the man before the Lord that riseth up and buildeth this city Jericho: he shall lay the foundation thereof in his firstborn, and in his youngest son shall he set up the gates of it." This prophecy was fulfilled in the days of King Ahab, when Hiel the Bethelite, an apostate Jew, rebuilt Jericho. He actually "laid the foundation thereof in Abiram his firstborn," and set up the gates thereof in his youngest son Segub (1 Kings 16:34).

This city, along with its nearby village of Gilgal, later had a school for the prophets and was visited by Elijah and Elisha just before Elijah's translation on the other side of the Jordan. On returning to Jericho, Elisha turned the brackish waters of the spring into good water, and became head of the school of prophets (2 Kings 2:19-22). The school grew so rapidly that it had to be enlarged.

237

It was here that Naaman came to Elisha, seeking a cure for his leprosy—which he received after going, in obedience, to the nearby Jordan where he dipped seven times. Other notable characters visited the city from time to time.

Lying as it did in a semitropical clime in one of the world's richest areas, the plain was so developed by the Maccabean rulers that when the Romans took over under Pompey in 63 B.C., its vast date palm industry, its world-famous balsam groves, and its well-cultivated fruit orchards, along with its splendid climate, made it a coveted winter resort. Like a rich pawn in international politics, it passed from one royal person to another. Mark Antony gave Jericho and its plain to Cleopatra, and Cleopatra farmed its revenues to Herod. And it was under Herod the Great that the region enjoyed its greatest prosperity during the last few decades before the birth of Christ.[1]

In the northern section, where grew 49 varieties of dates and "extremely sweet" wine grapes, two important villages named *Archelais* and *Phasaelis* were built. The first was built by Archelaus, son of Herod, and the other was erected by Herod the Great as one of the impressive memorials for his older brother. Outlines of the central buildings remain—the palace, a temple, a marketplace, and the remains of small shops. Water for these two villages was brought in an aqueduct from *Ain Fusail,* five and one-half miles up the Jordan Valley.

Looking across the verdant Plain of Jericho

Other important improvements in the way of buildings and roads, along with aqueducts and canals and farming projects, were carried out in the central portion of the plain and in the area of Elisha's Spring. But the most phenomenal of all undertakings was Herod's Jericho, south of Wadi Kelt, which he transformed into a magnificent Roman city.

Here, in what we now call "Roman Jericho," Herod built for himself a magnificent winter palace, fully equipped "with the conveniences and luxuries of swimming pools, baths, etc., that made it both a suitable place to entertain his friends and a place which he could show off with some pride to his political guests such as Cleopatra of Egypt."[2]

On his journey to Jerusalem a few days before the Passover, Jesus came into Roman Jericho where Zacchaeus, the small but wealthy tax collector, climbed a sycamore tree to see the Messiah. When the two met, Zacchaeus repented of the evil in his life, and his entire being was changed and illumined by the transforming power of the Christ who took lodging that night in the elegant home of the "rich little tax collector" (Luke 9:1-10). Likewise the blind man, Bartimaeus, met the Master in Jericho, and by persistent faith "received his sight, and followed Jesus in the way" (Mark 10:51).

Gilgal, where Israel set up their camp after crossing the Jordan and arranged 12 stones from the riverbed for a memorial, where they also renewed the rite of circumcision, and where the Tabernacle remained for a time, is thought by many to have been at *Tell en Nitleh.* It is on a slight elevation some three miles east of Jericho. In this area stone pottery and flint knives have been reported found. Dr. Kelso's excavations have revealed the remains of five Byzantine churches, which would indicate that the Early Church supposed this to be Gilgal.

Today, on the Jericho Plain, there are gardens and groves, fruits and nuts, grapes, melons, bananas, oranges, lemons, and Siamese pumelo, which not only grow unusually well here, but possess a flavor that is superior. Jericho oranges, for example, are larger, and bring a third more on the Jerusalem market.

However, only a small fraction of the plain is now in production. Here are some 60,000 acres that with the proper planning and development could well become one of the world's foremost garden spots and furnish food for multiplied thousands of people.

CHAPTER 24

The Dead Sea

The Dead Sea is the strangest and most unusual body of water known to man. To the Jew it is the "Salt Sea"; to the Arab it is *Bahr Lut,* "Sea of Lot." It lies 1,292 feet below sea level and forms the lowest point in the Great Rift Valley. The sea measures 47 miles long, has an average width of 9½ miles, and a maximum water depth near the north end of another 1,308 feet—making the bottom of the sea 2,600 feet below sea level. Its great depth is further enhanced by the mountains of Moab and Judea which rise steeply from the water line, on either side, to a maximum height of 3,000 to 4,000 feet. On the Moab side red sandstone and hard limestone rise abruptly and precipitously, while on the Judean side chalky marl, salt and gypsum cliffs somewhat more terraced and receding jut out near the water's edge.

Into this inland sea the Jordan, the Arnon, and other smaller streams dump an average of 6 million tons of chemical-laden water a day. There is no outlet, except by evaporation. Thus through many millennia the waters that these streams have emptied into this abyss of a sea have evaporated into the air, leaving the mass of chemicals which they had held in solution to accumulate. The chemical stock now constitutes about 26 per cent of its liquid contents. This means that the solution is so dense and buoyant that a man can lie on its waters and not sink. It has a peculiar, bitter taste.

The color of the water is a deep blue, tending toward the leaden. At times the surface is flecked with white wave crests as the wind rises and laboriously whips up a light foam which floats on the surface. During the summer, when evaporation is most rapid, there is a thin, almost transparent vapor which rises from

Looking north along the western shore of the Dead Sea

the sea. "When seen from a distance," says Lynch, "its purple tinge blends with the leaden color of the waters and gives it the appearance of smoke from burning sulphur. At times this is so accentuated as to give the sea the appearance of a vast cauldron of metal fused but motionless."[1]

In the rather distant past the Dead Sea was often described as a place of deep and fearful gloom, "where death reigned supreme, where no life might exist, where no beauty ever appeared, and where the body of Mrs. Lot stood encased in a pillar of salt."

However, for many centuries travelers have visited there, and 10 or more special expeditions have studied the various aspects of the sea. The first modern attempt seems to have been made in 1835 by Mr. Costigan, an American, who descended the Jordan in an open boat and traversed the sea to its extreme southern point. He crossed and recrossed it several times, only to be overcome by hunger, heat, and fatigue. He was carried back to Jerusalem, where he died and was buried in the Christian cemetery there.

A second attempt was fitted out by the British Admiralty in 1837 and led by G. H. Moore and W. G. Beke. They spent 19 days exploring the shoreline. In 1841, another British expedition under Major Scott and Lieutenant Symonds was sent. They sounded the maximum depth of the sea. Lieutenant Molyneux led an expedition in 1847, which added much to our knowledge of the sea; but soon after returning to his ship, he was overcome by fatigue and passed away.

A fifth expedition was equipped by the United States government in 1848, and commanded by Lieutenant Lynch. Their researches were of the highest scientific value. In 1924, another expedition (mostly by land) was led by Dr. Albright, Dr. Kyle, Mr. Day, and Mr. Densmore—archaeologists, geologist, and botanist. Meanwhile the commerical possibilities of the Dead Sea had been investigated in 1911 and 1920-21 by Mr. M. A. Novomeysky, a well-known British chemist.

The accrued knowledge gained by these and other studies have shown the Dead Sea, and the landscape of the surrounding area to be, in many respects, a place of rare beauty, endless variety, and one of health and fabulous wealth.

Contrary to popular supposition, however, there is more than salt in the waters of the Dead Sea. This had long been suspected and had been shown in part by an analysis made as early as 1854; but when, in 1911, Mr. Novomeysky began official tests by which the waters were carefully analyzed, he found that the greater the depth, the heavier the waters were with chemicals.

An official estimate, based on these and other analyses furnished to the British Parliament, gives a reasonable idea of the amount and value of chemicals in the Dead Sea:

Potash	1,300,000,000 tons	$ 70,000,000,000
Salt	11,900,000,000 tons	27,500,000,000
Bromine	853,000,000 tons	260,000,000,000
Gypsum	81,000,000 tons	120,000,000
Calcium Chloride	6,000,000,000 tons	85,000,000,000
Magnesium Chloride	22,000,000,000 tons	825,000,000,000
	42,134,000,000 tons	$1,267,620,000,000

This incredible valuation may now be even much greater with inflated world prices. Also, there is asphalt or bitumen of an undetermined amount. The chemicals are now being extracted, yet with the incoming waters they are increasing faster than they can be taken out.

From dawn to dark, illusions of color appear on the water and in the nearby cliffs which nature has piled about the depression. One has called it "the most imposing and beautiful lake which exists on the earth." Yet another has declared its beauty to be "the beauty of death. For," says he, "no vegetable life is found along its dazzling white shores, except heaps of driftwood carried down by the river, which are stripped and bleached like bones and incrustated with a layer of salt. No flocks graze beside it, no wild beasts come hither to drink, no fish swim in its depths."[2]

All of this is quite true, yet a few rods back from the beach are plants such as the Spina Christa, a thornbush which bears

244

245

Cave Four near Qumran where some of the first Dead Sea Scrolls were found.

piercing thorns and small fruit similar to scrawny crab apples. There is also the Osher, or "Apples of Sodom," a tropical-looking plant which bears a large, smooth apple or orangelike fruit which hangs in clusters of three or four together. When completely ripe, its fruit is yellow and looks very attractive; but if pressed, it bursts with a crack and crumbles away in the hand like soot and ashes. Then there is the oleander, the acacia, the castor bean, and a few wild palms which grow or did grow in the small oases on the east shores of the sea.

For a trip about the Dead Sea, one may leave Kallia, at the northwest end, and, either by motorboat on the water or by car on the splendid new highway, travel safely along the west coast. The rugged cliffs of the Judean Wilderness run alongside the sea in some places as much as a half mile back and in other places very near the sea.

Only three miles south, on a spur of land some 250 feet above the level of the Dead Sea, lie the ruins of *Qumran* where, during the middle of the second century B.C., a group of Essenes "retired from the evils of the world" to pursue a simple way of religious life and teaching. They built their center partly on the foundations of a seventh-century B.C. fort, but extended their buildings considerably on the south and west. They installed an elaborate water supply system, built potters' quarters and kilns, a bakery, a confectionary, a dining hall, an assembly room, and a Scriptorium where they made multiplied thousands of copies of the Scriptures—all of the Old Testament books except the Book of Esther.

When Rome's 10th Legion came in A.D. 68, Qumran was sacked and burned, and the inhabitants massacred or scattered. But they left behind them hundreds or even thousands of scrolls of the Scriptures hidden away, as if by intent, in nearby caves, to be discovered nearly 2,000 years later (1947) and publicized to the world as the Dead Sea Scrolls.

The excavated village, along with its cemetery, may now be visited, and the caves inspected. But not all the caves are in the immediate vicinity, for scrolls were found in caves as far south as Ain Jidy, where lived other Essenes.

Two miles south of the Qumran monastery, just near the seaside, is *Ain Feshkha,* an abundant, freshwater spring and stream which forms a fine oasis around which reeds, marsh grasses, and other vegetation now grow in abundance. Here the Essenes had an irrigation system and grew such fruits, vegetables, and other produce as they needed. Nearby were found the ruins of farm buildings, stables, toolsheds, and what appeared to be rooms for preparing leather for its various uses—including the parchment on which they were to write the scrolls.[3]

Some eight miles farther south are two important springs—*'Ain el-Ghuweir* and *'Ain et-Turaba*—which form another oasis in an otherwise barren landscape.[4] Ten miles farther on is a hot sulphur spring near the coast, and three miles beyond that is En-Gedi, previously described. Ten miles farther down the shore is mighty Masada, "the Gibraltar of the Dead Sea," also referred to earlier.

Four miles south of Masada the tracks of an ancient Roman road approach the narrow point of the Dead Sea and reappear on the eastern side at the southwestern tip of El Lisan. This means that 2,000 years ago the waters of the sea were much lower than they are today.

The eastern shores of the Dead Sea are vastly different from the western side. The rugged sandstone, basalt, and limestone cliffs approach the water's edge so near that no highway may be built there, so a trip along the upper eastern shore means taking a motorboat. For nine miles south of the Jordan, along the Moab coastline, red sandstone, black basalt, and gray limestone cliffs rise abruptly 900 to 1,000 feet and recede steeply eastward to a plateau 4,000 feet above the sea.

The first break in the towering coastline comes with **Wadi Zerka-Ma'in** (by some called the river Callirrhoe), a broad mountain stream rushing into the sea through a picturesque mountain gorge 122 feet wide with wild palms, tamarisks, and a jungle of cane and other vegetation on either side. Here one's eyes feast on the red, gray, and black stratified stone cliffs 900 feet high, rising perpendicularly on either side and sometimes seeming to meet.[6] About seven miles eastward, up through the gorge in the highlands, this torrent receives much of its waters from the 10 mineral-laden hot springs of *Callirrhoe,* where during the last year of his life, Herod the Great, at the advice of his physician, sought relief from his fatal malady.

Three miles south of Wadi Zerka-Ma'in are the scant ruins of **Zira,** the ancient Hebrew town of *Zareth-shahar,* where there are strange tropical shrubs, tall grass, canebrakes, and warm sulphur springs. Some suppose Herod bathed here, and he may have done so, for in seeking a cure for his sickness he visited most of the known mineral springs.

Ten miles farther south, along one of the world's most colorful and charming coastlines, one comes to the **river Arnon,** now known as *Wadi el Mojib,* where the 82-feet-wide and four-feet-deep stream flows into the sea through an impressive gorge of red sandstone cliffs which, on either side, rise sheer and steep some 400 feet and form a scene so romantic as to be called *"Arnon's Rock Gate."* The color of the cliffs is the same as in the rose-red city of Petra and forms a striking contrast with the silvery stream of the river, the leaden blue waters of the sea, and the patch of green vegetation in the miniature delta at the estuary. A unique experience awaits all who wade up this clear, cool, rock-shaded stream a few hundred yards to the waterfall, and return in the late afternoon to see the entrance of the gorge shot through by the gorgeous shafts of sunlight—a scene which one never cares to forget.

Motoring on some 10 miles southward from the Arnon gorge, one soon comes to a bold, broad peninsula called **El Lisan** ("The Tongue"). From the east shore this strange, tonguelike peninsula extends more than halfway across the sea, then breaks off in a towering, wall-like shoreline 40 to 60 feet high and 9 miles long, with a steep white ridge 20 feet higher running like a spine down the center. Most of the peninsula is bordered by this gray white, wall-like, chalky-marl formation that looms up white and dazzling in the sun, presenting "the appearance of a wall of sawn ice or newcut carbonate of lime" rising out from the leaden blue waters. At one place near the south end, this peninsula rises out, tier upon tier, to a height of some 300 feet. At the foot of the surrounding cliff is a beach of washed-up sand, which varies in length and breadth according to the season—wider in summer than in winter. The northern point of this tonguelike promontory is called Point Costigan, and the southernmost is called Point Molyneux, after the two explorers who lost their lives about the middle of the 19th century while leading expeditions to study the sea.

South of El Lisan is a baylike area, irregular in shape, but some 16 miles long and 8 miles wide, where the water is exceedingly shallow—3 to 17 feet deep.

Almost all who have made a serious study of this baylike area have been led to believe that it now covers the well-watered and fertile "land of the plain," where in Abraham's and Lot's day was located *Sodom and Gomorrah,* on which "the Lord rained brimstone and fire out of heaven, and overthrew those cities, and that which grew upon the ground" (Gen. 19:24-25).

The picture given in the Bible seems to favor a location at the southern end of the sea for the "vale of Siddim" where the "cities of the plain" were located (Gen. 13:10-12; 14:1-3, 10; 19:20-23). The late Greek and Latin writers—Diodoros, Strabo, Josephus, and Tacitus—agree on the southern location.[7] And it seems natural to come to this conclusion when the surrounding physical features of this shallow southern bay of the Dead Sea are examined. Note the indications:

1. Stretching for miles along the east shore of this embayment and extending up along the east side of El Lisan is the *Ghor Safieh,* a broad, luxuriant plain which in ancient and medieval times was a fertile oasis where orchards, dates, wheat, barley, indigo, cotton, sugarcane, and vines grew. Today it is cultivated in places. Five clear streams course down from the mountains of Moab and flow through this long, narrow, fertile area into this very Dead Sea basin. Some of these streams are sizeable, have gravelly beds, and are tapped by little conduits, so that the whole area can be turned into a watered garden or meadow. In some places even now there are patches of corn, barley, millet, and indigo growing. In other places there are trees, shrubs, cane, date palm, and swampland. Much of this area swarms with wild-

life, including the wild boar. Apparently there was a mountain stream for each of the five "cities of the plain." The city sites are thought to be now buried under the shallow water, but the outer fringes of the oasis of Ghor Safieh remain.

2. Higher up in the foothills above the remaining portion of this oasis Drs. Albright and Kyle discovered extensive ruins of a well-fortified "open air settlement with enclosures, and hearths for individual family units." East of the fortified camp was a group of fallen monoliths (mazzeboth) or sacred cult pillars, "at which the religious rites of the community of Bab edh-Dhra were performed." The absence of debris indicated that it was not continuously inhabited, but "a place of pilgrimage, where annual feasts were celebrated, and to which people came, living in booths and merry-making for several days of the year." The pottery indicated that the place began to be used about 2,300 B.C., and ceased to be occupied around 1,900 B.C., which accords with the Bible narrative and chronology as to when the "cities of the plain" were destroyed.[8]

3. Alongside this shallow, southern end of the Dead Sea area, on its west, is Jebel Usdum (Mount Sodom)—a mountain of salt five miles long, three miles wide, and rising 742 feet above the water. The mountain is underlaid by a solid mass of greenish-white, crystalized rock salt 50 to 200 feet thick. Above this salt stratum the mountain has a crust of salt, marl, and clay, topped with a limestone cap-rock. Within this mountain are caves in which are beautiful, cavernlike rooms with stalagmites and stalactites, all composed of pure, crystalline salt.

On the east slope of Mount Sodom, about 40 to 60 feet above the water, rises a lofty, round pillar of salt, capped with carbonate of lime. Tour guides point this out as the "pillar of salt" into which Mrs. Lot was turned for her disobedience. Josephus, Clement, Irenaeus, and some modern historians and explorers mention such a pillar as having been there when they visited this area. Perhaps not the same one, for climatic and geologic factors seem, at times, to change these pillar formations. At least some think that the ancient pillar has been washed into the sea and replaced by the present pillar. Others think the same pillar stands. An occasional salty mist arises in this area and encrustates every object on which it settles.

New potash works have been established on land near Jebel Usdum. Here they pump Dead Sea water into huge earthern "pans" and extract the chemicals by evaporation. It is then purified in the mills and sent out to the world markets. These are now being expanded at a cost of $100 million. Significantly, the new city which serves as a center for these activities is named Sodom. It is rated as "the lowest post office in the world."

Two modern Jewish colonies—new *Zohar* and *En Bokek*—lie just north of Jebel Usdum. Then a bit farther north, we return to the now submerged Roman road which once led across to El Lisan.

Divers have searched many parts of this southern embayment of the sea for ruins of the cities of Sodom and Gomorrah, but none have yet been located, either here or elsewhere. Probably they were so thoroughly destroyed that they will never be found.

CHAPTER 25

The Arabah or "Valley of the Desert"

Beginning at the southern end of the Dead Sea, and extending southward for 110 miles to the eastern arm of the Red Sea, is a depression—the continuation of the Great Rift Valley. From ancient Bible times it has been known as the *Wadi el Arabah,* or "Valley of the Desert." This remarkable valley or depression begins at 1,292 feet below sea level at the Dead Sea and gradually ascends as it goes southward for 62 miles to reach its highest point of 650 feet above sea level near *Jebel er-Rishe.* From here it quickly descends until 48 miles farther southward it reaches the Gulf of Aqabah (the arm of the Red Sea) at Ezion-Geber. The Arabah is from 6 to 12 miles wide and is bordered on either side by towering and forbidding mountains, especially on the east by the mountains of Edom.

An ancient caravan route entered this "Valley of the Desert" at Ezion-Geber and passed along northward to a point south of the Dead Sea, then one road branched northwest toward Palestine and another northeast toward the Jordanian countries. Where parts of this arterial highway now run, the children of Israel once "passed . . . from Elath, and from Ezion-gaber" on their way to the Promised Land (Deut. 2:8). Along this same way came the queen of Sheba on her way to Jerusalem to know more of Solomon's wisdom, and Solomon's men travelled to his mines in the Arabah and to his southern seaport at Ezion-Geber. Here also the Romans established fortified stations to protect their trade.

Surface explorations along with minor digs, carried on by Dr. Nelson Glueck and others, have revealed ancient caravan stations and fortresses at intervals along the valley. There are also ruined villages, mining camps, slag heaps, and remains of copper and silver mines from which ore was dug in the time of Solomon (1000-900 B.C.) and during the time of the Nabateans (300 B.C. to A.D. 200).[1] All of which gives substance to the words of Scripture which spoke of a "land whose stones are iron, and out of whose hills you can dig copper" (Deut. 8:9).

These remnants of ancient mining operations stimulated an interest on the part of the Jews; and when their mining engineers made tests, they were convinced that the mineral deposits in the Wadi Arabah were "far from exhausted," despite the intensive mining by Solomon and the Nabateans. Considerable money and equipment would be necessary in order to carry out modern mining operations, but the Jews met the challenge sufficiently that by 1965, the output from the mines at Timna, near Solomon's mines, was 23 million tons of copper and manganese. The operations have continued, with few interruptions, from year to year. 253

The major portion of the Arabah is made up of shifting sands and salty, brackish soils and gravel, and is extremely hot and dry during much of the year. Rainfall is less than two inches annually. A few spring-fed oases, such as the more famous one at *Ain Ghudyan* in the southwest part of the valley, furnish an abundance of water, both from a strong spring and from a subterranean flow of water which is easily reached with wells. In other places there are swamps with dark loam which cracks into up-rolled scales when drying. Also there are small areas where fresh-water brooks come down, creating habitable lands, where there were small towns in ancient times. For long centuries, however, it has been mostly wasteland occupied at intervals by only a few Bedouin Arabs.[2]

With the magnificent obsession of salvaging the desert, the Jews, in 1948, began their first farming efforts in the Arabah by founding the colony of *Yotvatah* at the *Ain Ghudyan* oasis. After extensive landscaping, drainage, and reducing the salt and alkaline content of the soil, fertilizing the land, planting shelter-belt avenues of trees around the fields, building access roads and homes, they began to plant crops. Through the years there have been many complicated battles with the soil, and with harnessing the water resources; yet by patient toil and unceasing effort they have shown that fruits, vegetables, melons, and flowers may be grown here the year around. These can be exported to Europe at a time when they are in short supply, thus creating an important source of foreign currency.

Other colonies have settled in the valley—*Ein-Yahav,* near the central part of the valley, and *Hatzeva* farther north toward the Dead Sea, and five more at strategic points. Thus, today, rising out of the desert like mirages, are eight oases of life. Neat houses come into view, surrounded by green gardens; date plantations heavy with fruit; fields ready for crops; sprinklers stilling the thirst of the soil. Eight man-made miracles. Eight new names on the map. Eight villages on land wrested from desolation. The hum of the tractor is broken by the laughter of children, the voices of men, and the singing of women. The caravan route of old is being turned into a highway of progress.

Natural sculptures abound in the southern Arabah, among which are the two delicately formed, yet huge mineral-encrusted rock formations known as the Pillars of Solomon which stand guard over Solomon's Mines at Timna, 16 miles north of Elat. Seldom is there found such variation, delicacy, and beauty combined with massiveness; yet in the nearby mountain passes of Edom eastward and the Paran plateau on the west are corresponding types of rock formations with a delicate blending of rich reds, light browns, and pale yellows.

Elat (Elath) and *Ezion-Geber,* at the southern tip of the Arabah, on the shores of the Red Sea, were stations on the route of the Exodus of Israel from Egypt (Deut. 2:8; Num. 33:35). Here ancient Israel later had its southern port—her gateway to Arabia, Africa, and India. Here King Solomon maintained a navy and sent and received his ships from Ophir, laden with gold, silver, ivory, apes, peacocks, and other exotic treasures (1 Kings 9:26-28; 10:11, 22). Here the queen of Sheba and her retinue are said to have landed when she came to Jerusalem to see Solomon and "commune with him all that was in her heart," and here Jehoshaphat's navy was destroyed (1 Kings 22:48). This was one of the main ports

The Jordanian city of Aqaba on the Red Sea at the southern end of the Arabah.

in the Nabataean and Arabian spice trade; from here Roman ships set sail for the east, and now since 1967, Elat has been built into a first-class port city—a veritable "Gateway to Africa and Asia." Phosphates, potash, copper ore, salt, cement, and other commodities are exported from here. Oil tankers dock farther south at the terminal of the oil pipeline.

The smooth, blue waters of the Red Sea (Gulf of Aqaba), the Coral Beach, the glass-bottom boat to the coral reefs, the deep-sea fishing and the maritime museum, along with the all-but-rainless days and pleasant nights throughout the year make Elat one of the finest winter resorts in the Near East.[3] There are many ultramodern hotels and 15,000 permanent residents, most of whom are there to serve the state, the shipping companies, and the needs of tourists. Across the bay on a curve of perfect beach is the Jordanian port city of Aqaba dazzling white "in a blaze of desert sand and partly shaded by rings of date palm trees." Biblical Elath was near where Aqaba now stands. The Crusaders built a castle there, and Col. T. E. Lawrence had a base of supplies at Aqaba. Here three countries meet—Saudi Arabia, Jordan, and Israel. The whole area is heavy with history—especially that history which is tinged with sacredness.[4]

While excavating the ruins of ancient Ezion-Geber, Dr. Glueck was deeply moved by the significance of the geographic and historic setting as represented by the "mighty past" which again "rode supreme" at Ezion-Geber and its environs. He says:

> On days of storm in springtime I have seen enormous clouds hurtling across from Sinai to Arabia. I have heard the thunder roar and have almost felt the ground shake beneath my feet. At such moments it seemed as if I could almost see Moses and his weary people emerging from the wilderness on their way to the Promised Land.
>
> Above them hovered the God of Sinai, who in the midst of such thunder and lightning had spoken to Moses with the sound of a loud trumpet and to Elijah with a still small voice that was stronger than wind, earthquake or fire.
>
> At such thrilling moments a glow of the mighty past lay upon the parched and barren land.[5]

*

The Eastern Tableland

*

CHAPTER 26

Mount Hermon

Mount Hermon, the finest
and one of the most venerated mountains of Bible lands, forms
the southern extremity of the Anti-Lebanon Mountain Range,
and is separated from the Anti-Lebanons only by the deep gorge
of the river Barada (Abana) which flows eastward to Damascus.
It is a gigantic mountain, 5 miles wide and almost 20 miles long,
which culminates in three peaks about a quarter of a mile from
each other. The tallest of these peaks is in the center and is made
up of a small plateau about 435 yards in diameter and is 9,166 feet

258

above the Mediterranean Sea, which is only 30 to 40 miles away. Its noble majesty filled the ancients with veneration and awe, as it rose high above the sources of the Jordan, the city of Damascus, and the Valley of Lebanon. It could be seen from most all parts of Palestine, Syria, and Trans-Jordan.

The Sidonians called it Sirion, the "glittering breastplate"; the Amorites called it Shenir; while the Baal worshipers considered it the very abode of the god Baal-Hermon—the Quibla or focal point of all Baal worship. Today the Arabs call it *Jebel esh Sheik*, the "Chief of the Mountains," or "the mountain of the white-haired."

The geological formation of Mount Hermon is limestone and Nubian sandstone, with occasional veins of black basalt. Nearer the base it is strewn for miles with large boulders of traprock. The lower slopes are well wooded partly with fir, partly with fruit, and here and there stretches of oak and shrubs. On its northern slopes groves of olives and mulberry trees can be found as far up as 5,000 feet. Above this are found only a few scattered oaks, almonds, and dwarf juniper trees.

259

Snow-crowned Mount Hermon, elevation 9,166 feet

One of the striking things about Hermon is the "shadow mountain" effect which on clear days is seen morning and evening. On rising in the morning, the sun casts Hermon's shadow far out across the Lebanons into the Mediterranean Sea. The evening shadow is impressively thrown back eastward across Damascus and the desert beyond.

The winter snowline begins at an elevation of about 3,250 feet, and piles higher and higher to the very summit which causes Hermon to stand out against the skyline like a great white ghost. The summer sun melts most of the snow away, except in the coves and deep clefts with here and there long, deep drifts on the northern slopes. Three-fourths of this water finds its way down the deep gorges of the Great Rift Valley of the Jordan. The other one-fourth drains through the Abana and Pharpar rivers which slake the thirst of Damascus and its great surrounding basin. All these rivers rise and fall according to the amount of snow and rain which falls on Mount Hermon.

Some years ago the writer took Rev. Bud Robinson all the way around Mount Hermon, taking care to point out the drainage. When we had completed the circle, his cryptic reply was, "Well, Mount Hermon is the waterworks of Palestine."

During summer months, when no rain falls, most vegetation throughout Palestine depends on dew for moisture, and Mount Hermon with its high, cold elevations enhances the supply of distilled dew. In Ps. 133:3 the happiness of brotherly love is compared to the "dew of Hermon which descendeth upon Mount Zion." In no other known place in the world is the dew as heavy. It is a natural phenomenon caused by the moisture from the Mediterranean Sea coming in contact with the cold atmosphere of the mountain. The evaporating dew of the morning produces a heavy cloud of mist, which drifts along, forming ribbons of filmy white on a background of green. These dews and mists plus other advantages of Mount Hermon make it the source of many blessings to the land over which it so proudly lifts its form.

260   The height of Hermon along with its isolation and location makes it a promontory second to none from which to view the Holy Land. From its summit a great part of Palestine and Syria can

be seen. To the east lies Damascus, one of the oldest cities in the world, a paradise in the midst of the desert. To the southeast the plain of Bashan is visible, dotted everywhere with ruins. The Huleh Basin, where were the "waters of Merom" of Bible times, lies almost at the foot of Hermon. Further south is the Sea of Galilee, while 95 miles below is the Dead Sea. Between these is the length of the Jordan River in its vast chasm from 6 to 12 miles wide. West of Jordan, one can see peak after peak and many of the sacred sites of western Palestine, such as Nazareth, the Mount of Olives, Mount Carmel, and other notable points; while the expanse of the Mediterranean, which stretches away to the sky, seems almost boundless.[1]

No one point in Palestine acquaints one with the country and with the old forms of worship as does Mount Hermon. It seems to have been the chief of the high places dedicated to Baal before Abraham passed this way preaching the doctrine of one God.

The great confession of Peter, when he boldly acknowledged that Jesus was "the Christ, the Son of the living God," was made at Caesarea Philippi just before the Transfiguration, and the healing of the afflicted child was just after "they came down from the mountain" (Matt. 16:16). Therefore it follows that the "high mountain" must have been Mount Hermon. It also seems reasonable, as many suppose, that Christ would go to this mountain to be transfigured. It is believed that He went to the southernmost peak of the mountain rather than the highest one because of the pagan temple then occupying that most eminent peak. At the transfiguration of Christ there were five representatives with Him: Moses, Elijah, Peter, James, and John. Moses represented the law; Elijah, the prophets; Peter represented persistence; James, administration; and John, love. What a place for such an event! What a company to be present when the Eternal broke through in revelation, attestation, and encouragement.

The Greeks dedicated Mount Hermon to their god Pan, and the village of Caesarea Philippi was called *Panias;* later the Arabs changed it to *Banias.* Jerome, who lived from A.D. 340 to 420, tells us that in his time there was a remarkable temple on the summit of Mount Hermon in which the heathen from the region of

Panias and Lebanon met for worship. In A.D. 420, when suffering from the ravages of wild beasts, the inhabitants about Mount Hermon summoned Simeon Stylites to aid them. He counselled them to give up their idolatry. Soon after this, Theodosius the Younger made a law enjoining the destruction of all heathen temples in default of their being turned into Christian churches. In the 10th century Hermon became a center of the Druse religion when its founder retired there from Egypt, but we have no record of their ever having worshiped on the summit of Mount Hermon.

During the summer of 1934, Dr. J. Stewart Crawford and the present writer led a small expedition in which we studied the ancient Baal shrines surrounding Mount Hermon. We located many ruined shrines, and in each case they were so oriented that, when officiating at the altar, the priests faced the chief Baal sanctuary, or *Quibla,* on the highest of the three peaks of Hermon. We then ascended the mountain and found the ruined temple of Baal, constructed of Herodian masonry, which dated its construction just previous to and during the early Christian era. In a low place near the northwest corner of the temple, we dug up literally loads of ashes and burnt bone which had been dumped there as the refuse from the sacrifices of the Baal temple, which was in full use while Jesus Christ was transfigured on the summit to the south.

CHAPTER 27

Damascus, "Pearl of the East"

Damascus, the paradise of the Arab world, and the "Pearl of the East," lies on the Plain of Damascus (known as Al-Ghutah), two miles east of the foothills of Mount Hermon, and 133 miles northeast of Jerusalem. Modern Damascus, with its surrounding villages, is a city of over 1 million people. Its white buildings, broad domes, and towering minarets shine with an iridescent sheen under the oriental sun. The plain on which it is located is a dark, islandlike mass of green, 2,000 feet above sea level, more than 150 square miles in extent, and 30

263

miles in circumference. Shaped and nourished by the life-giving waters of the Abana and Pharpar of Scripture, it has been a garden oasis of marvelous beauty and fertility for 5,000 years.[1]

The Abana River, now known as the *Barada,* is a cold, swift stream which springs from the northern foothills of Mount Hermon and the Anti-Lebanon. After hurrying through its tree-lined gorge and over its cascades, it enters the plain just west of the city and soon divides fanlike into seven branches. These in turn divide and subdivide into literally hundreds of canals which carry water everywhere until every garden, orchard, grove, public park and quiet, retired nook is irrigated. Every mosque, khan, hotel, restaurant, home, and court has its fountain or fountains.

Almost any place you go in Damascus you will see a stream of running water or hear a gurgling fountain—even in the restaurants and dining rooms where you eat. Orchards, gardens, groves, meadows, and plantations about the city and on the nearby plain receive an abundance of water for irrigation, after which the remains of the Abana flow across a vast meadowland, and at last sink into the desert sands of Lake Atebeh, east of the city.

The Pharpar River, now called the *Awaj,* rises among the eastern foothills of Mount Hermon in three forks which soon merge and flow eastward into the plain some seven miles south of Damascus. After irrigating miles of fields, gardens, and groves of the southern part of the plain, it reforms into two small streams which wind their way into Lake Hijaneh.

Thus the waters of the Abana (Barada) and Pharpar (Awaj), which are so pure, clear, and cool, have given this desert plain its groves of apricot and olive and lime and lemon and orange trees; along with its grape arbors, its date palms, its pomegranates, and its gardens of vegetables and flowers and fruits. It is quite understandable that Naaman, before his healing in the Jordan, regarded these rivers as "better than all the waters of Israel" (2 Kings 15:12).[2]

264   It is little wonder that when seen from afar, the misty white and gold and blue city of Damascus, sitting among all this "gorgeous grove and garden tapestries of purple and green," is

regarded by the Orientals as one of the most beautiful and luxuriant regions in the world. This is especially true when the almonds and plum and apricot orchards are in bloom, and a cloud of pink and white blossoms brood over the oasis. It then appears as a veritable "paradise on earth." When seen at close range, however, it appears more earthy.[3]

Damascus is known for the charm of its winding narrow streets, yet the street called Straight, where Saul of Tarsus received back his sight (Acts 9:11-18), runs in a fairly straight line across the city to the Eastern Gate. It has its long, covered arcade with little windows in the roof, high above the street, dimly lighting the ornate, oriental bazaars and shops below. But it is narrow and can hardly be said to resemble the mile-long 100-foot-wide, arcaded Roman street called Straight which in Paul's day lay 15 feet below the present street level. Here, and in al-Hamidiyah, most famous of the Damascus bazaar streets, you may purchase silks, swords, sandals, saddles, fine oriental rugs, inlaid woodwork, glass and silver ware, brass, copper engravings with gold and silver inlaying. The design may be ancient or traditional, yet it will be the finest of Old World craftmanship. Or you may purchase your trophy in a factory shop where the ancient art of brass and copper engraving, and gold and silver inlaying is completed before your eyes. In the produce market there is almost every kind of fruits, vegetables, and nuts that grow, and they are almost all produced locally. Here is a city that comes as near to being self-sustaining as any city on the face of the earth.[4]

In the very center of Damascus stands the famous *Grand Mosque,* one of the most interesting buildings of the Near East. It has been in turn a heathen temple, a Christian church, and a Mohammedan mosque. Now it is the fourth most holy sanctuary of Islam. The building is 429 feet long and 125 feet wide, has a spacious court, and is surmounted by three lofty towers and a dome 50 feet in diameter and 120 feet high. Its gorgeous interior is very impressive with its many arched colonnades, richly colored mosaics, ornate carvings, and its thousands of waxed candles. The marble floors are covered with expensive carpets and small prayer rugs, some of which are beautiful while others are quite ordinary. In worshiping here, the people kneel wher-every they wish. The imam, or leader of the mosque, raises his face to heaven and cries, "Allahu akbar" ("God is great"), and 1,000 voices echo the affirmation, "God is great."[5]

In the courtyard is the tomb of Saladin, which bears the inscription: "O God, receive this soul, and open to him the doors of paradise, that last conquest for which he hoped."

One of the three minarets towering above this mosque is the minaret of Jesus, who, it is said, will descend upon this min-aret, and with Mohammed and John, judge the world at the last day. Over one of the portals of the Great Mosque, (once a Chris-tian cathedral), may still be seen the significant, prophetic words: "Thy kingdom, O Christ, is an everlasting kingdom, and thy dominion endureth to all generations."[6]

CHAPTER 28

The Land of Bashan

Bashan, "the Land of Giants," has from the earliest times had something of mystery and of "strange wild interest" connected with it. It was known for its oaks, its fruits, its sheep, its cattle, its giants, its rich men and their pampered wives. The oaks of Bashan were used by the Phoenicians of Tyre in building their ships in early Bible times, while the rams and "bulls of Bashan" were sought for as the sires of the choice herds throughout the Middle East. The vine and fig flourished here in luxuriant fashion in the days of Bashan's glory as the

267

winter and spring streams irrigated and enriched the slopes and filled the great cisterns and reservoirs in every city and in the countryside.

The whole country was praised by the Hebrew poet-prophets for the strength and grandeur of its oaks, the beauty of its mountain scenery, the unrivaled luxuriance of its pastures, the fertility of its wide-spreading plains, and the excellence of its cattle (Ps. 68:15; Jer. 50:19; Ezek. 27:6; Mic. 7:14).

Bashan is that broad upland *east* of the Sea of Galilee and the Lake Huleh Basin. Its southern boundary line is formed by the deep gorge of the river Yarmuk, and it extends to the foothills of Mount Hermon on the north. Eastwards, it extends to *Selkhad* in the Druze Mountains. Its elevation ranges between 1,600 and 3,000 feet above sea level.

The land of Bashan is divided into four fairly well defined districts, each having a description peculiar to itself. These districts are: *Jedur, Golan,* the *Hauran,* and *El Leja.* El Leja is so unusual that we will describe it separately.

Jedur extends from the foothills of Mount Hermon and the Pharpar River southward to the latitude of the northern end of Lake Huleh area, and eastward to the Hauran.

The district is thought to have derived its name from Jetur, one of the 12 sons of Ishmael, whose descendants appear to have inhabited that region. During the period of the monarchy of Israel, King David married Maachah, the daughter of Talmai, king of Geshur (Jedur), of whom Absalom was born. It was to Geshur that Absalom fled and remained seven years following the slaying of his brother Amnon. In Greek and Roman times this district was called Iturea (2 Sam. 13:37-39).

Owing to its high elevation and rough terrain, the northern portion is often covered with snow in the winter, which melts and provides moisture for pastures in spring and summer. In the south it spreads out into a broad plain and is a rich pastoral region where many camels, cattle, sheep, and donkeys feed most of the year. There are ruins of 30 or more ancient towns and deserted villages. Less than a dozen are inhabited.

Golan district takes its name from the city of Golan, one of the three "cities of refuge" east of the Jordan (Deut. 4:43). Researches have not found the certain location of that city, but the district of Golan is that broad strip of rich plateau in the central and western portion of Bashan. The western border is made up of the rugged hills and narrow, fertile valleys overlooking the lower Huleh Basin, and the Sea of Galilee. These hills of conflict have been widely publicized in recent years as the *Golan Heights,* where Syria and Israel are occasionally in conflict. In elevation it rises northward by a series of terraces 1,000 to 3,000 feet above sea level, and its plains stretch eastward to *Nahar Allan.*

The topography of Golan, in general, is made up of wide stretches of lava, sandy plains, grazing lands, and black basalt twisted into fantastic shapes and rimmed with limestone. There are some conelike peaks of extinct volcanoes, and a few oak trees grow here and there. The soil is rich, and flourishing wheatfields cover most of the plain. Olives grow well in the hollows, and camels, cattle, and sheep thrive throughout the region.

The many ruined towns and villages found in the district indicate that it was once thickly populated. One of these largest ruins was Golan itself—a strong fortress for defense and a welcome refuge for the oppressed.

It was down the western slopes of Golan's high tableland that demons, expelled by Jesus from the poor man, chased the herd of swine into the Sea of Galilee. It was on the grassy slopes of Golan's lower plains near the sea that the multitudes were twice miraculously fed by the Master. *Kunetra* is now the largest city of this district. A number of new Jewish colonies have recently been located here.

The Hauran, or "hollow," is the name given to the great, all but treeless area between Golan and the Leja, and southeastward to the Jebel Druse Range. The south central and southern portions of Bashan deepen slightly, in basinlike fashion, with the curving downward of the Yarmuk valley. It was called *Auranitis* by the Greeks, and is a great plain about 50 miles long and 20 miles broad in its central area; and about 50 miles wide in the south where it begins northwest of Edrei and extends eastward to Selkhad in the Druze Mountains.

269

The surface of the district forms a prairielike plain of rich, red soil, broken in a few places by shallow watercourses, and an occasional outcropping of basalt. Springs are rare in the Hauran, but cisterns of enormous dimensions are seen in every village. Where springs are found, there are aqueducts to direct the water to the cities. Most of the oaks of Bashan, for which the district was once famous, have long since perished, but "the bulls of Bashan" and "rams of Bashan" are easily recalled in the herds of cattle and flocks of sheep which graze in the lush grass which grows in the unplowed portions of the plain.

The great plain owes its extraordinary fertility to the fact that its soil is composed of disintegrated lava, which makes it some of the richest of the whole country. Selah Merrill says, "Hauran is like the richest prairie of the west. . . . The natural wealth of the soil here is a constant surprise to me. I have seen men on this plain turning furrows which are nearly one mile in length, and as straight as one could draw a line. The finest wheat in all Syria comes from these old plains of Bashan."[1] Wheat is now the chief crop, and it often yields 80-fold, and barley is said to yield 100-fold. The semitransparent "hard wheat" is very highly valued, and during the season thousands of camel loads of grain are exported to other sections of the country.[2]

The basaltic stones of the district of the Hauran are some of the hardest and best in Near Eastern countries and are ideal for the forming of handmills for the grinding of grain. A handmill is usually from 18 to 24 inches in diameter and is made up of an "upper" and "nether millstone." The top of the "nether millstone" is slightly convex, and the lower portion of the "upper" stone—called "the rider" or "chariot"—is formed so as to fit directly onto the convex or dome-shaped top of the "nether" or lower stone. The "nether millstone" is usually formed of a denser or harder kind of stone than the upper one. The basaltic stone, found in such abundance in parts of the Hauran, possesses the extreme hardness and durability necessary for the manufacturing of these stones. Mills made from them are in such great demand that they are transported by camel and mule caravan to various parts of the Near East.

There are a number of strange, ancient cities built of black basalt. Some of these old cities have homes, temples, and churches kept so well that they appear ready to be occupied—and have been at intervals through the centuries. The majority of these date from the Graeco-Roman period, but some partly buried cyclopean structures date much farther back—perhaps to the time of King Og. Once the writer sat on an eminent point for a long while watching one of these cities with walls, towers, and gates of stone. All this time no sentry moved on its walls, no one came or went from its gates—the city was completely abandoned.

The habits and state in which the people of Hauran live are much the same as in the days of Abraham and Joshua. Dr. Porter says:

> I could scarcely get over the feeling, as I rode across the plains of Bashan and climbed the wooded hills through the oak forest, and saw the primitive ploughs and yokes of oxen and goads, and heard the old Bible salutations given by every passer-by, and received the urgent invitations to rest and eat at every village and hamlet, and witnessed the killing of the kid or lamb, and the almost incredible dispatch with which it is cooked and served to the guests . . . that I had been somehow spirited away back thousands of years, and set down in the land of Nod, or by the patriarch's tents at Beersheba. Common life in Bashan I found to be a constant enacting of early Bible stories. . . . Away in this old kingdom one meets with nothing in dress, language, or manners, save the stately and instructive simplicity of patriarchal times.[3]

Sheikh Meskin is usually thought of as the present capital of all the Hauran, being the central city and residence of the chief of the sheikhs. Yet *Edrei* (now called Der'a)—famous for its ancient underground city, with streets, complete with shops, houses, and marketplaces—is a busy center. It will ever be thought of as the chief city because of the Battle of Edrei. It pitted Og and Moses against each other. Og was the king of Bashan and a giant—the only one of the big fellows left among the rulers. His kingdom stretched from Mount Hermon in the northwest to Salkhad, high in the Druze Mountains in the southeast. The prosperous twin cities of *Ashtaroth* and *Edrei* he doted on, for

Ashtaroth was his capital and Edrei his far-famed underground fortification with its network of streets and avenues. Og's name inspired fear more than almost any ruler of his time. His reputation and the strength of his cities reached the Israelites. Yet after destroying Sihon of Heshbon, Moses turned and went marching to Bashan—straight toward Edrei.

Giant Og was so confident that he left his almost impregnable city of Edrei and with his army went out on the broad plain to meet Moses to whom the Lord had said, "Fear him not: for I have delivered him into thine hand, and all his people." Just when the battle was in the process of being joined, a strange, wild, confused consternation entered all the ranks of Og. Hornets swarmed in and stung the big soldiers and drove them wildly about in dismay, while Moses' forces "smote him, and his sons," routed his army, pillaged his cities, and carried away his huge iron bedstead to Rabbath-Ammon as a trophy of war (Num. 21:33-35; Deut. 3:11; Josh. 24:12).

Bozrah, 25 miles to the east and somewhat south of Der'a, was the strongest center of Bashan during both the Greek and Roman rule in Syria. It is not known when the city was established, although its fine natural springs would indicate a very ancient date for a city in this location—perhaps as early as, or earlier than, the time of Joshua. One tradition pushes it back to the time of Job. One strong spring, named Gahier, at Bozrah, has above it a sign in Aramaic which says, "This spring was used 2,000 years before Christ." A splendid underground street runs from this spring directly to the old capital building. Considerable Early Bronze I and II band-slip pottery has been found throughout this area, which means that it was inhabited during the early part of the third millennium B.C.—3000 to 2600 B.C.

In pronouncing the doom of cities across the Jordan, the prophet Jeremiah (ca. 590-80 B.C.) seems to mention Bozrah —associating it with *Beth-Gamul* (probably the present Ummal al-Jamual) and Keiroth, which were only a few miles in either direction (Jer. 48:15-24). However, our earliest certain records extant show it as a Greek military center. (The Bozrah of biblical fame was in Edom.)

In A.D. 105, the Romans made Bozrah a colony, and thereafter for many centuries it ranked as one of the most important commercial, political, and religious cities of the Near East. It attained a population of 100,000, and Christianity became its leading religion. At one time it was the seat of an archbishop, to whom 33 bishops were subject. One or more councils were held here, over which Origen presided. There are now 13 Christian church buildings in Bozrah, one of which bears the date of A.D. 512. Others are much older. Two of these are now used as mosques. The population of Bozrah is now estimated at 100,000.

Tradition says that Mohammed, when a young man, visited Bozrah while directing a commercial caravan for Khadijah (who afterwards became his wife). While there he became acquainted with John Boheira, a Christian monk of the Nestorian faith, who not only taught Mohammed of Christianity but, it is said, accompanied him back to Mecca and became his instructor while writing much of the Koran. The traditional home of Boheira is now shown in Bozrah.

Bozrah instituted a new system of reckoning time, dating from the Bostrian era, which commenced A.D. 105. It was used for some time in a large portion of the country east of the Jordan, but gave way to the Christian date.

The castle fortress is of great size and strength. In its basements were immense reservoirs and numerous cisterns—enough to last a garrison, it is said, for 10 years. One reservoir alone is 390 feet square and 15 feet deep. Bozrah was once a great caravan city, from which radiated great highways connecting it with Damascus, Beirut, Amman, and the port city of Acre. One went eastward, straight as an arrow to the Castle of Salkhad, 12 miles away, then on across the desert to Baghdad.

Salkhad, one of the most remarkable cities east of the Jordan, was known in Bible times as "Salcah," and was the farthest east of all the cities of Bashan—"All Bashan unto Salcah" (Josh. 13:11). Located on a graceful, conical hill, 500 feet in elevation, near the very highest and most striking summit in the beautiful Druze Mountains, its fine old castle fortress rises over intervening peaks until the watchman on the wall could on a clear day view scores

273

(Above) The remote fortress of Salkhad in Bashan, and (below) some of the ancient dwellings as well as modern structures on the southeastern slopes of the hill.

of surrounding cities, villages, and distant places—some as much as 40 and 50 miles away.

On the north lay the black basaltic district of El Leja, "the Refuge"; eastward was Philippopolis, built by Emperor Philip, and beyond was the road leading on through the desert to Baghdad. Southward were mountains and plains and ruined cities, and the road that led to Azraq at the head of Wadi Sirhan, a main route into Arabia. To the west an old Roman road led straight to Bozrah; and northwestward, the eye could sweep across the vast plains of Bashan, even to Mount Hermon.

Immediately below the great old fortress of Salkhad, on its eastern and southern slopes, are a large number of ancient dwellings with their massive stone walls, stone roofs, stone doors, and stone windows—some 800 houses, or enough homes for ample accommodation of hundreds of families.

The city was impressive enough in appearance and in its strategic location to gain the attention of the planning commission in Joshua's day, and the present huge towering fortress and massive private dwellings could have, from all appearances, stood there then, but probably the majority of the structures we now see were built later. Nabatean inscriptions indicate that the place was captured by their King Milik in A.D. 17. Numerous inscriptions from Greek and Roman times have been found, and one of Saladin, the great Arab leader of Crusader times.

There were two ancient moats for defense, and through the centuries the city has had an ample water supply, as attested by the large reservoirs on the east side of the castle, and the many cisterns in connection with the ancient stone homes. New homes have been built during the past few decades, and they are constructed of the same black basalt blocks and slabs.

At present some 3,000 to 4,000 people live in Salkhad, most of whom are the tall, stalwart, hardy mountaineers known as Druse. Their origin and the exact nature of their religion is unknown, yet they believe in the unity of God, and that He was manifest in Jesus, Mohammed, and Hakim. Hakim, the sixth Fatimite caliph of Egypt (who lived in the 11th century), proclaimed himself an incarnation of God, but disappeared while walking in the vicinity of Cairo. His followers believe he will return to this earth to reign and propagate his faith. Druzi, one of his most notable missionaries, proclaimed Hakim's tenets with such zeal in Lebanon that his followers came to be called "Druse." Sultan Atratsh, the president of all the Druse of Lebanon, Mount Hermon, southern Syria, and Palestine, lives in the small town of Kraie, eight miles south of Soueida. The Druse have three chapels of worship.

A hundred or more evangelical Christians live in Salkhad. They have their own pastor and hold church services each Sunday. The few Roman Catholics are visited on occasion by a priest who says mass for the group. There are no Moslems in Salkhad, but many Bedouin Arabs live in tents surrounding the city, and have the entire care of the camels, cattle, donkeys, sheep, and goats belonging to the Druse and Christians who live in Salkhad.

When the Druse took possession of this mountain area in 1860, it appeared barren and unproductive. But the tribesmen with infinite pains laid out terraces on the slopes, carried up fertile earth from the valleys below, set out vineyards, and planted mulberry, lime, pomegranate, apricot, fig, and other fruit-bearing trees. They founded a silk industry and made of the area a practical and profitable place to live.

Being on the rim of the desert, Salkhad has long been a marketplace to which Arab tribes come from the desert, bringing for sale horses, donkeys, lambs, hides, and wool. In turn they purchase clothing, saddles, bridles, dried olives, figs, dates, onions, potatoes, and other supplies. Few market scenes are quite so picturesque, and they are much the same as in ancient times.

CHAPTER **29**

El Leja or "The Refuge"

The Leja, which makes up the fourth section of Bashan, is a most unique land. It is a vast 350-square-mile, oval-shaped lava plateau, 22 miles long and 14 miles wide, located some 20 miles south of the city of Damascus. Its elevation is 20 to 40 feet above the surrounding plains, rising up sheer, like a black wall.

Being made up of vast fields of wavy, congealed lava, often twisted into fantastic shapes, with a labyrinth of passages through its volcanic vastness, this area was known as Argob to the Greeks,

Trachonitis to the Romans, and El Leja, "the Refuge," to the Arabs. It is rough, stony, and inaccessible—so wild and out of the way that it is little known to the outside world.

Almost the entire area is made up of a strange basalt lava, so black or dark brown, as to appear more like steel than stone. Like an island, whose irregular edge rises out like a rocky coast, it occasionally sends out long arms of black basalt into the surrounding plains. Through this irregular shoreline there are a few openings into the interior, but for the most part there are no roads except those which have been excavated to the towns within the Leja.

This great, rough, jagged island of basalt has the appearance of a sea when it is in heavy motion beneath a dark, cloudy sky. But its large waves have no white crests of foam—all is of a dull black cast and motionless. In the process of cooling, this lava often cracked and left great layers of black basalt, between which there are countless fissures and chasms which cannot be crossed. In other sections the lava has the appearance of a great, black, rolling prairie, and between the hillocks of lava there are small intervals of surprisingly fertile soil.

At many points in this strange area there are splendid springs of cool water, a few small lakes, and some fields. At strategic places there are ruins of round watchtowers, especially near the ancient roadways. And, most interesting of all, there are ancient cities, towns, and villages. A list of 71 city names was collected by Professor Ewing in 1895. On one city wall you can stand and see as many as 18 to 20 other cities, some of which are as much as three miles in circumference and have massive black walls and heavy square towers. Their gates, including the hinges on which they swing, are made of the same black stone. Within are temples, houses, and marketplaces. All these, too, are made of stone. Their walls, their floors, and their roofs are blocks of well-hewn stone, the latter being formed of slabs, closely joined, and resting on corbels, or supported in the interior of the rooms by means of arches. In most cases, the doors and windows, including the hinges, are intricately carved and show the amazing skill of the architects and artisans.

These are the "Black Cities" of the *Arabian Nights,* which hung so heavy with weirdness and mystery—because of their black massiveness, the absence of men, and the awful silence that filled the sable ruins; and because "there was never a face, nor a flower, nor a flutter of a robe" in the streets, nor a sentry to walk these city walls, nor guard to keep the gate, and no one to live in these impressive homes. Once people lived there and children played in those streets, but now, in most instances, the entire environs are deserted, standing just as the former occupants left them.[1]

In giving the description of one fine old home, Dr. Porter said:

> It seemed to have undergone little change from the time its old master had left it, and yet the thick nitrous crust on the floor showed that it had been deserted for long ages. The walls were perfect, nearly five feet thick, built of large blocks of hewn stones, without lime or cement of any kind. The roof was formed of large slabs of the same black basalt lying as regularly, and jointed as closely as if the workman had only just completed it. They measured twelve feet in length, eighteen inches in breadth, and six inches in thickness. The ends rest on a plain stone cornice, projecting about a foot from each side of the wall. The room was twenty feet long, twelve wide, and ten high. The outer door was a slab of stone four and a half feet high, four wide, and eight inches thick. It hung upon pivots formed of projecting parts of the slab, working in sockets in the lintel and the threshold, and though so massive, I was able to open and shut it with ease. At one end of the room was a small window with a stone shutter. An inner door, also of stone, was of fine workmanship, and not quite so heavy as the other. It admitted us to a room of the same size and appearance as the other. From it a much larger door communicated with a third room, to which there was a descent by a flight of stone steps. This was a spacious hall, equal in width to the two rooms and about twenty-five feet long by twenty wide. A semicircular arch was thrown across it, supporting the stone roof, and a gate so large that camels could pass in and out, opened on the street, the gate being of stone and in its place. Such were the internal arrangements of this strange old mansion. It had only one story; and its simple, massive style of architecture gave evidence of very remote antiquity.[2]

279

Ancient stone door entrance to a castle in the forbidding Leja region

Whence came this vast lava district, these black stone cities, these massively designed homes, this dread silence? Complete and altogether satisfactory answers cannot be given. When the curtain lifts, however, and we get our first general view, this *Argob* ("rocky district") was being wrested away from Og, the last of the great monarchs (Deut. 3:4-6). It was assigned by Moses to the tribe of Manasseh, and was conquered by Jair the son of Manasseh (Deut. 3:13-14), including all 60 of its cities.

El Leja, "the Refuge," is just what the place seems to have been in the beginning of the first century before Christ—a sanctuary for political outcasts, a refuge for the oppressed, and a rendezvous for robbers. Josephus speaks of the place as habitually inhabited by robbers: "The inhabitants of those places lived in a mad way and pillaged the country of the Damascenes. . . . It was not an easy thing to restrain them since this way of robbery had been their usual practice."[3] For whatever purpose they came here, however, they found a ready-built home of stone awaiting them, and a safe retreat in its rocky recesses. They were jealous of strangers, so much so that no guide will to this day take travelers into the area.[4]

Once the Nabateans occupied the district, but with the coming of Rome, in 64 B.C., one Zenodorus ruled the district. When he failed to sufficiently control the lawless element, Augustus Caesar ordered the area given to Herod the Great, who established a garrison of 3,000 Idumeans in Trachonitis to keep the peace.[5]

While Christ was on earth, the Leja prospered, and afterwards for many decades. New buildings such as temples, churches, homes, and theaters were constructed in the older cities. New cities and villages were established until the Arab invasion of A.D. 634-638. Then the curtains were drawn and little more is known until this last century when intrepid explorers like Burckhardt, Porter, Merrill, and Ewing began to tell of this mysterious region.

Inscriptions cut in the indestructible basalt of the Leja (and throughout Bashan) are numerous and in many cases remarkable. A few are in Hebrew, more in Nabataean, some in Aramaic and

Latin, but the majority are in Greek which was the written language used throughout the Roman and Byzantine periods. The majority of the buildings seem to date from 100 B.C. to A.D. 600, but there are other half-covered buildings, along with underground caves and cellars which are much older—perhaps many go back to the time of Moses and Joshua. Excavations are yet to be carried out here.

CHAPTER 30

The Land of Gilead

Gilead, that great upland cattle country, which played such a large part in the lives of so many biblical characters, was located between the Yarmuk River on its north, and the Wadi Heshbon on the south—50 miles from north to south. It had Ammon on its east.

Gilead seems to have always been thought of as *two* regions: the northern half and the southern half. This division was occasioned by its being cut through just a bit south of its center by the main stream of the Jabbok River (now called Zerka, or Blue

283

River). Each of these regions had its center—its focal point of interest. Those centers were not necessarily the same as at the present, but today they are Ajlun in the north and Es Salt in the south. Each place is built near the top of the highest mountain in its district.

It is a pleasant country with piled-up mountains, spread-out plains, lush valleys, and wadis that run down to the Yarmuk and Jordan. It appealed to the tribes of Gad and Reuben so well that they said to Moses, "The country is a land for cattle, and thy servants have cattle. Wherefore let this land be given unto thy servants for a possession. . . . Our little ones, our flocks, and our cattle shall be there in the cities of Gilead" (see Num. 32:1-22).

The name "Gilead," however, comes from the occasion when Jacob and Laban "made an heap" of stones to seal their covenant, and Jacob called it Gal-haed, the heap of witness, and from this came the name *Gilead.* Then came the "Mizpah," for Laban graciously said, "The Lord watch between me and thee, when we are absent one from another."

Here Jacob took his last farewell of Laban, the father-in-law; and as he went on his way, "the angels of God met him"; and when Jacob saw them, he said, "This is God's host." The place was ever afterward called *Mahanaim.*

On the brink of the Jabbok River one of the angels focused Jacob's attention on his inner self, and his relation to God and man. All night long Jacob wrestled with the angel of God. At the break of day the climax came, and the sun rose on a changed man. No longer was he to be Jacob "the schemer, the trickster," but "Israel"—a prince, who had spiritual power with God and with man (Gen. 32:24-30).

There was a wild grandeur about Gilead, for it was a rugged, fertile country; famed for its plains so well suited for cattle ranges, for its grain, its noble forests of oaks and pine, its olive yards, its grape vineyards, its palms, its glades with oleanders, and its widely sought-for "balm of Gilead." As for its men, there was a hardiness, a dash, a daring, and a dependableness such as one would think of as characterizing the Texas Rangers of the last generation. For example, there was *Jair,* the judge and ruler of

Israel for 22 years, who had 30 sons who rode 30 donkeys and had the oversight of 30 cities. There was *Jepthah,* who was a general, a judge, and a man who made a vow and implicitly trusted God; and *Jehu,* that speedy driver who stamped out Baalism by beginning at the top with Queen Jezebel. And, of course there was *Elijah,* that sun-bronzed, untutored prophet who wore "a girdle of leather about his loins," burned with indignation at religious compromise, challenged the king and the people to a test between Baal and God on Mount Carmel, rode in a chariot of fire as he was translated to heaven in a whirlwind, and appeared with Moses on the Mount of Transfiguration representing that dynamic breed ·of men known as "the prophets of God." O Gilead, what men, under God, thou didst produce!

Gilead has played a historic role as a place of refuge. Being far removed from the central orbit of men who specialized in politics, in religion, and in war, it has opened wide its arms of welcome to individuals, families, and political or religious groups who, in emergencies, needed a place of retreat where they could continue normal life undisturbed by the pressures which had beset them.

Ishbosheth, the son of Saul, took shelter here when he sought to reestablish the rule of his father's house (2 Sam. 2:8).

David found sanctuary here when he was forced to flee from his rebellious son Absalom. And when he arrived at Mahanaim, the people brought him all manner of supplies: beds to sleep on, utensils with which to eat, along with "wheat and barley, and flour, and parched corn, and beans, and lentils, and parched pulse, and honey, and butter, and sheep, and cheese." For, said they, "The people are hungry and weary, and thirsty" (2 Sam. 17:24-29).

It was here in the thick woods that Absalom lost the battle and, when fleeing upon a mule, went "under the thick boughs of a great oak, and his head caught" in the forks of a limb; and Joab "took three darts and thrust them through the heart of Absalom" and slew him. He then "cast him in a great pit in the wood, and piled a very great heap of stones upon him."

It was here at Mahanaim that David sat on the tower of the

city gate and heard the tragic news of Absalom's death and took up the sad lament: "O my son Absalom, my son, my son Absalom: would God I had died for thee, O Absalom, my son, my son" (2 Sam. 18:33).

It became a refuge for Jesus when the high authorities of Judaism sought to stone Him because He said, "I am the Son of God" (see John 10:32-42; 11:1-16).

In the beginning of his ministry, John the Baptist wore a camel's hair coat and a leather belt, and "preached repentance in the wilderness of Judea"—on the Judean side of the Jordan River. But the ruling Jews sent priests and Levites from Jerusalem, asking him, "Who are you?" He merely replied that he was but a voice crying in the wilderness. He then moved those enormous mass meetings across the river on the Perean or Gilead side—the territory where Herod Antipas was the ruler. Therefore, John the evangelist says, "These things were done in Bethabara beyond Jordan, where John was preaching" (John 1:28). John had come "in the spirit and power of Elijah," and the major portion of his ministry was near the place where Elijah had been caught up by a whirlwind into heaven.

It was from the Perean or Gilead side that Jesus entered Jordan to be baptized. And after John had finished his rugged ministry, Jesus returned here and spoke as man never spoke. Here He gave the parable of the great supper, the rich man and Lazarus, the Pharisee and the publican, the lost coin, the lost sheep, the prodigal son, and other such illustrations.

It was here that they "brought young children to [Jesus], that he should touch them . . . And he took them up in his arms, put his hands upon them, and blessed them" (Mark 10:13, 16). And it was here that the rich young man ran and kneeled to him and said, "Good Master, what good thing shall I do, that I may have eternal life?" Jesus gave him his answer but "he went away sorrowful," not willing to pay the price. Jesus then said to His disciples, "How hard is it for them that trust in riches to enter into the kingdom of God!" (cf. Matt. 19:16-23; Mark 10:17-24). So the rich young man did not follow Jesus, but thousands of others did, and the countries of Gilead and Bashan became a great strong-

286

hold for Christianity, as attested by church history and archaeology. Most of the cities had one or more Christian churches. Eight have been found standing bold among the ruins of Beth Gemal, and 13 in the city of Bazra.

Gilead had many cities, towns, and villages—Arab, Greek, Roman, Israelite—and stone-circled tenting places of shepherds of an even earlier time. The names of many of these towns we know, and somewhat of the roles they played in making the histories of their day. Yet the uncertainty with regard to so many of their sites make it difficult to be altogether certain about their positions on the map, or to discuss them with exactness. A few of the more famous cities have, with some degree of certainty, been located:

Gadara (now called *Um Quais*) was the capital of "the country of the Gadarenes," and at one time the capital of Perea. It was located three miles south of the Yarmuk, and five miles east of the Jordan River. Its ruins are over two miles in circuit, through which there runs a well-paved Roman street with the bases of colonnades on either side, and ruts worn by chariot wheels in the center. The rich ornamental work in marble, granite, and basalt scattered over the mound, along with the remains of an amphitheater, a theater, a marketplace, and a Christian cathedral, indicate the existence of a city of great wealth and magnificence.

People have often been left to wonder when they read authorities who said, "In the immediate vicinity of this town, the scene of the healing of the fierce demoniac and the destruction of the herd of swine took place" (cf. Matt. 8:28; Luke 8:26). On studying this section of the country more carefully, however, one discovers Gadara to be a member of the Decapolis and the capital of "the country of the Gadarenes." In the north its territory extended beyond the Yarmuk River to the east side of the Sea of Galilee. It was here that the miracle took place—some eight miles north of the city proper where a small mountain ridge rises up in "the country of the Gadarenes, which is over against Galilee" (Luke 8:26).

Jabesh-gilead, is identified with the twin sites of *Tell el-Maqbereh* and *Tell Abu Kharaz,* located on a hilltop overlooking the Wadi Yabis (River Jabesh) just across the Jordan Valley east of Beth-Shan.

This is the city which an Israelitish army of 12,000 attacked because they would not join their brethren in the war against Benjamin, and took maidens to become wives of the Benjamite men who were left without companions (Judg. 21:8-15). Afterwards Saul went to the rescue of Jabesh-Gilead with an army of 330,000 when the men of the place were about to lose their right eyes in a capitulation to the Ammonites (1 Sam. 11:1-11). The men of Jabesh-gilead afterwards showed their gratitude for King Saul's timely relief by traveling all night and taking down the bodies of the king and his sons from the walls of Beth-Shan, where they had been placed by the Philistines after the fatal battle of Gilboa.

It is probable that Jabesh-gilead was the home of the prophet Elijah.[1]

Abel-Meholah, the home of the prophet Elisha, who succeeded Elijah, has been identified with *Tell el-Maqlub,* on the river Jabesh, some five miles east of Jabesh-gilead. If these identifications are correct, then Elijah and Elisha would likely have known each other for years before either of them became prophets.

Ramoth-gilead, one of the six cities of refuge, has been identified with *Tell er-Rumeith,* located some 10 miles southwest of Edrei. Here Jehu, the swift charioteer, was anointed to be king. He rid Israel of the idolatrous Queen Jezebel and gathered in baskets the heads of 70 of the king's sons.

Ahab came here to fight against Ben-Hadad and to recapture Ramoth-gilead, but, in harmony with the prophecy of Micaiah, "a certain man drew a bow at a venture" and smote Ahab so that the blood ran down in the chariot, and the king died with the going down of the sun. They carried him to Samaria where they removed his body, washed the bloody chariot, whereupon "the dogs licked the blood of Ahab" in keeping with Elijah's prophecy (1 Kings 22:37-38).

Pella is identified with *Tabaqat Fahil,* two miles north of Jabesh-gilead. It is now a great fortress mound, high up in the hills, situated like an eagle's nest on a ledge overlooking the Jordan Valley. "It occupies a unique position with regard to the Jordan Valley, being neither a part of it nor completely separated from it." Pella abounds in clear springs "and a track winds past it, once good enough to carry chariot traffic and donkey trains. . . . It was inevitable that men should settle by this gathering of waters and build houses and temples and strong fortifications."[2]

It was to Pella that the Christians of Jerusalem withdrew just before the destruction of the city by Titus in A.D. 70. The place became a great Christian center and prospered until it was destroyed by the Saracens during the Crusades.

Peniel, or Penuel, is located on the banks of the Jabbok at a place now called *Tell edh-Dhahab* (the "Hill of Gold"). The river bends around the base of this mound on three sides, and in flood season cuts it off altogether from the mainland as if to say, "This is a particularly important place, not to be associated with the ordinary, mundane world." Dr. Glueck says, "My Arab companions were very loath to have me sleep there alone, but would on no condition accompany me there to spend the night. They made their camp at the foot of the hill, warning me that if I persisted in my intention to sleep on top of it, a spirit (jinni) would seize me during the night, and that if indeed I did survive the ordeal I would wake up in the morning *majnun,* that is, possessed by the spirit. But here Jacob had wrestled during the night, . . . being left alone until the break of dawn. And here I would sleep or sit out the night, with the living past breathing its vivid tale into my ears. What would happen to me before I crossed the Jordan again?"[3]

Succoth, to which Jacob journeyed after leaving Esau, and where he "built him a house, and made booths for his cattle," is identified with the imposing ancient mound known as *Tell Deir'alla.* It is in a very rich section, located in the edge of the Jordan Valley just where the Jabbok River enters the valley. A pleasant place for Jacob and his family to live for a while after his inner change and his forgiveness by Esau.[4]

Jerash (or Gerasa), one of the 10 cities of the Decapolis which sprang up across the Jordan after the conquest of Alexander, was located in the heart of the mountains of Gilead, on

the west banks of one of the northern tributaries of the Jabbok. Its ruins, which include a columned street that runs the city's length, arches, gateways, massive walls, theaters, amphitheaters, churches, a temple, a forum, and villas that rise like a dream attest that it is probably the most perfect Roman city left above ground. Destruction came first from the Persians, then the Arabs, then earthquakes. There is nothing visible now that dates before the Christian era. The ruins of Jerash were rediscovered to the west by the German traveler Seetzen in 1806, and since that time the numbers of visitors, scholars, and travelers have steadily increased.[5]

Ajlun, 20 miles north of Jerash, is not a known biblical site, but has a very fine specimen of a medieval Arab castle which the natives call *Kalat al Rabadh*. It is located on a prominence of north Gilead's highest mountain range—a rocky cliff 3,400 feet above sea level, and overlooking the Jordan Valley 4,300 feet below. Its lofty position made it an ideal *beacon station* and *pigeon post* by which news could be sent along a line of message stations extending from Egypt to the Euphrates.

The castle was built in 1184-85 by Azz al Din Ausama, a cousin of Saladin. Its chief purpose was to hold in check the Christian barons of Belvoir Castle (across the Jordan), and Karak Castle (east of the Dead Sea), and to maintain communications with Damascus. The nearby town of Ajlun evidently grew up with the castle, for it was spoken of in 1300 by Dimisishqi, an Arab writer, who found "fruits of all kinds and provisions in plenty." In 1355, Ibn Batuta described it as "a fine town with good markets and a strong castle; a stream runs through the town and its waters are sweet and good."[6]

Jebel Osha (the "mountain of Hoshea") is the most prominent peak of the Gilead mountain range. It is on the southern side of the Jabbok River, and rises 3,597 feet above sea level—one of the highest mountains in Palestine, aside from Mount Hermon. Far up toward the peak is the traditional tomb of the prophet Hosea which the Arab guides show with great respect and veneration.

Standing on top of this peak, one enjoys a commanding view

The Roman theater at Jerash, one of the best preserved of all ancient Roman cities.

all the way from Mount Hermon to the south end of the Dead Sea. The view is so astounding that some verily believed it to be "the mountain . . . over against Jericho," from which Moses viewed the Promised Land (Deut. 34:1-3). A more natural vantage point from which to view the land could not be found east of the Jordan. Yet the topography hardly fits the place where God took Moses for his last earthly look.

Es Salt, with its white buildings and contented people, rises tier upon tier on its hill terraces at the southern base of Mount Osha. It is one of the most highly populated centers of Gilead, and is famous for its olives, figs, apricots, pomegranates, and its enormous crops of choice grapes and raisins which it furnishes for the markets of the Middle East. Native life is seen here at its best, especially on market days.

The "balm of Gilead" is proverbial with the land of Gilead. The Ishmaelites, to whom Joseph was sold, came from Gilead "with their camels bearing spicery and balm and myrrh" (Gen. 37:25). This balm, with its wonderful medicinal properties, was one of the "choice fruits of the land" which Jacob sent down to Egypt as a present to Joseph, who was then the governor of the land of the Pharaohs (Gen. 43:11).

The tree from which came the balm was only a small evergreen with scant foliage and small white blossoms.[7] Its value was in the balsam resin or juice which was drained out through a cut in the bark or obtained from the reddish black berries which, when thoroughly ripe, take the form of a nut with a pulpy case and fragrant yellow seed. An inferior quality of balsam is also obtained from the young wood by a bruising and boiling process. The rare and almost priceless balm was mixed with other ingredients and used internally as a medicine and externally for wounds and certain skin eruptions. It is now used in perfumery. The tree seems to have had its original home on the east coast of Africa, yet it has been found in a few other places, especially at Mecca.

292   There is a tradition that the queen of Sheba presented some of the young balm trees to King Solomon, who planted them at Jericho and En-Gedi. Cleopatra sent to Jericho for some of the

plants for her garden at Heliopolis. Twice this balm tree was paraded in the triumphal processions at Rome: once in 65 B.C. when Pompey returned from his trip to the East and his conquest of Judea, and a second time after the destruction of Jerusalem by Titus in A.D. 70, when the balm tree was taken together with the golden candlestick and the other treasures of the Temple.[8]

Jeremiah said, "For the hurt of the daughter of my people am I hurt: I mourn; dismay hath taken hold on me. Is there no balm in Gilead; is there no physician there? Why then is not the health of the daughter of my people recovered?" (Jer. 8:21-22). The balm tree has been carefully sought for throughout modern Gilead, but none has been found there.

CHAPTER 31

The Land of Ammon

The Ammonites, descendants of *Ben-Ammi,* the son of Lot, by conquest displaced the southern branch of the ancient race of giants called Zamzummims—"The Lord destroyed them; and they succeeded them, and dwelt in their stead" (Deut. 2:20). This involved the territory from the Arnon to the Jabbok, and from the Jordan River eastward into the edge of the Arabian desert.

As their "royal city" and chief trading center, the Ammonites built or rebuilt Rabbath-Ammon, which came to be called "the

City of Waters," for it had a strong living spring, and was located on a conspicuous "Citadel Hill" in a narrow valley through which ran the main south-north tributary of the river Jabbok (Wadi Zerka). Its walls were high, its gates secure, and its markets enticing to desert men and managers of caravans who came from the desert and the south.

Later they were dispossessed of the western part of their territory by Sihon, king of the Amorites. Then during the Israelite conquest, Moses destroyed Sihon and took all his territory, but heard the word of the Lord, saying, "When thou comest near over against the children of Ammon, distress them not nor meddle with them: for I will not give thee of the land of the children of Ammon any possession; because I have given it unto the children of Lot for a possession" (Deut. 2:19).

The Ammonite kingdom, in its reduced form, was located around the headwaters of the Jabbok. Its exact boundary lines are somewhat uncertain, yet the western boundary line ran to the west of, or with, the south-north tributary of the Jabbok which arose near Rabbath-Ammon and flowed northward to the main

295

A Roman fort at Azrak, a military outpost of the kingdom of Jordan east-west Jabbok (Josh. 12:2). Eastward it extended far out into the edge of the Arabian desert, including the unusual oasis town of *Azrak,* 60 miles southeast of Amman, where Lawrence of Arabia had his headquarters during the latter part of the Arab war against the Turks.[1]

Thus, the kingdom of the Ammonites was only moderately extensive, yet it was prosperous and pleasant—an ideal range for vast herds of camels, cattle, donkeys, sheep, and goats. Gazelle, bustard, partridge, and other game were in plentiful supply, and there were vast stretches of land along the various tributaries of the river Jabbok for gardens, grains, and olive groves.

The Ammonites might have exploited all these resources and been a contented and happy people, but they were not. They lost the territory to Sihon, and later Moses took it from him. They always looked on it as "our land" and blamed their neighbors for being in possession of what they themselves had lost to Sihon. This inordinate claim fed a hostile attitude and prompted them to go to war many times in the coming generations. Always they lost, grew steadily weaker, and settled back with less incentive.

In the time of Jephthah, the Ammonites made war against Gilead with the intent of regaining a great part of the country which had formerly been theirs before the Amorites under Sihon had possessed it. But Jephthah sent messengers to the king of Ammon, assuring them that Gilead had not taken their lands from them, and urged them to be content with what Chemosh, their god, had given them to possess. Instead they resisted all overtures of peace and marched their army against Gilead. The "Spirit of the Lord came upon Jephthah, he vowed a vow unto the Lord," and mightily led the Gileadites as they defeated the Ammonites and forced them back east of the encircling Jabbok (Judg. 11:1-33).

In the beginning of Saul's reign, Nahash, king of the Ammonites, attacked Jabesh-gilead, forcing it to capitulate; but he would accept no conditions other than that the inhabitants submit to having every man's right eye plucked out. This would disqualify them as soldiers and "lay it for a reproach upon all Isreal." The leaders at Jabesh asked for seven days in which to consider the matter. Before those seven days were up, Saul gathered his forces and came with an army of 330,000 and delivered the people from the intended barbarity and scattered the Ammonite army "so that two of them were not left together" (1 Sam. 11: 1-11).

On coming to the throne, David lived on friendly terms with Nahash, king of Ammon, and endeavored to continue the friendship with Hanun, Nahash's son and successor. But Hanun grossly insulted David's messengers when he "shaved off the one half of their beards, and cut off their garments in the middle . . . and sent them away" in shame and disgrace as though they had been spies. The next spring the Ammonites attacked, but David's army under Joab laid siege to Rabbath-Ammon, took over their water supply, and forced their capitulation. It was during this siege engagement that David suffered the shameful spiritual downfall with Bath-sheba. When unable to longer conceal it, he had Uriah, her husband, sent to "the forefront of the hottest battle," where he lost his life under the very walls of Rabbath-Ammon (2 Sam. 11:1-21).

Bands of the Ammonites joined Nebuchadnezzar in the destruction of Jerusalem in 586 B.C., and afterward Baalis, king of Ammon, sent Ismael, an Ammonite, to assassinate Gedaliah, the new governor of Judea appointed by Nebuchadnezzar (Jer. 40: 14—41:10). Judas Maccabaeus broke almost the last semblance of Ammonite power in fulfillment of Ezekiel's prophecy, as the Nabataeans overran their country. It is not known what became of King Og's iron bedstead (size 6 by 13 feet)—the first "king-size" bed of which we have a record—but the Ammonites became extinct as a nation and were gradually blended with the Arabs.

Rabbath-Ammon was rebuilt in grand style by Ptolemy Philadelphus of Egypt, in the third century B.C., and named Philadelphia. It became one of the cities of the Decapolis (the 10 important Greek cities, mostly east of the Jordan which were linked together for defense, trade, and culture). During early Christian times it was a near-desert outpost of the Roman Empire. Its remains of antiquity are now represented by the well-pre-

Amman, Jordan's capital city, has many beautiful modern buildings but also this well-preserved Roman theater.

served ruins of the Graeco-Roman theater in the valley east of the acropolis which was cut in the hillside and built to accommodate about 4,000 people.

Amman, now the modern capital city of the kingdom of Jordan, was only a small village when it became capital of Transjordan in 1921; now a third of a million people live here. It retains its splendid springs of water and is an important marketplace. It has interesting ancient ruins, but also has many beautiful modern buildings and is the home of King Hussein, ruler of the kingdom of Jordan. Yet it is not old Rabbath-Ammon, but Philadelphia, the Graeco-Roman city among whose prostrate ruins you grope your way.

Zerka, built on the site of the Roman town of Gadda, is about 15 miles northwest of Amman. Traces of an ancient roadway have been found coming from Amman through Zerka. In recent years the city has had a rapid growth.

The country of Jordan in general, however, is unlike most

298

other countries on the face of the earth. In most areas it appears sterile, yet it is amazingly fruitful; in appearance it is inhospitably wild, yet it is one of the quietest, most homelike of lands. The way of life is much as it was in ancient times, in color, in content, and in dress. No Jews live here, only Arabs and Carisians, with a sprinkling here and there of Crusader blood cropping out in those native to the land. Here the Bedouin, the camel, the horse, the donkey, cattle of all kinds, and wildlife in great variety are all at home. Here the Arab has a country and an atmosphere in a setting to his tastes, emotions, and manner of life. Yet hard by is Israel with its metropolitan, agricultural, and industrial stride.

This, then, has long been Jordan. Now a new nation with a solid future is being built upon the ancient heritage of an old country—a new irrigation system, increased agriculture and industry. Of that future, His Majesty King Hussein has said:

> We have given ourselves the goal of economic self-sufficiency. That is a difficult assignment. I am well aware. But with the determination that inspires our people, we will achieve it.
>
> Along with economic independence, we have parallel goals in health, education, and social welfare. While it will take time to reach complete maturity in these areas, steady progress is being made with each passing year. Within a decade I am confident that Jordan will have become with the help of God, a strong, resourceful, and still reverent nation.

CHAPTER **32**

The Land of Moab

$\mathbf{T}$he mention of *Moab* stimulates thoughts of Moses, Elimelech, Naomi, and Ruth; and of David, who in time of trouble, trusted his aged parents to the king of Moab (1 Sam. 22:3-4). Also, it starts visions of camel trains, Bedouin tents; of flowing robes and white turbans, and everything that is usually supposed to make up a patriarchal retinue.

As a land primitive in its ways, it was famous for its upland pasturelands, its vineyards, its grainfields, its threshing floors, its

300

wildlife, its medicinal hot springs, its inaccessible mountains, and its deep, dark chasms through which its streams rushed to the Dead Sea. It was sufficiently prominent to be mentioned 158 times in the Old Testament.

Moab lay east of the Dead Sea, with boundary lines shifting with the growth of its people, and with the ebb and flow of conquest. Yet during its major history it began in the south with the brook Zered (Wadi Hesa), and extended northward to the river Heshbon. Its known history is mainly related to Israel, to the Nabataeans, and to the Crusades.

Moab is, for the most part, a broad, almost treeless plateau, averaging some 3,000 feet above the sea level and 4,300 feet above the Dead Sea. The crest or ridge is formed by the Abirim mountain wall which towers above the Dead Sea, then gently slopes away eastward to the Arabian desert. This wall-like mountain range is cleft almost to its base by the two deep, narrow gorges of the Callirrhoe *(Wadi Zerka Ma'in)* and the river Arnon *(Wadi Mujib)*. *Wadi Heidan* cuts diagonally through central Moab and joins the Arnon near its mouth, and *Wadi Kerak* in the south augments its drainage. The streams in each of these impassable gorges flow westward into the Dead Sea.[1]

The Moab Plateau is higher than the Judean hills and receives more or less reliable winter rainfall, which makes grain, fruit, farming, and grazing superior to many other sections. In the Book of Ruth the family of Naomi migrated from Bethlehem to Moab, which had not suffered from the drought as much as Judea. On going to Bethlehem, Ruth was experienced in working in the harvest fields. Moab's uplands were so famous for their variety of wild game, for cattle, and for the countless thousands of sheep which grazed its ranges, that even Mesha, the king of Moab, "was a sheepmaster," and at one time rendered an annual tribute to Israel of "an hundred thousand lambs, and an hundred thousand rams with wool" (2 Kings 3:4).

The Plains of Moab, which merge with the southern plain of Gilead, lie below sea level and are about 15 miles in length and 8 in breadth. They are now known as "the Meadow of the Acacias." Four streams traverse the plain, and a number of towns and villages were there in biblical times. "And they [the Israelites] pitched by Jordan, from Beth-jesimoth even unto Abel-shittim in the plains of Moab" (Num. 33:49).

The Moabites called for help from the armies of the Amalekites, yet fear prevailed to the extent that Balak, king of Moab, attempted to have the prophet Baalim to curse the Bene-Israel encamped below in the Plains of Moab. But alas, for while the savory odors ascended from the sacrifices on the seven rock-hewn altars on Moab's mountain heights, the venerable old prophet broke forth in those exceedingly significant words:

> How shall I curse, whom God hath not cursed? or how shall I defy, whom the Lord hath not defied? For from the top of the rocks I see him, and from the hills I behold him: lo, the people shall dwell alone, and shall not be reckoned among the nations. Who can count the dust of Jacob, and the number of the fourth part of Israel? Let me die the death of the righteous, and let my last end be like his! . . . How goodly are thy tents, O Jacob, and thy tabernacles, O Israel! *(Num. 23:8-10; 24:5).*

While encamped here on this plain, Moses, the man of God who had marvelously led them for 40 years, heard God calling time on him. With a brave heart the mighty leader committed the people to God and to Joshua, "made an end of writing the words of this law in a book," gave his valedictory address, then, bidding farewell to the people, "went up from the plains of Moab unto the mountain of Nebo, to the top of Pisgah, that is over against Jericho." There the Lord showed him the Promised Land across the Jordan but told him, "Thou shalt not go over thither." So, with this glorious vision fresh in mind, "Moses the servant of the Lord died there in the land of Moab, according to the word of the Lord," and the Lord "buried him in a valley in the land of Moab, over against Beth-peor: but no man knoweth of his sepulchre unto this day" (Deut. 34:1-6).

This was the bravest warrior
That ever buckled sword;
This was the most gifted poet
That ever breathed a word;

And never earth's philosopher
Traced with his golden pen
On deathless page, truths half so sage
As he wrote down for men.

No intelligent clue has been advanced as to which of the nearby deep, wild gorges might be graced by Moses' mortal remains. However, tradition and the most careful of researches have persisted in pointing out a nearby, round mountaintop as being Pisgah, a prominent point on Mount Nebo, as the place from which he obtained his last view. It juts westward from the Moab Plateau, 3,930 feet above the Dead Sea, and commands a most unusual view of the Jordan Valley, the Dead Sea, and the Judean mountains. Even Bethlehem and the towers on the Mount of Olives may be seen on a clear day. Nearby are the excavated ruins of a small church and monastery, the accounts of which may be traced by pilgrim reports as far back as A.D. 394.

In a valley just to the northeast are a group of very fine springs, long known as *Ain Musa* (Moses' Springs). And, four miles east is Heshbon, now called Hasban, the capital of the Amorite king, Sihon, who lost it to Israel. Later it came into the possession of the Moabites.

Five miles south is the city of Madeba, famous as the traditional home of Ruth, and for its large mosaic pictorial map, the oldest original map known. Some think it to be a fitting memorial to Moses' last view of the Promised Land. In ancient times Madeba was a well-known center for northern Moab (Num. 21:30; Josh. 13:16), and it flourished during the early Christina centuries. In more modern times, however, Madeba became only a city mound "on the plain of Madeba." Albeit, the mound contained the ruins of many buildings, including 12 Christian churches.

In 1880, a group of Christians from Kerak founded a new colony about the mound. The Latins and others followed, each building its place of Christian worship. In 1884 the Greek Orthodox people chose for their church site the ruins of an old basilica to the northwest of the mound. While cleaning the foundations,

A large, mosaic pictorial map at Madeba, possibly the oldest original map known.

they discovered a most interesting mosaic pavement comprising the entire floor of the ancient Byzantine church.

A Greek monk living east of the Jordan wrote a letter to the Greek patriarch of Jerusalem, telling him of the mosaic pavement covered with names of cities such as Jerusalem, Gaza, Neapolis, etc. Patriarch Nicodemus made no reply. Six years later, after he was exiled, the new patriarch found the monk's letter and sent a master mason with orders to save the mosaic for the new church, if the mosaic seemed worthwhile.

In building on the foundation of the ancient church, the master mason drove a pilaster through the map, and damaged or destroyed other parts of it—all with the trivial explanation that the mosaic did not possess the importance which had been attributed to it. In January of 1897, Father Cleopas, librarian of the Greek Patriarchate, went to Madeba and made notes and sketches of the 65- by 26-foot mosaic map with its "amazingly

304

exact and impressive rendering of landscape features" such as hills, rocks, trees, watercourses, flora, fauna, etc., along with villages, towns, and cities of the Holy Land—all based on the invaluable list of place-names compiled earlier by Eusebius in his *Onomastikon.*

What a surprise and a delight was the news to the outside world! Draftsmen, photographers, and archaeologists hastened to rescue the mosaic. Now thousands journey to Madeba to view the remnant of the map in deep admiration, yet they wonder why such an invaluable geographic and historic treasure should not have been preserved complete.

From Madeba a road runs southwest to the hot springs of *Callirrhoe,* within the wild gorge of the *Wadi Zerka Ma'in,* known in ancient times as "the Valley of God," by Beth-peor, where the body of Moses was said to have been buried. All along its seven miles to the Dead Sea, this deep, narrow gorge is bordered by palm trees and cane, and passes by peaks and through walls of sandstone, limestone, and black basalt. In many places they are almost perpendicular, and as much as 1,000 to 1,700 feet high.

The 8 or 10 springs of Callirrhoe burst from the north cliffs of sandstone and limestone and dash down the sulphur-deposited precipice in numerous cascades and rapids to join the main stream of cool water which flows along the bed of the chasm. The two principal springs are about a half a mile apart, and each sends forth a volume of water sufficient to run a mill. The springs vary in temperature, the one farthest west having a temperature of 143° and the other 130°.

Above the springs and some distance to the south, on an almost inaccessible mountaintop, are the ruins of the ancient fortress-castle of *Machaerus,* built by Alexander Jannaeus. It was destroyed by the Roman general Gabinius and rebuilt on a larger scale and fortified with massive walls and towers by Herod the Great. Here lived Herod, at brief intervals, during the latter part of his life, and, as Josephus says, "bathed himself in the warm baths of Callirrhoe" in the vain attempt to cure himself of his loathsome disease.[2]

Sometime after Herod had died, his son, Herod Antipas,

moved south to Machaerus, bringing his new wife, Herodias, and her daughter Salome. John the Baptist was conducting revival meetings and baptizing farther north along the Jordan. Thousands from Judea "and all the region round about Jordan" heard those weighty words "Repent ye: for the kingdom of heaven is at hand," and "were baptized of him in Jordan, confessing their sins" (Matt. 3:2-6). King Herod attended the meetings and became so deeply interested that "he did many things, and heard him gladly," but never qualified for baptism, for John "reproved . . . him for [having] Herodias his brother Philip's wife, and for all the evils which Herod had done" (Mark 6:18-20; Luke 3:18-20).

For this reason Herodias chalked up a grudge against John and wanted to kill him, "but she could not." However, she had Herod arrest John and put him in prison in the dungeon at Machaerus. On Herod's birthday, when the party was gay with drink, Salome came in and danced to the great delight of Herod and his guests. He was so pleased that he promised her anything she asked, to half his kingdom. At her mother's instigation Salome "came in with haste to the king" and asked that he would give her on a charger the head of John the Baptist. Herod was aghast, yet because of his oath and the presence of his guests, he sent one of his palace guardsmen, who beheaded John in the prison beneath the castle and brought back his head on a broad dish and gave it to Salome, who handed it to her mother.

"Thus," says George Adam Smith, "Moses and John, the first and the last of the prophets, thirteen centuries between them, closed their lives almost on the same spot. Within sight is the scene of the translation of Elijah."[3] The homegoing of three of the greatest men of all time—all near the same area, and each brought here for that purpose. What a land, and what a Providence!

Twelve miles below Callirrhoe is the *Arnon* (Wadi Mojib)—the deepest gorge and largest river on the east side of the Jordan Rift. The channel of this river is never more than 60 to 100 feet wide, but runs through a narrow valley of rich verdure, whose multicolored sandstone cliffs frequently tower 2,000 feet.

Dibon, the capital city of Mesha, king of Moab, is located on the west side of the highway three miles north of the river Arnon, and 13 miles east of the Dead Sea. It was here that the famous stele of Mesha, known as "the Moabite Stone," was discovered by Rev. F. A. Klein in 1868. It is a black basalt slab three feet 10 inches high, two feet in breadth, and 14 inches thick. The inscription is dated about 850 B.C., and consists of 34 lines of alphabetical script which in dialect, style, and content resembles and supplements the account in 2 Kings 3 of Mesha's revolt against Israel's oppression.

The American School of Oriental Research conducted annual excavations here between 1950 and 1956, and discovered many things of interest, among which was "one of the most impressive pieces of ancient city walling to be seen anywhere in Jordan."[4]

Kerak, the biblical city known as Kir of Moab, is perched high on a rocky plateau 4,407 feet above the Dead Sea, 17 miles south of the Arnon. The general character of the country in which it is located is wild and grand, and the city is separated from the surrounding hills by chasmlike ravines from 800 to 1,000 feet deep. An ancient road led from Kerak down to the Dead Sea.

Arranged in triangular form, and measuring a half mile on each of its three sides, the city occupies the entire summit, with a high, well-built wall surrounding the brow of the precipice on every side. The ancient entrances to the city were by four rock-hewn tunnels, two of which are yet preserved. The one on the west is still used, and is approached by a zigzag path along a very steep, rugged slope of some 1,500 feet. When near the top, the path abruptly turns into an 80-yard-long rock tunnel which leads to the gate and into the marketplace. Here, guarding this entrance, is the "castle of Bibars," while behind and above the complex arises the 27-foot-thick walls of the great Castle of Kerak, one of the strongest castles of the Near East. The chapel within the castle is 90 feet long.

This immense castle, and other fortifications as we now know them, were built by the Crusaders about 1131-36, but they were constructed on Roman and Nabataean ruins, and are "on the wreckage of the Moabite fortress."[5]

Many interesting and some tragic events have taken place at Kerak. It was here that Mesha, king of Moab, retired with the remnant of his army when he was being attacked by Israel and Judah (2 Kings 3). In his extreme circumstance, Mesha offered his eldest son as a sacrifice on the wall. Israel and Judah withdrew in horror, and Mesha carved his version of the war, and his praise of Chemosh, on the "Moabite Stone."

The most famous of Kerak's Crusader rulers was Reginald of Chatillon, who married the lady of Kerak and thus became lord of Kerak. He was handsome and venturesome, yet his rashness frequently prejudiced the cause of the Crusades. Eventually he broke the truce between the Moslems and Christians when he intercepted and plundered a rich caravan on its way from Damascus to Mecca. The treasures were seized and many attendants and pilgrims slain.

Saladin, with due regard for the existing treaty, sent a message to the king of Jerusalem, demanding redress for the outrages committed by Reginald. When nothing was done about the matter, Saladin proclaimed *Jihad,* or holy war, which had its climax in the decisive Battle of Hattin, on July 3, 1187, after which Reginald was slain and Kerak passed into Moslem hands.

The houses in Kerak are close-built, and the city is well populated with many people of both Moslem and Christian faiths—even a strong Protestant group.

The view from Kerak westward is sublime. Far below, only a few miles away, lies the deep cleft of the Arabah, and the waters of the Dead Sea; then tier upon tier is the gray Judean Wilderness; and 50 miles away, on a clear day, one can see Jerusalem and the buildings on the Mount of Olives.

CHAPTER 33

Colorful Edom and Petra

Edom denotes the land ocu-
pied by Esau's descendants, formerly the land of Seir which was
originally occupied by the Horites (Gen. 14:6; Deut. 2:12-22).
Esau and his descendants intermarried with the Horites and eventually gained the ascendancy so that the country came to be
known as Edom (red). Apparently the term "red" derived from
Esau's being "red all over like a hairy garment" and the singular
harmony of the red sandstone cliffs which are so characteristic
of the country.

The land of Edom stretched from the Brook Zered (Wadi el Hasa) to the Gulf of Aqaba, about 100 miles south. The Zered is 35 miles long and has a fall of 3,900 feet, which gives an idea of the wild, rugged, mountainous terrain of the country. Some areas, however, are suitable for cultivation, and for the grazing of cattle and camels. Edom is known as "the Land of Passage," due chiefly to the fact that in Bible times the "king's highway" passed along its central plateau (Num. 20:14-18)—much as the highway passes now. Long stretches of the fine Roman road of Trajan can be seen beside the modern road. It is part of the great paved highway which ran from Damascus to Aqaba. Viewing some of these sections of ancient roadways suddenly jerks us up, and time stands still—momentarily. Eastward is the north-south "desert road," which in part the children of Israel traveled as they "went around Edom." It comes up from Aqaba to Maan, then continues northward past the headwaters of the brook Zered (Wadi el Hasa) and of the river Arnon (Wadi Mojeb).[1]

The places of particular interest in Edom are: Khirbet al Tannur, Bozrah, Shobak, Teman, and Petra.

Kirbet al Tannur is the ruined remains of an impressive Nabataean temple complex which stands on a high plateau on the southern edge of brook Zered 40 miles north of Petra. It was in use 150 years (from 25 B.C. to A.D. 125) and was one of the chief attractions of the Nabataeans. Excavations by the American School of Oriental Research in conjunction with the Jordan Department of Antiquities revealed the plan of the temple. They unearthed considerable fine painted, eggshell-thin pottery, much carved sculpture and a whole pantheon of hitherto unknown Nabataean deities, of which Dushara and Allat seemed to be the chief. The nature of the ruins and the position of the fallen stones led the excavators to believe that the temple was destroyed by an earthquake.[2]

Bozrah, the capital of ancient Edom, is identified with modern Buseirah, 20 miles southeast of the Dead Sea and 25 miles north of Petra on the west of the high road to Petra. Built on a high, flat mountain spur, and shut in by wild canyons, it was considered practically impregnable. The reference "Who is this that cometh from Edom, with dyed garments from Bozrah?" (Isa. 63:1), has been usually considered a Messianic scripture, and also indicative of the grape and sheep industries of ancient Bozrah. Its full import, however, is yet to be fully understood.

Shobak, an important Crusader stronghold, known as Mont Reale, was built by Baldwin I in 1115 to control the road from Damascus to Egypt. It was captured by Saladin in 1189, and restored by the Mamelukes in the 14th century. A village occupies the site today. The only worthwhile ancient remains is a great rock-cut well shaft with 375 steps leading down to an underground water supply.[3]

Teman, the district and town in Edom, was named after the grandson of Esau (Gen. 36:11). Amos names it along with Bozrah, and Eusebius in his *Onomastikon* mentions a Roman garrison by this name 15 miles from Petra. Job and Jeremiah leave us to believe that wise men lived in Teman, and that it was an important center of Edom (Job 2:11; Jer. 49:7).

With these and other bits of information in mind, Dr. Nelson Glueck made extensive researches and eventually located a city mound between *Ain Musa* and the Siq leading to Petra which he considered to be Teman. It is now called *Tawilan,* and is situated a few miles east of Petra, in the heart of a fertile, well-watered area. Here was the meeting point of important trade routes where there could be the benefits of the caravan trade without the caravans passing through.

Petra, "the rose-red city, half as old as time," was known in Bible times as Sela ("the Rock"). As ancient Edom's place of safe refuge, the Nabataeans' formidable commercial and administrative center, and Jordan's most magnificent tourist attraction, Petra has long been known as a unique place, the like of which cannot be found anywhere else in the world. It has been quite correctly designated as one of the greatest wonders ever wrought by nature and man.

Located 50 miles south of the Dead Sea, and 180 miles south of Amman, the city is built within a high mountain basin, surrounded on every side by brilliantly colored granite and

The "Treasury of Pharaoh" sculptured out of the solid cliff walls at Petra

sandstone cliffs—a veritable amphitheaterlike city. Its chief allurement lies in its color, its isolation, and its unique structure.

The only entrance to the city is from the east, by a mile-long waterworn cleft known as "the Siq"—a narrow, winding gorge with high, forbidding, red sandstone walls and mysterious side canyons. On entering the "Gate of the Siq" from the blinding light of the desert sun, one very soon acquires a sense of detachment and is struck with awe as the shadows deepen into a perpetual twilight and the sky becomes a thin blue line above the towering cliffs. The scenery gets wilder and more unlike anything else on earth as on and on the ancient gorge-road meanders between 100- to 300-foot cliffs which overhang to such a degree that in places the sky is completely shut out for brief intervals. The gorge road averages 12 feet wide, but in places the steep side walls are so close that you can almost touch them with your outstretched hands. Yet, you instinctively ride on and on until, as you round a turn in the ravine, suddenly the Siq ends (momentarily). One can hardly believe his eyes as there stands before him in dazzling sunlight the magnificent *Khazneh al Faraun*, or "Treasury of Pharaoh."

It is a 90-foot-high and 60-foot-wide royal temple-tomb, artistically carved from the face of the rose-colored mountain. Its two stories are adorned with gorgeous sculpture, and 12 or more beautifully carved columns of the Corinthian order. On its very apex, high above its attic story, is a massive, yet artistically carved urn which carries the marks of many bullets fired at it in the hope of shattering it and releasing the treasure which local tradition says is hidden there. Within the temple is a moderate size twin-loculi tomb-room which is without ornamentation.

The "Treasury of Pharaoh" is the most perfectly preserved monument of this area, and in its purity and refinement probably the best Petra possessed in the zenith of her power. But its architectural style is so unique, and it is so detached with respect to adjacent monuments, that no one knows exactly when it was 313 carved or to whom it belonged. Archaeologically it is generally regarded as the tomb of a Nabataean king of the late Hellenistic period—perhaps King Aretas the Philhellene (87-62 B.C.). "Aretas" was the Hellenized form of Harith.

Continuing for a time in the Siq, one comes next to a large, rock-hewn Roman theater, with 33 rows of seats, accommodating approximately 3,000 spectators. In the background can be seen fronts of early tombs, partly cut away in making the theater, and leaving the inner chambers now open to the sunlight.

When inside the city, one's eyes may turn almost any direction for a mile and see columned streets, paved roadways, arches, forums, theaters, temples, palaces, dwellings, a banqueting hall, a high place of worship, and hundreds of tombs carved with meticulous care from multicolored Nubian sandstone cliffs towering 200 to 300 feet in the air. In all parts of Petra it seems almost every available rock surface has been sculptured as the front of a temple, a shrine, a palace, or a dwelling.[4] Engrained in these sandstones are surprising shades of reds, pinks, violet, blue, yellow, ivory, raspberry, crimson, and coral—each adding a fresh brightness.

One tomb near the entrance has four pyramidal obelisks towering high above its entrance. The so-called Palace Tomb, with a facade imitating a Roman palace of three stories, contains enormous mausoleums and vaults in which were buried many of the kings of Petra. Nearby, there is the tomb of the Roman governor, Sextus Florentinus, whose name is given in Latin inscription above the portico.

Ed-Deir, one of the largest of all the monuments, is a huge two-story temple of reddish-brown stone 130 feet high and 150 feet wide. It has an altar set in a niche at the back of its one room. Some think it could have been a very fine tomb which was reworked and subsequently used as a monastery and place of worship. It stands at the extreme west portico of the city.

Petra has a 20-foot-wide colonnaded street which runs along the southern bank of the wadi and divides the city into two parts. At the end of the street is a triple monumental gateway, which some regard as a Triumphal Arch. To the west of the triple gateway is the *Kasr al Bint Faraun* (the Palace of Pharaoh's Daughter), which is one of Petra's most beautiful and best preserved monuments.

Just a little north of the citadel, on a leveled-off crag or tableland which rises high above the city, is a *High Place* which is about 47 feet long by 24 feet wide. It is approached by a flight of steps cut in the rock. At the top of the steps, on the high place is an altar 9 feet long, 6 feet wide, and 3 feet high. On top of the altar is a hollow, panlike area for the fire, and just south of the altar is where the animal victims were slain for sacrifice. Here the Nabataeans worshiped the god Dushares, whose emblem was a black stone. In 1934, this great High Place was excavated by the Melchett Expedition in collaboration with Dr. Albright.

In recent years surveys and excavations have been going on in Petra, and it is gradually giving up its secrets and treasures. It is now estimated that there are 800 to 1,000 temples, tombs, shrines, and monuments in Petra. In describing the place, writers use such terms as "rugged beauty," "fantastic," "awe-inspiring."

A city of importance must have long existed here. And Petra almost came into the dim twilight when "Chedorlaomer and the kings that were with him . . . smote the Horites in their Mount Seir" (Gen. 14:5-6). Again it seemed to be in the dim historical background when "Esau took his wives, and his sons, and his daughters, and all the persons of his house, and his cattle, and all his beasts, and all his substance, . . . and went" and "dwelt . . . in mount Seir" (Gen. 36:6, 8). And in the time of the Exodus, when the city was the evident stronghold of the biblical Edomites, they refused to permit the Hebrews to pass through their country on the way to Canaan.

Its known history begins in 312 B.C., when the forces of Antigonus I unsuccessfully attacked the city. In the second century B.C., the Nabataeans, a remarkable Arab tribe (identified with Nabioth of the Old Testament), moved in from Arabia and not only occupied Petra, but soon dominated the great caravan routes that stretched from the Red Sea to Damascus. They planted their outposts throughout this region and amassed a fortune by collecting tolls from the caravans in exchange for a guarantee of safe conduct. This wealth they lavished on their

315

capital, which to them was always a place of safe retreat. Among Petra's citizenry were princes, elders, horsemen, architects, doctors, and bards.

The city reached its height between 100 B.C. and A.D. 100 while the Nabataean Arabs ruled the country as far north as Damascus. In A.D. 106 the Nabataean Kingdom was incorporated into the Roman Empire, but Petra continued to flourish as the Romans built the colonnaded street, the Triple Gate, and carved the theater, the forum, and countless temples in the crimson walls of the sandstone canyons. In the fifth century Christianity penetrated Petra and had a bishop stationed there. The Crusaders under Baldwin I took it over at the beginning of the 12th century, and Baybars visited it between 1260 and 1277; then it was lost to history and the Western world until John L. Burckhardt rediscovered it in 1812.

It is only since about 1925, however, that any except the very intrepid and wealthy have visited Petra—and they under heavy guard. It is now very safe, and many thousands go each year to see the strange city. Some come by train, most by car, and a few fly, yet all must walk or ride a horse the last mile or two. But to visit the mountain fastness of Petra is such an unusual experience that anyone who has been there is quick to say, "I have been to Petra." Of Petra, Dr. Nelson Glueck says, "Even in its present condition of dilapidated elegance, Petra continues to be an unforgettable monument" to the "creative abilities" of the ancient Edomites, and later to the Nabataeans.

Some are anxious to return for a second trip, because of the endless sights and the grandly rewarding spell it casts over the whole self. Mr. G. Lankester Harding, former director of the Jordan Department of Antiquities, says:

> I have visited Petra many times, but always that first breathtaking vision remains in my mind. Nor does familiarity breed contempt here, for at every visit one has to rein up the horse or stop in one's tracks and gaze astonished, as if seeing it again for the first time, at the sharpness and purity of line, of the carving and the glowing brilliance of the rock. . . . Petra is astonishing and fantastic. . . . Before one is a vast panorama of rugged sandstone peaks, white, brown and red in color,

316

while in the distance to the west can be seen the blue haze of Sinai. Trees cling to the slopes of the crags wherever they can find a foothold and sufficient water to keep them alive, and the whole effect is strangely like looking at a Chinese land-scape painting.[5]

> *It seems no work of man's creative hand,*
> *By labour wrought or wavering fancy planned;*
> *But from the rock, as if by magic, grown*
> *Eternal, silent, beautiful, alone.*
>
> *Match me such marvel save in Eastern clime:*
> *A rose-red city half as old as time.*

Reference Notes

(Complete bibliographical data will be found in the bibliography.)

Chapter 1

1. Excavations at Byblos (Gebal), Ras Shamra (Ugarit), and Megiddo attest these early civilizations. The families or tribes were known as the Hittites, the Jebusites, the Amorites, the Girgashites, the Hivites, the Arkites, the Sinites, the Arvadites, the Zemarites (Zerarvites), and the Hamathites. Some failed to become famous, but five or six of them were frequently mentioned as inhabiting Palesine and Syria.

Other tribes lived in Palestine and were occasionally referred to as "Canaanites," but were not of that stock. Among these were the Giants, the Philistines, the Perizzites, and the Moabites. They were not descendants of Canaan, but were called "Canaanites" because they lived in the land of Canaan.

2. Gen. 10:15-20; Herodotus, *The Histories,* Book One, 1:2.

3. In the Tell El Amarna correspondence of the 14th century B.C., the land of "Kanahhn" is referred to as the northern portion of the Mediterranean coast, and from a technical point of view that is usually considered correct.

Even during Augustine's day, he says that if the Carthaginian peasants were asked of what race they were, they would answer, "Canaanites." Greek literature and the Nuzi documents refer to the purple dye obtained from certain species of shellfish found on the Eastern Mediterranean coast.

4. George Adam Smith, *Historical Geography of the Holy Land,* p. 75.

5. Heusser, *The Land of the Prophets,* pp. 32-35.

6. 1 Kings 5:6.

7. *Iliad,* 23:741.

8. Acts 27:3.

9. Matt. 15:21-28.

10. Isa. 23:7.

11. Josh. 19:29.

12. Tyre is now called *Sur,* which in Arabic means "rock." The Hebrews called it *Tzor,* which also meant "rock."

13. Ezek. 27:3.

14. Ezek. 27:12-24.

15. Ezek. 26:2.

318

16. Ezek. 29:18.
17. Ezek. 26:12.
18. Acts 21:2-6.
19. Ezek. 26:13-14.

Chapter 2

1. Gen. 49:13.
2. *Palestine Annual,* 3:90.
3. Acts 21:7.
4. Bentwich, *A Wanderer in the Promised Land,* p. 74.
5. Gen. 49:13.
6. 1 Macc. 13:12-30

Chapter 3

1. Smith, *Historical Geography of the Holy Land,* p. 338.
2. Song of Sol. 7:5.
3. 1 Kings 17:1.
4. 1 Kings 18:22-24.
5. 1 Kings 18:46.

Chapter 4

1. Some geographers call this narrow, 20-mile-long plain "The Coasts of Dor," and do not begin the Plain of Sharon until the Crocodile River is reached.
2. This bowl is now preserved in the Cathedral of Saint Lorenzo in Genoa, Italy.
3. *Mikveh Israel,* the first agricultural school in Palestine, was established by French Jews in 1870, on land granted by the Turkish Government. Through the school gates you see red-roofed buildings, tall palm trees, and fruit orchards. Better yet to go inside and see what may be done with the fertile acres of the Plain of Sharon. The writer can never forget a day and a half spent here in 1934 while making a survey of the educational institutions of Palestine.

Chapter 5

1. Gen. 10:14; Amos 9:7; *Quarterly of the Palestine Department of Antiquities,* vol. I, no. 4, p. 156.
2. Deut. 2:23.
3. Stewart, *The Land of Israel,* p. 88.
4. Judg. 1:18-19.
5. Amos 9:7.
6. Breasted, *Ancient Records of Egypt,* 4:38, 64.
7. McGarvey, *Lands of the Bible,* p. 22.
8. *Dagon* seems to have at one time been the national god of the Philistines. The image had the face and hands of a man, and the body and tail of a fish. Some are wont to say that it was the "fish-god" which the people were led to believe had risen from the sea.

9. Amos 1:8.
10. Isa. 20:1.
11. Sachar, *A History of the Jews,* p. 56.
12. Duff, *Palestine Picture,* p. 34.
13. 1 Macc. 5:68; 10:83-84.
14. Acts 8:40.
15. Duff, *Palestine Picture,* p. 33; 1 Sam. 6:4.
16. 2 Sam. 1:20.
17. Marston, *New Bible Evidence,* p. 117.

Chapter 6

1. Josh. 10:40.
2. Smith, *Historical Geography of the Holy Land,* pp. 197-99.
3. 1 Chron. 27:28; 2 Chron. 26:10.
4. Smith, *Historical Geography of the Holy Land,* p. 202.
5. Josh. 10:8-14.
6. 1 Sam. 6:1-18.
7. 1 Sam. 17:12-54.
8. Judg. 13:15-20.
9. Judg. 18:1-2.
10. Judg. 14:5-18.
11. Mic. 7:19.

Chapter 7

1. Wilson, *Picturesque Palestine,* 2:18.
2. Song of Sol. 3:9; Hos. 14:5; 2 Kings 14:9; 2 Chron. 2:16.
3. *National Geographic,* Dec., 1946, p. 736.
4. Isa. 2:13; Ps. 92:12.
5. The notation of the exact location of this quotation has been misplaced.

Chapter 8

1. Stewart, *The Land of Israel,* p. 111.
2. Josephus, *War,* 3:3.
3. Hamilton, *Put Off Thy Shoes,* p. 73.
4. *Ibid.,* p. 72.

Chapter 9

1. Payne, *The Splendor of Israel,* pp. 133-34.
2. See our article "Mt. Tabor," in Zondervan's *Biblical Encyclopedia.*
3. Owen, *Abraham to Allenby,* pp. 250-52.

Chapter 10

1. Comay, *Israel: An Uncommon Guide,* p. 283.
2. Rev. 16:16.

3. Smith, *Historical Geography of the Holy Land,* pp. 393-95.

4. Judg. 5:19-21.

5. I first inspected Nahalal in the spring of 1934. Then it was prosperous. The improvements in the past 40 years are all but startling.

Chapter 12

1. Stewart, *The Land of Israel,* pp. 148-50.

2. Wilson, *Picturesque Palestine,* 1:234.

3. Owen, *Abraham to Allenby,* pp. 38-39.

4. *Ibid.,* p. 77.

5. Smith, *Historical Geography of the Holy Land,* p. 214.

6. *Ibid.,* p. 54.

7. *The Story of the Bible,* 1:369.

Chapter 13

1. This book is published jointly by the Beacon Hill Press of Kansas City, Mo., and Baker Book House, Grand Rapids, Mich.

2. The holy family spent about two months in Bethlehem. The presentation in the Temple, which took place 40 days after the birth, and the adoration of the Magi who probably arrived soon afterwards, must have occurred before the flight to Egypt, where they remained till the death of Herod, and then returned directly to Nazareth, their proper home (Matt. 2:22-23).

3. Wilson, *Picturesque Palestine,* 1:139.

4. Josephus, *Antiquities,* 8. 7. 3.

5. Vilnay, *Guide to Israel,* p. 188; McGarvey, *Lands of the Bible,* p. 240.

6. Smith, *Historical Geography of the Holy Land,* pp. 240-41.

Chapter 15

1. Wilson, *Picturesque Palestine,* 1:142.

2. Josephus, *Wars of the Jews,* 8. 9. 1.

3. Erskin, *The Vanished Cities of Arabia,* pp. 126-27.

Chapter 16

1. See Glueck's *Rivers in the Desert* for extensive research on the Negeb.

2. Lowdermilk, *Palestine: Land of Promise,* pp. 49-50, 180-200.

Chapter 17

1. Stanley, *Sinai and Palestine,* p. 3.

2. *Palestine Exploration Fund Quarterly Statement for 1886,* pp. 41-46.

3. Glueck, *Rivers in the Desert,* pp. 283-84.

Chapter 19

1. Wilson, *Picturesque Palestine,* 1:357.

Chapter 21

1. Comay, *Israel: An Uncommon Guide,* p. 295.
2. Glueck, *The River Jordan,* pp. 53-54.
3. Josephus, *The Jewish Antiquities,* 17. 2. 1.
4. Fromer, *Israel and Its Holy Land,* pp. 242-43.
5. *Ibid.,* p. 242.
6. *Ibid.,* p. 237.

Chapter 22

1. Magregor, *Rob Roy on the Jordan,* p. 406.
2. The writer has studied the Jordan River from three of its sources at the foot of Mount Hermon down through the Rift Valley to the Dead Sea, but only from its banks. However, I have received considerable information directly from Mr. John D. Whiting, who with Rev. R. J. E. Boggis, Mr. Spafford Whiting (23), and Mr. John Vester (21), went down the river in rubber boats. Also, have read his article in the *National Geographic,* "Canoeing Down the River Jordan."
3. Glueck, *The River Jordan,* p. 156.

Chapter 23

1. "Settlements in the Jericho Valley During the Roman Periods," by Lucetta Mowry, *Biblical Archaeologist,* vol. 15, May, 1952.
2. *Ibid.,* p. 34.

Chapter 24

1. Lynch, *United States Exploring Expedition,* p. 324.
2. Leary, *The Real Palestine,* p. 138.
3. Trever, *The Untold Story of Qumran,* p. 151.
4. Baly, *The Geography of the Bible,* p. 203.
5. *World of the Bible Library,* vol. 5.
6. McGarvey, *Lands of the Bible,* pp. 370-71; Tristram, *Land of Moab,* p. 300.
7. Harland, *The Biblical Archaeologist,* May, 1942.
8. *Ibid.,* p. 27.

Chapter 25

1. Glueck, *The River Jordan,* p. 146.
2. Kroeling, *Rand-McNally Bible Atlas,* p. 27.
3. Comay, *Israel: An Uncommon Guide,* pp. 203-6.
4. Hamilton, *Put Off Thy Shoes,* pp. 47-50.
5. Glueck, "On the Trail of King Solomon's Mines," *National Geographic,* Feb., 1944, pp. 234-35.

Chapter 26

1. Tristram, *The Land of Israel: A Journal of Travels in Palestine,* p. 614.

Chapter 27

1. Porter, *Five Years in Damascus,* p. 10.
2. *Ibid.,* pp. 96-97, 119.
3. Hamilton, *Both Sides of the Jordan,* pp. 248-50.
4. *Ibid.,* p. 12.
5. *National Geographic,* April, 1974, p. 516.
6. Porter, *Five Years in Damascus,* pp. 22-25.

Chapter 28

1. Merrill, *East of the Jordan,* p. 333.
2. Wilson, *Picturesque Palestine,* 1:82.
3. Porter, *Bashan and Its Giant Cities,* p. 18.

Chapter 29

1. Smith, *Historical Geography of the Holy Land,* p. 644.
2. Porter, *Bashan and Its Giant Cities,* pp. 26-28.
3. Josephus, *Antiquities,* 15. 10. 1; 17. 2. 1-2.
4. Porter, *Giant Cities of Bashan,* pp. 92-93.
5. Josephus, *Antiquities,* 15. 10. 1; 16. 9. 1; 17. 2. 1.

Chapter 30

1. Glueck, *The River Jordan,* p. 170.
2. *Ibid.,* p. 175.
3. *Ibid.,* pp. 112, 117.
4. *Ibid.,* pp. 147, 151.
5. Harding, *The Antiquities of Jordan,* pp. 63-89.
6. *Ibid.,* pp. 42-43.
7. Its botanical name is "Balsamodendrois Gileadensa"—Balsam Mecca.
8. Wild, *Geographic Influences on Old Testament Masterpieces,* pp. 102-3.

Chapter 31

1. Glueck, *The Other Side of the Jordan,* p. 139.

Chapter 32

1. Orni and Efrat, *Geography of Israel,* p. 111.
2. Josephus, *Antiquities,* 17. 6. 4.
3. Smith, *Historical Geography of the Holy Land,* p. 600.

4. Harding, *Antiquities of Jordan*, p. 921; Owen, *Archaeology and the Bible*, pp. 261-63.
5. Glueck, *The River Jordan*, p. 35.

Chapter 33
1. Harding, *Antiquities of Jordan*, p. 19.
2. Glueck, *The Other Side of the Jordan*, pp. 178-98.
3. Harding, *Antiquities of Jordan*, p. 98.
4. Cottrell, *The Past*, p. 366.
5. Harding, *Antiquities of Jordan*, p. 100.

Bibliography

Balmforth, H., et al. *The Story of the Bible,* 4 vols. New York: Wm. H. Wise and Co., 1952.

Baly, Denis. *The Geography of the Bible.* New York: Harper and Brothers Publishers, 1957.

Bannister, J. T. *Pictorial Geography of the Holy Land.* Bath, England: Binns and Goodwin, n.d.

Breasted, James H. *Ancient Records of Egypt.* 4 vols.

Burckhardt, John Lewis. *Travels in Syria and the Holy Land.* London: John Murray, 1822.

Comay, Joan. *Israel: An Uncommon Guide.* New York: Random House, 1969.

Conder, C. R. *Tent Work in Palestine.* London: Richard Bentley & Son, 1878.

Cottrell, Leonard, ed. *The Past A Concise Encyclopedia of Archaeology.* New York: Hawthorn Books, Inc., 1960.

Erskin, Mrs. Steuart. *The Vanished Cities of Arabia.* New York: E. P. Dutton and Co., 1925.

Fodor, Eugene. *Fodor's Israel, 1972.* New York: David McKay Co., Inc., 1972.

Fulton, John. *Palestine, the Holy Land.* Philadelphia: Henry T. Coates and Co., 1900.

Geikie, Cunningham. *The Holy Land and the Bible.* 2 vols. New York: James Pott and Co., 1888.

Glueck, Nelson. "King Solomon's Copper Mines," *Illustrated London News.* July 7, 1934.

———. *Rivers in the Desert.* New York: Farrar, Straus and Cudahy, 1959.

———. *The Other Side of Jordan.* New Haven, Conn.: American School of Oriental Research, 1949.

Graham, William C., and May, Herbert G. *Culture and Conscience.* Chicago: The University of Chicago Press, 1936.

Hamilton, Elizabeth. *Put Off Thy Shoes.* New York: Charles Scribner's Sons, 1957.

Hamilton, Norah Rowan. *Both Sides of the Jordan.* New York: Dodd, Mead and Co., n.d.

Harding, G. Lankester. *Antiquities of Jordan.* New York: Thomas Y. Crowell Co., 1959.

Harland, J. Penrose. *The Biblical Archaeologist*. May, 1942.

Herodotus. *The Histories*. Baltimore: Penguin Books, 1955.

Josephus, Flavius. *The Works of Flavius Josephus*. Philadelphia: David McKay Publishers, n.d.

Leary, Lewis Gaston. *Syria: The Land of Lebanon*. New York: McBride, Nast and Co., 1913.

Libbey, William, and Hoskins, Franklin E. *The Jordan Valley and Petra*. 2 vols. New York and London: G. P. Putnam's Sons, 1905.

Lieber, Joel. *Israel and the Holy Land on $5 and $10 a Day*. New York: Arthur Frommer, Inc., 1972.

Lowdermilk, Walter Clay. *Palestine: Land of Promise*. New York: Harper and Brothers Publishers, 1944.

Lynch, W. F. *Expedition to the River Jordan and the Dead Sea*. Philadelphia: Lea and Blanchard, 1850.

MacCoun, Townsend. *The Holy Land in Geography and in History*. New York: Townsend MacCoun, 1897.

MacGregor, John. *Rob Roy on the Jordan*. New York: Harper and Brothers, 1875.

Marston, Sir Charles. *New Bible Evidence*. New York: Fleming H. Revell Co., 1934.

McGarvey, J. W. *Lands of the Bible*. London: J. B. Lippincott and Co., 1882.

Merrill, Selah. *East of the Jordan*. New York: Charles Scribner's Sons, 1883.

Mowry, Lucetta. *Biblical Archaeologist*, vol. 15, May, 1952.

Owen, G. Frederick. *Abraham to Allenby*. Grand Rapids, Mich.: Wm. B. Eerdmans Publishing Co., 1943.

―――. *Archaeology and the Bible*. Westwood, N.J.: Fleming H. Revell Co., 1961.

―――. *Jerusalem*. Kansas City: Beacon Hill Press of Kansas City, 1972.

Palestine Annual, vol. 3.

Palestine Exploration Fund Annual, London, 1927.

Palestine Exploration Fund Quarterly Statement for 1886.

Payne, Robert. *The Splendor of Israel*. New York: Harper and Row, 1963.

Porter, J. L. *Five Years in Damascus*. London: John Murray, 1870.

―――. *Giant Cities of Bashan*. New York: Thomas Nelson and Sons, 1884.

Sachar, Abram Leon. *A History of the Jews*. New York: Alfred A. Knopf, 1930.

Smith, George Adam. *Historical Geography of the Holy Land*. Magnolia, Mass.: Peter Smith, Publisher, Inc., n.d.

Smith, William Walter. *Students' Historical Geography of the Holy Land*. New York: George H. Doran Co., 1924.

Survey of Western Palestine. London: Palestine Exploration Fund, 1881.

The City and the Land. London: Palestine Exploration Fund, 1892.

Thompson, W. M. *The Land and the Book*. London: Thomas Nelson and Sons, 1910.

Thornbeck, Ellen. *Promised Land*. New York: Harper and Brothers, 1947.

Trever, John C. *The Untold Story of Qumran*. Westwood, N.J.: Fleming H. Revell Co., 1965.

Tristram, H. B. *The Land of Israel: A Journal of Travels in Palestine*. London: Society for Promoting Christian Knowledge, 1886.

Trumbull, H. Clay. *Kadesh-Barnea*. Philadelphia: John D. Wattles and Co., 1895.

Trumper, Victor L. *Historical Sites of Palestine*. Cairo: Nile Mission Press, 1921.

Vilnay, Zev. *Guide to Israel*. Jerusalem: Hamakor Press, 1970.

Vincent, John H. *Earthly Footsteps of the Man of Galilee*. New York: N. D. Thompson Publishing Co., n.d.

Wild, Laura H. *Geographic Influences on Old Testament Masterpieces*. Boston: Ginn and Co., 1915.

Wilson, Colonel. *Picturesque Palestine*. 2 vols. New York: D. Appleton and Co., 1883.

Wolf, Betty Hartman. *Journey Through the Holy Land*. Garden City, N.Y.: Doubleday and Co., 1967.

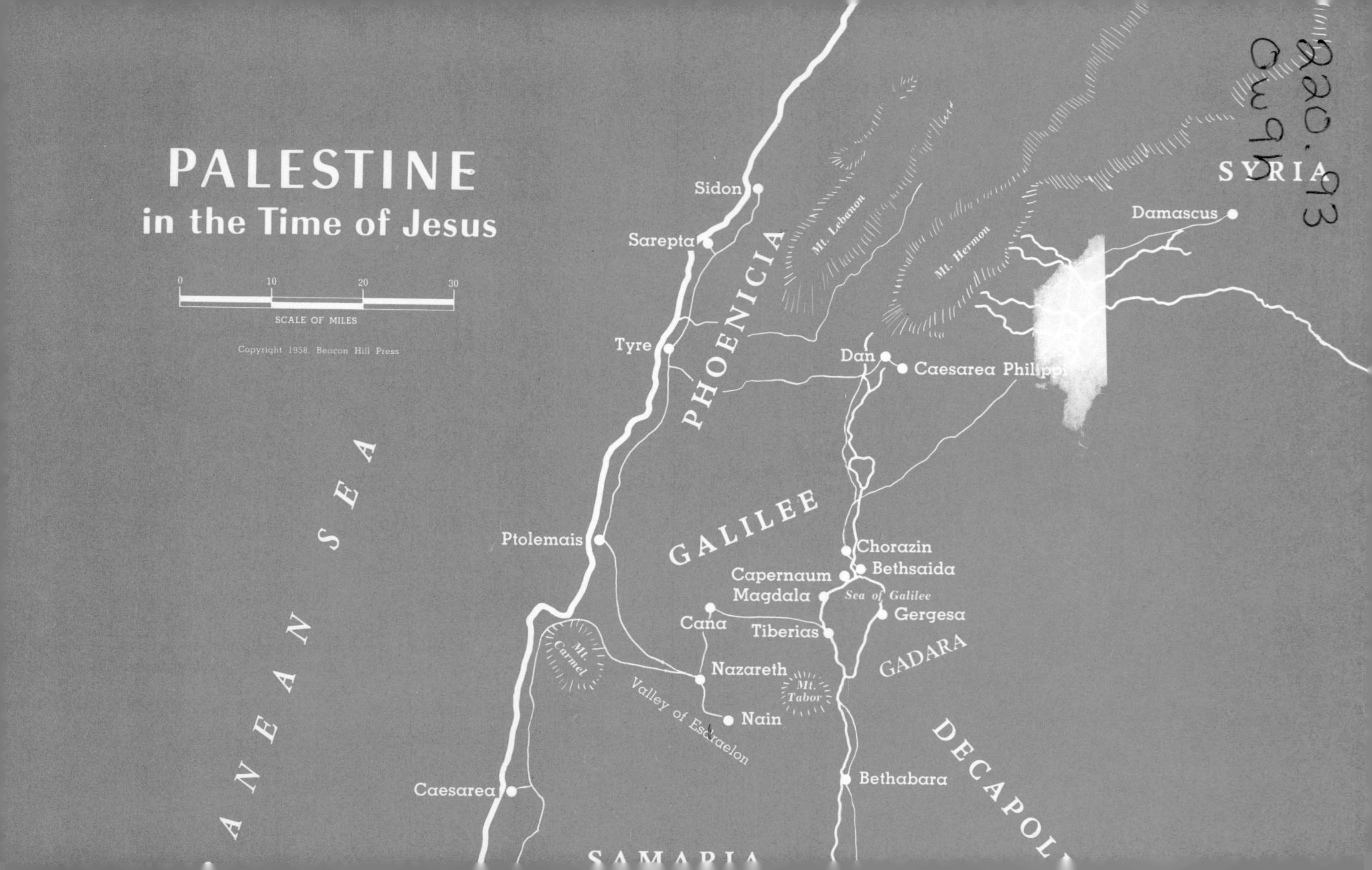
PALESTINE
in the Time of Jesus
0
10
20
30
SCALE OF MILES
Copyright 1958, Beacon Hill Press
SYRIA
Damascus
Sidon
Sarepta
Tyre
PHOENICIA
Mt. Lebanon
Mt. Hermon
Dan
Caesarea Philippi
GALILEE
Ptolemais
Chorazin
Bethsaida
Capernaum
Magdala
Sea of Galilee
Gergesa
Cana
Tiberias
GADARA
Mt. Carmel
Nazareth
Mt. Tabor
Valley of Esdraelon
Nain
DECAPOLI
Bethabara
Caesarea
SEA
ANEAN
SAMARIA